U0129723

[美国]埃里克·H.克莱因 著　付满 译

牛津通识读本·

特洛伊战争

The Trojan War

A Very Short Introduction

译林出版社

图书在版编目（CIP）数据

特洛伊战争 /（美）埃里克·H.克莱因（Eric H. Cline）著；付满译.
—南京：译林出版社，2022.8
（牛津通识读本）
书名原文：The Trojan War: A Very Short Introduction
ISBN 978-7-5447-9170-0

I.①特…　II.①埃…　②付…　III.①特洛伊战争－研究　IV.①K125

中国版本图书馆 CIP 数据核字（2022）第 086866 号

The Trojan War: A Very Short Introduction, First Edition by Eric H. Cline
Copyright © Eric H. Cline 2013
The Trojan War was originally published in English in 2013. This licensed edition is published
by arrangement with Oxford University Press. Yilin Press, Ltd is solely responsible for this
bilingual edition from the original work and Oxford University Press shall have no liability for
any errors, omissions or inaccuracies or ambiguities in such bilingual edition or for any losses
caused by reliance thereon.
Chinese and English edition copyright © 2022 by Yilin Press, Ltd
All rights reserved.

著作权合同登记号　图字：10-2018-429 号

特洛伊战争　[美国]埃里克·H.克莱因 /著　付　满 /译

责任编辑　郑　丹
特约编辑　茅心雨
装帧设计　景秋萍
校　对　蒋　燕
责任印制　董　虎

原文出版　Oxford University Press, 2013
出版发行　译林出版社
地　址　南京市湖南路 1 号 A 楼
邮　箱　yilin@yilin.com
网　址　www.yilin.com
市场热线　025-86633278
排　版　南京展望文化发展有限公司
印　刷　江苏扬中印刷有限公司
开　本　890 毫米 ×1260 毫米　1/32
印　张　9
插　页　4
版　次　2022 年 8 月第 1 版
印　次　2022 年 8 月第 1 次印刷
书　号　ISBN 978-7-5447-9170-0
定　价　39.00 元

版权所有·侵权必究

译林版图书若有印装错误可向出版社调换。质量热线：025-83658316

序　言

王以欣

　　二十年前，为了完成我的博士论文，我来到牛津大学的古典中心，在阿什摩尔博物馆的图书馆里徘徊寻觅，顺便询问一位牛津学者：哪里能够找到特洛伊研究的藏书？他将我引到古希腊研究的书架前。我随之提出一个幼稚的问题："特洛伊研究也算古典学吗？""当然啊！它不仅是古典语言学的研究对象，也是古典考古学的重要分支。"在馆内的一个有趣的角落，书架上摆放着整整一排特洛伊研究的专著，从施里曼的发掘报告、布雷根的四卷本《特洛伊》，直至最新出版的一部图文并茂的德文考古专著，后者汇集了美德联合考古队于世纪之交在特洛伊遗址发掘的最新成果。这里的古典藏书犹如一座宝山，有取之不尽的宝藏。当时国内的研究资料极度匮乏，深入调查特洛伊课题几无可能，多赖牛津的藏书和古典期刊，我的研究需求才得到满足。2002年回国时，我将大量爱琴考古复印资料海运回国，但登机时还是因携带资料过多，行李超重而被罚款。

　　二十年过去了，国内的研究环境有了显著改善。古典资料不必远赴重洋去搜寻求索；国外攻读古典学的年轻学子也陆续学成归国；古希腊语和拉丁语的教学在文科重点院校渐趋普及；在特洛伊战争研究方面的进展亦复如是。德国图宾根大学与美国辛辛那提大学的联合考古队自1989年以来对特洛伊遗址展开大规模考察，发现了一个比特洛伊古堡大10倍的青铜时代晚期的特洛伊下城遗址。2016年以来，土耳其的考古队重新考察特洛伊遗址，荷兰阿姆斯特丹大学的考古家们也随之加入考察的行列。希沙利克山丘的遗址上始终活跃着各国考古家的身影，新的考古报告不断出炉；特洛伊研究的新成果也不时涌现，其中不乏知识性和学术性兼顾的作品。美国古典考古家、乔治·华盛顿大学古典学和人类学教授埃里克·克莱因于2013年出版的专著《特洛伊战争》堪称其中的佳作，经付满先生翻译，今以汉英对照形式由译林出版社付梓出版。这是古典爱好者的福音，对专业学者而言也是裨益无穷。

古希腊人冲冠一怒为红颜，为夺回被特洛伊人劫持的斯巴达王后海伦，不惜动用千艘战舰，十万之众，远征小亚细亚西北角的特洛伊古城，苦战十年，终于焚毁了那座雄伟坚固的古堡，抱得美人归来。这个发生在英雄时代（考古学上的迈锡尼时代晚期）的神话叙事，借助于盲诗人荷马炉火纯青的口传史诗，成为古希腊文化传统的集大成者，是古希腊人生活中须臾难离的精神食粮，古希腊文学和历史的摇篮，也是古希腊人留给后世的一笔最为丰厚的文化遗产，历经三千余年的王朝兴替、文化变迁和世事更迭，始终植根于民间文化的沃土中，在地中海世界世代传诵，成为一幅世界文化史的奇观。早在迈锡尼文明崩溃后无文字的"黑暗时代"，特洛伊的传奇故事就在希腊民间口耳相传，被职业化的游吟歌手改编吟诵，历时三百余年。在希腊历史曙光初照之际，即公元前8世纪后期，经某位或多位天才口传诗人（传说的荷马）的整理加工，两部传世的英雄史诗《伊利亚特》和《奥德赛》最终问世。在随后的世纪里，特洛伊战争的其他故事也被陆续加工成英雄史诗，形成一套完整的特洛伊战争史诗诗组，从帕里斯的裁判、劫海伦等战争起因讲起，历经十年战事，最后靠木马计攻陷并焚毁特洛伊，以及英雄返乡和后续的故事，洋洋洒洒，气势磅礴，蔚然大观。尽管这些后期编成的史诗失传，但仍有摘要和残篇存世。公元前6世纪至公元前5世纪，特洛伊传奇成为希腊抒情诗人反复吟诵的主题，也是悲剧诗人钟爱的戏剧素材。史家们将特洛伊战争的故事当作真实的"古史"记录下来，或写入其通史著作中；神话编纂者将其编入散文体的神话故事集，后者被当作神话指南或工具书供人查阅；埃及亚历山大里亚图书馆的学者们则致力于史诗的研究和校勘工作；奥古斯都时代的诗人维吉尔模仿荷马的叙事风格，用拉丁文创作了英雄史诗《埃涅阿斯纪》，讲述特洛伊王子埃涅阿斯率领族人逃离被希腊人焚毁的家园，在地中海四处漂泊，最终在意大利登陆并定居的故事，并预言其后代创建阿尔巴隆加城和罗马城的传奇，将历史上的罗马人说成特洛伊人的后裔，从而在希腊人和罗马人之间搭建起某种文化桥梁，并为后者最终征服前者提供了神话理据。即使是在罗马天主教主宰的西欧中世纪，拉丁文版本的特洛伊战争传奇依旧流传，蛮族国家的王室也纷纷以特洛伊人的后代自居；而在拜占庭帝国统治的东正教世界，古典传统从未中断，荷马史诗仍是研习希腊文法的必读课本；文人雅士，包括东正教的主教们，仍在从事荷马研究并校注其史诗。

君士坦丁堡陷落之前，拜占庭学者们将古希腊文的典籍，包括荷马史诗的抄本带到西欧，引发古典文化的复兴热潮，也为欧洲未来古典学的建立奠定基础。文艺复兴时期的诗人、作家和艺术家对古希腊神话题材钟爱有加，各种特洛伊战争主题的诗歌、小说和艺术作品应运而生，也引发欧洲旅行家寻访特洛伊古迹的兴趣。

古希腊罗马时代的新伊利昂城（特洛伊VIII、IX城）是一座真实存在的古典城市，那里的居民相信，他们的城池就坐落在特洛伊古遗址之上。古代很多名人都曾探访过这座古城，包括东征波斯的亚历山大大帝、罗马的恺撒大帝、奥古斯都、哈德良、卡拉卡拉、"背教者"朱里安皇帝等。近代旅行者的探访和考察逐渐确定了古遗址的准确方位，即小亚细亚西北角达达尼尔海峡附近的希沙利克山丘。1871—1873年，德国富商海因里希·施里曼在此发掘，发现了古堡、城墙、城门、塔楼、宫殿、街道和战火破坏的迹象，于是声称找到了被希腊人焚毁的普里阿摩斯国王的城堡，还发现了著名的"普里阿摩斯宝藏"，证明了特洛伊战争的历史真实性。1893—1894年，施里曼的助手，德国考古家威廉·德普菲尔德在施里曼发掘的城堡南侧继续发掘，发现了一座更大更雄伟的城堡遗迹。进一步的调查显示：史前特洛伊共有七座相互叠压的城堡（I-VII），施里曼发掘的古堡属于特洛伊II城，存在于公元前2600—前2300年间的铜石并用时代，不可能是迈锡尼时代晚期被希腊人焚毁的城市；德普菲尔德发现的古堡，即所谓的特洛伊VI城，在迈锡尼时代晚期可能毁于战火，与荷马描述的特洛伊古城在时间上颇为吻合。1932—1938年，美国考古家卡尔·布雷根再次发掘特洛伊遗址，其结论是：特洛伊

VI城可能毁于地震，其废墟之上重建的VIIa城才是被希腊人焚毁的特洛伊城。三位考古家皆断言，特洛伊战争是历史上真实发生的史实。然而，废墟上的石头毕竟不会讲话，无法证实城池的摧毁者就是迈锡尼时代晚期的希腊人。迈锡尼时代晚期的希腊虽有线形文字B档案出土，但都属于宫殿账目管理文献，与历史、文学和外交无涉。同期小亚细亚的赫梯帝国王室档案也引发学界兴趣。相关研究显示，赫梯楔形文献确实记录了小亚细亚西北角存在一座名叫维鲁萨的古城，很可能是伊利昂城（特洛伊别名）的古称，其王阿拉克山杜本是赫梯诸侯，与神话中的特洛伊王子帕里斯的别名亚历山德罗斯（亚历山大）雷同。此外，赫梯文献中还浮现出一个古国，即阿希亚瓦王国，常与赫梯帝国争夺小亚细亚西海岸的控制权，彼此保持外交书信往来，时有军事摩擦发生。赫梯与古典学者如今已形成共识，这个阿希亚瓦王国应是爱琴海西面的阿卡亚人的国家，即考古学上的迈锡尼希腊人的某个王国。遗憾的是，并无直接证据显示，阿希亚瓦王国曾攻打过维鲁萨城。因而，迄今为止，特洛伊战争尚无法获得同期历史文献的证实，依然是个历史悬案。

特洛伊城在希腊人点燃的熊熊烈火中被付之一炬，化为焦土，但诗人荷马在后人心中点燃的燃烧三千年的好奇探究的热情之火却从未熄灭。它促成了古希腊人的荷马研究，诞生了最早的荷马学；它带来了西欧中世纪的文艺复兴；它导致了近代的古典语言学学科的创立；它推动了19世纪后期爱琴考古的热潮，由此导致了古典考古学的建立。至今，特洛伊战争仍是文学艺术再创作的灵感之源，众多影视作品的素材。它留下的千古谜团仍然吸引着一批批虔诚而专业的学者为之奉献毕生的学术才华和精力，让众多的古典爱好者为之心驰神往，不断探究。从这个意义上讲，古典爱好者们不妨读一读这部译著。它不是神话故事的简单汇集，而是严肃的学术史探讨。通过深入阅读，你心中的很多谜团将被解开。

2013年，我曾有幸参观特洛伊古遗址，追寻旧迹，发思古之幽情，并填写了一首怀古词，就用这首词作为本序言的尾声吧：

贺新郎 特洛伊怀古

烈焰焚城处，望荒墟，菁菁草色，断墙高仁。冉冉流光天将暮，落日苍凉满目。深井畔，乱石堆路。蔓草侵阶庭芜绿，冷灶台，不见炊烟户。暮云紫，笼轻雾。

冲冠只为红颜怒，起刀兵，爱琴海上，千帆争渡。十载他乡征夫泪，未见家园归路。断送了，英魂无数。累累坟丘埋枯骨，千古怨，知向何人诉。听旧事，问盲瞽。

献给我的母亲，是她让我在七岁时
发现了特洛伊战争的奇妙之处。

目 录

1

特洛伊战争

致 谢

本书简明扼要地介绍了特洛伊战争以及发现和发掘特洛伊/希沙利克的过程，是根据我在乔治·华盛顿大学多次讲授的研讨会课程所编写。此前我就写过特洛伊战争，包括各种学术文章、与吉尔·卢巴尔卡巴合著的一本年轻人读物——《探究特洛伊：从荷马到希沙利克》（2010），以及配合我音频讲座的一本课程导读——《考古学与〈伊利亚特〉：荷马史诗与历史中的特洛伊战争》（2006）。本书是对以上这些内容的更新，也是对这一广受研究的主题的重新调查与解读。

感谢我的编辑南希·托夫和她的助手索尼娅·蒂科一直以来付出的巨大努力。感谢我的妻子黛安·哈里斯·克莱因、我的父亲马丁·克莱因以及两名牛津大学出版社的匿名读者，他们阅读了整个手稿，并就编辑情况提出了修改建议。感谢录书出版社《现代学者》音频书系的埃迪·怀特允许我使用并重新制作最初与我的音频课程一起出版的材料。感谢辛辛那提大学的埃里克·山诺威尔、克里斯托夫·豪斯纳、特雷沃·布莱斯、卡罗尔·赫申森和古典学部。感谢图宾根大学的彼得·雅布隆卡和特洛伊项目为本书提供插图。感谢卡罗尔·贝尔、约翰·本尼特、约书亚·坎农、欧文·库克、奥利弗·迪金森、彼得·雅布隆卡、苏珊·谢拉特、里克·维森和埃里克·凡·东根为本书提供了参考书目和PDF格式的文章。感谢我在乔治·华盛顿大学的学生们,在过去的几年中,他们耐心等待我尝试提炼新的资料。最后,感谢我的家人给予我一如既往的宽容。

特洛伊战争

图1　约公元前1250年，青铜时代晚期的爱琴海和西安纳托利亚地区，涵盖了希
腊大陆、克里特岛、基克拉泽斯群岛和土耳其西海岸（安纳托利亚）的主要城市

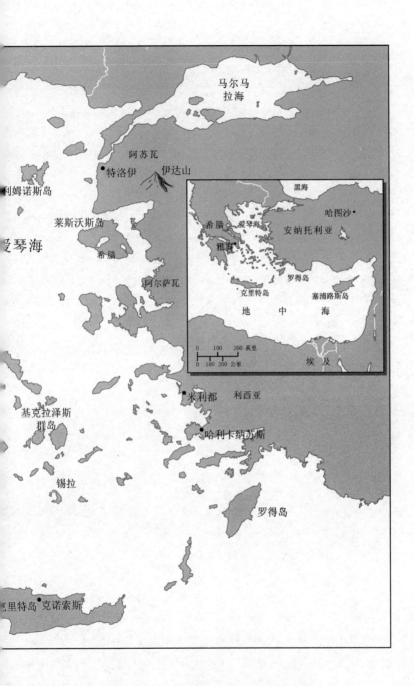

马尔马拉海

阿苏瓦

特洛伊· 伊达山

利姆诺斯岛

莱斯沃斯岛

爱琴海

希腊

阿尔萨瓦

黑海

希腊 爱琴海

哈图沙·

安纳托利亚

雅典

克里特岛

罗得岛

塞浦路斯岛

地 中 海

0   100   200 英里

0   100   200 公里

埃 及

米利都 利西亚

基克拉泽斯
群岛

哈利卡纳苏斯

锡拉

罗得岛

克里特岛·克诺索斯

导　言

　　上古时代是否发生过某场冲突，从中产生了关于特洛伊战争的传说？那场冲突中的战斗是否发生在我们现在称之为特洛伊的地方？古希腊人和古罗马人当然认为这场冲突发生过，而且他们认为他们知道这些战斗发生的地点，就在安纳托利亚（今土耳其）西北部。后来，他们在相同的地点分别建立了自己的城市，希腊人和罗马人都称之为"伊利昂"。据说亚历山大大帝甚至在睡觉时头枕着亚里士多德注解的《伊利亚特》的抄本，而且在公元前334年出征亚细亚时参观了当时推测的特洛伊的遗址。

　　希腊人和罗马人认为，特洛伊战争不仅是真实事件，而且是世界历史上的一个关键时间点。公元前5世纪，希罗多德和修昔底德在各自撰写的著作开篇中简要阐述了特洛伊战争。然而，后来希腊和罗马的学者及作家中没有一人能完全确定这场战争真实发生的时间。包括希罗多德在内，多数人估计这场战争发生在公元前1334年到公元前1135年，但这些估计通常缺少足量

1

的实质性证据。有些人提出将这场战争发生的时间描述为"亚历山大大帝参观（特洛伊遗址）前一千年"或"希罗多德时代前八百年"。最终，虽然也是主要基于猜测，但公元前3世纪希腊地理学家埃拉托色尼估计的时间——公元前1184年（"第一次奥林匹克运动会前407年"）得到了最多的支持。

中世纪至近代早期的古典学者对此更加持怀疑态度，并经常极力贬低特洛伊战争的重要性，甚至完全不屑一提，认为其是虚构之事。只有到被称为迈锡尼考古学之父的海因里希·施里曼声称在19世纪70年代再次找到了特洛伊遗址时，人们才认真关注起来，认为其可能具有历史现实基础，从而重新把兴趣集中于施里曼在希沙利克（土耳其语为Hisarlık，意为"要塞之地"）新近发掘出的遗址上。自那时以来，相关学术讨论一直没有减弱，争论点集中在几个领域，包括有关荷马、青铜时代的希腊、特洛伊和特洛伊战争本身是否存在的文献证据和考古数据，以及与之相关的具体细节（见图2）。

由于公元前8世纪的荷马以及后续几个世纪的其他古希腊诗人和剧作家的著作中提及了特洛伊战争，有关这场战争的传说中所包含的主题世代流传。基本内容很容易讲述，这就是一部关于爱情与战争、竞争与贪婪、英雄与懦夫的永恒史诗。它围绕着几个核心主人公和众多配角展开。故事中的核心人物主要分为两方，一方是斯巴达国王墨涅拉俄斯的妻子海伦、墨涅拉俄斯的哥哥迈锡尼国王阿伽门农、来自色萨利的几乎所向无敌的迈锡尼勇士阿喀琉斯以及伊塔卡国王奥德修斯；另一方包括特洛伊国王普里阿摩斯的儿子帕里斯、普里阿摩斯本人以及普里阿摩斯年龄稍长的儿子赫克托。

图2　结束成功的商业生涯后，富裕的海因里希·施里曼把毕生精力投入到寻找和发掘特洛伊遗址上

　　几个世纪以来，特洛伊战争的故事一直令人们心驰神往，并且催生出无数的学术文章和著作、大量的考古发掘、史诗电影、电视纪录片、舞台剧、艺术和雕塑以及纪念品和收藏品。在美国，除了南加州大学的体育队被称为"特洛伊人"之外，还有十所四年制的学院和大学的体育队也叫"特洛伊人"。此外，还有

3

三十三个州的城镇名也叫"特洛伊"。特别令人着迷的是对"特洛伊木马"的描述，这一大胆的计划结束了特洛伊战争。"特洛伊木马"还进入到现代术语当中，催生出了一句谚语——"小心带着礼物的希腊人"，并且暗指意图通过向计算机系统中植入"特洛伊木马"从而使其遭受严重破坏的黑客。

但是，荷马的故事令人信服吗？当然，阿喀琉斯、赫克托等英雄们都被刻画得如此可信，以至于人们很容易相信这个故事。但这确实是基于真实事件的描述吗？而且那些主人公是真实存在的人物吗？无论一个女人有多么漂亮，难道古代世界中的整个希腊就会因为她而开战，并且持续十多年之久吗？难道阿伽门农真的是万王之王，能够集合那么多人参加这样一场远征吗？而且，即使有人认为曾经真实发生过特洛伊战争，这是否意味着荷马史诗《伊利亚特》和《奥德赛》中的具体事件、行动和描述，以及《史诗集成》中的其他片段和注解符合史实而可以信以为真？荷马所描述的事情真实发生过，而且是按照他所描述的那样发生的，这可信吗？

简而言之，要想了解更多，需要认真探究以下几个主要问题：我们有什么证据可以证明特洛伊战争确实发生了？如果真的发生了，那么它是在哪里发生的，何时发生的？战争原因是什么？最重要的主人公是谁？（关于特洛伊战争的）传说应该放在什么历史背景下？迈锡尼人和特洛伊人的传奇事迹中是否存在真理的内核？我们是否需要将与青铜时代晚期属于同一时代的其他族群，例如安纳托利亚中部的赫梯人，纳入考量范围？

不断涌现的谜团以及人们对于这些问题答案的持续探索，使得近代对于特洛伊战争的研究直到今天（据推测战争发生时间距今已超过三千年）依然活跃且引人入胜。因此，尽管特洛伊战争的传说非常简单，但要写一本有关特洛伊战争的书却并不像它初看起来那样简单。其复杂性以及对于细节的关注必然会超出人们的预期，而复述荷马讲过的故事只是冰山一角。希腊和赫梯的文献中都记载了多次特洛伊战争，因此必须确定哪一场战争是荷马所记录的战争（如果它确实发生过）。此外，由于希沙利克（古代特洛伊）遗址上先后建有九座城市，因此必须确定哪座城市是普里阿摩斯建造的（如果它确实存在过）。但是在讨论这些之前，必须先讲述故事本身，并根据希腊文献查明我们已知的有关特洛伊战争的信息。 5

第一部分

特洛伊战争

《伊利亚特》、《奥德赛》和《史诗集成》中记载的传说

那些在高中或大学里阅读过《伊利亚特》或《奥德赛》的人,阅读过近年来出版的一部或多部译著的人,或者看过好莱坞电影《特洛伊》的人,都对特洛伊战争的故事十分了解。奇怪的是,尽管它们篇幅很长,也描述了很多细节,但《伊利亚特》和《奥德赛》都没有着重描述现代读者所熟悉的许多事件,包括在古代土耳其一处小山坡上发生的决定性遭遇战,使用中空木马的计策攻陷特洛伊,以及后来除奥德修斯之外的古希腊勇士跨海返家的漫长旅途。举个例子,"特洛伊木马"只在《奥德赛》第四卷中墨涅拉俄斯描述其旅程及辛劳时被提及过一次。在《伊利亚特》中则完全没有被提及。

要想了解特洛伊战争及其后果的全部故事,我们必须通读由十二部叙事史诗共同组成的作品集——《史诗集成》,该作品集最有可能出现于公元前8世纪至公元前6世纪,大概是荷马所处时代或稍后不久。《伊利亚特》和《奥德赛》是作品集中仅存的两部完整诗集。其余的早期史诗大多随着时间的流逝而散

佚，只有部分内容因后世作家们的引用或者摘要才得以保留至今。一位自称为普罗克洛斯（现在一些学者认为他叫欧提基奥斯·普罗克洛斯）的人把这些文学作品片段收集到了一起，他是生活在公元 2 世纪的罗马皇帝马卡斯·奥里欧斯的语法学家和家庭教师。另有些人将这部作品集归功于另一位名叫普罗克洛斯的人，此人精通柏拉图哲学（一名"新柏拉图主义者"），生活在三百年后的公元 5 世纪。

但无论如何，其中一位普罗克洛斯将这些来自不同史诗的简短摘要和零星引用集合起来，出版了一本书，名为 *Chrestomatheia Grammatiki*。这本书的书名源自希腊语，意为"对学习有用"，是我们现代词汇中"诸家名文选集"的来源，通常定义为"选自一位或多位作者的精选文学作品集"。通过将这些零散的史诗结合起来，普罗克洛斯把此前迥然不同的多个故事创造成了一个似乎天衣无缝的传说。

荷马所描述的细节有时很少，而其他史诗的文学片段正好丰富了这些细节。这些文学片段集合起来之后，提供了有关特洛伊战争起源的信息。它们还描述了希腊人首次入侵特洛伊的失败尝试，并且完整介绍了特洛伊木马的故事。后来，公元前 5 世纪希腊古典时期的剧作家对特洛伊战争进行了论述，维吉尔、奥维德、李维和昆图斯·斯密尔奈乌斯等更后来的作家提出了不同版本的叙事，拓展并延续了这一传说，增添了更多细节，让这个传说变得有血有肉，从而形成了我们今天所知道的故事。因此毫不奇怪，这些后来增加的内容经常与最初的故事情节相矛盾，比如战争期间海伦是否真的在特洛伊等细节。

《塞普里亚》

　　《塞普里亚》是《史诗集成》的开篇，最初有十一卷（章），讲述了引起特洛伊战争的一系列事件以及特洛伊战争发生后九年间发生的事。《塞普里亚》目前只余一份概要存世，虽然冗长，但十分有价值。普罗克洛斯告诉我们，《塞普里亚》的原作者不是荷马，而是一个据说来自萨拉米斯岛的名叫赫格西亚斯的人，或者是一个据说来自塞浦路斯的名叫斯达西努斯的人。还有一种不同的传统观点认为，这部史诗实际上是由哈利卡纳苏斯（位于土耳其西海岸）的一个名叫塞普里亚斯的人所写，书名取自他的名字。书中所提到的这三位可能写作此书的人大概都生活在公元前6世纪。

　　《塞普里亚》刚开篇就告诉我们，（出于未指明的原因）宙斯密谋发起特洛伊战争。为此，他派遣纷争女神厄里斯去参加珀琉斯和海洋女神忒提斯的婚礼。珀琉斯不仅是一位战争英雄，而且是埃伊纳岛的王子。他们后来成为尚未出生的英雄阿喀琉斯的父母。

　　在他们的婚礼上，厄里斯在赫拉（宙斯的妻子）、雅典娜（代表智慧与战争的女神）和阿芙洛狄忒（代表爱与美的女神）之间主动挑起争论，争论主题是她们三人当中谁最美丽。后来的资料对这个故事进行了详细说明，指出厄里斯故意向一群宾客当中扔了一个刻有"献给最美丽的人"字样的金苹果，从而引发了争吵。由于赫拉、雅典娜和阿芙洛狄忒都认为自己当之无愧，所以她们无法自行解决争端。因此，宙斯命令信使之神赫尔墨斯带领这三位女神来到位于今土耳其西部（古代称安纳托利亚）

的伊达山，她们在那里遇到了一个年轻人。

书中把这个年轻人称为亚历山大，而后来一位注解者在一部最早的现存版本中所作的旁注指出，《史诗集成》中第一次出现的这个亚历山大，具体说来就等同于帕里斯。尽管荷马和早期的希腊诗人称呼他为亚历山大的频率更高，但现代读者更熟悉帕里斯这个名字，这或许是为了避免与后来的亚历山大大帝混淆。在荷马写作的时候，亚历山大大帝还没有出生。书中将亚历山大/帕里斯描述为"凡人中最公平的人"，他同意为三位女神做出裁决，这就是现在人们所熟知的"帕里斯的裁判"。彼得·保罗·鲁本斯的那幅画作——《帕里斯的裁判》为我们提供了令人印象深刻的视觉图像，展现了据说在伊达山上所发生的事。

尽管亚历山大/帕里斯是特洛伊国王普里阿摩斯的儿子，但他在还是新生儿的时候就被驱逐出了宫廷。据说普里阿摩斯做过一个梦，梦到他的妻子赫克犹巴生出的不是儿子，而是一把带有火蛇的火炬。火炬的火花点燃了特洛伊城周围的高草丛，烧毁了整座城市。当普里阿摩斯把解梦人召集到一起时，他们声称这个还未出生的孩子将成为这座城市及其父亲的祸端。他们建议，应当把他遗弃在森林里自生自灭，这样预言可能就不会实现。

刚一出生，这个孩子就被送到了普里阿摩斯的牧民那里。牧民把婴儿带到伊达山，并把他放在野外自生自灭。然而，一只熊救了他，并且养育了他。后来，牧民返回那里，发现这个男孩还活着，于是就把男孩带回了家，当作自己的儿子抚养。

在做出三个女神中谁最美丽的重要决定时，亚历山大/帕

特洛伊战争

里斯并没有意识到自己本身也有皇室血统。直到后来他去了特洛伊，才发现自己的真实身份，并与他的父亲、母亲和整个家庭团聚。可能是出于这个原因，他才有了两个名字。一个是在出生时或与家人团聚后获得的名字，另一个是牧民给他起的名字。当然，关于他为何会有两个名字，还有许多其他可能的解释，其中一种解释认为，特洛伊人和古希腊人使用了不同的名字；另一种解释认为，两个原本不相关的传说融合在了一起，其中一个传说刻画了帕里斯，而另一个则刻画了亚历山大。

　　第二种解释，也即我们今天看到的是类似故事合并的结果，似乎最有可能，因为正如前文指出的，在这些史诗中名字重复的例子数不胜数，有些名字重复两次，有些甚至会重复三次。不仅存在亚历山大和帕里斯这两个名字，特洛伊附近的一条主要河流也有两个名字（分别是"斯卡曼德罗斯"和"桑索斯"），对迈锡尼人也有另外三种不同称呼（亚该亚人、达南人和阿尔戈斯人）。比如，亚历山大和帕里斯这两个名字在《伊利亚特》第三卷中同时出现（可以参见第16、30行与第325、437行），因此我们轻而易举就发现了重复的情况。总体来看，《伊利亚特》共有七卷使用了帕里斯这个名字，共有五卷使用了亚历山大这个名字。《史诗集成》中对两个名字都有提及。

　　至于特洛伊城本身，它也有两个名字。尽管荷马和其他所有作者总是把当地居民称为特洛伊人，但在《史诗集成》中，他们所居住的城市有一次被称为特洛伊，有六次被称为伊利昂。在《伊利亚特》当中，荷马还交替使用了这两个说法。比如，在第一卷中（参见第71行与第129行），荷马既把这个城市称作伊利昂，也称作特洛伊。学者们早就知道，伊利昂（Ilios）这个名字用古希腊语书写时,原本的首字母在拼写和发音上都和"W"相近,因此原本是Wilios,而非简单的Ilios。随着时间的推移,首字母消失了,这个城市的名字简化成了Ilios。

不管怎样,这个相当令人难以置信的故事被认为是一种"建城神话",在上古时代,这一概念通常用来形容和解释某人意外登上王位或成为民族领袖的崛起故事。发生在古代世界其他地方最著名的例子(包括传奇人物和历史人物)有:公元前23世纪美索不达米亚的阿卡德王萨尔贡、公元前13世纪埃及的摩西、公元前8世纪意大利的罗慕路斯和瑞摩斯,以及尤为著名的公元前6世纪波斯的居鲁士大帝。在某种程度上,这些故事都与亚历山大/帕里斯的故事相似。

根据《塞普里亚》中的说法,以及其他古希腊神话和著作中重复讲述的内容,亚历山大/帕里斯选择阿芙洛狄忒作为三位女神之间选美比赛的获胜者,原因在于阿芙洛狄忒承诺他将赢得海伦的爱并娶到海伦。海伦被描述为世界上最美丽的女人。其他两位女神(智慧女神雅典娜、财富与力量女神赫拉)提供的贿赂显然不如娶到美丽海伦的前景那么诱人。

《塞普里亚》略去了亚历山大/帕里斯与家人团聚并搬回特洛伊的旅程,直接讲述了他在那之后穿越爱琴海前往希腊大陆的远航。在那里,他受到斯巴达国王墨涅拉俄斯和他美丽的妻子海伦的热情款待。

墨涅拉俄斯要么是过于轻信别人,要么就是不怎么聪明,因为他在亚历山大/帕里斯到达后不久便前往了克里特岛。尽管当时他仍在款待亚历山大/帕里斯及其随行人员,但《塞普里亚》中没有讲清楚他为何会离开。为什么他不带海伦去克里特岛?

特洛伊战争

这个摘要用语谨慎，只是简单写道："墨涅拉俄斯离开后，阿芙洛狄忒将海伦和亚历山德罗斯（亚历山大/帕里斯）带到了一起，两人成婚之后将大量珍宝装上船，并在夜间航行离开了。"当然，希腊人声称海伦是被绑架的，而特洛伊人则声称她是自愿与亚历山大/帕里斯一起离开的。无论如何，墨涅拉俄斯都有充分理由以"挑拨感情"提出控诉，或者与希腊人交战夺回海伦。

这可能不是海伦第一次被"绑架"。后来，生活和写作于公元300年前后的希腊作家瑙克拉提斯城的阿特纳奥斯曾经写过报告称，海伦在还是年轻姑娘的时候就被英雄忒修斯绑架过。让忒修斯更为出名的或许是，他在杀死克里特岛上的弥诺陶洛斯（人身牛头怪物）之后，与克里特岛国王米诺斯的女儿阿里阿德涅交往的故事。

有趣的是，《塞普里亚》没有说亚历山大/帕里斯和海伦直奔特洛伊，而是说赫拉由于被拒绝依然有点恼火，掀起了一场暴风雨拦截他们，以至于他们的船被刮到了西顿，即现在的黎巴嫩境内。亚历山大/帕里斯并没有轻易下船，而是暂时停止了他与海伦之间的调情，攻击并占领了这座城市。在那之后，这对情人才继续前进并返回了特洛伊。荷马同意这种说法，认为他们在到达特洛伊之前曾在西顿停留，他在《伊利亚特》中写道：

> 那里摆放着西顿妇女精心制作的绸缎长袍，这是神明的亚历山德罗斯（亚历山大/帕里斯）从西顿带回家的。在那次穿越广阔大海的旅程中，他也带回了身为显贵后裔、光彩照人的海伦。
>
> （《伊利亚特》VI：289—292）

不管怎样，《塞普里亚》只是简短提及了这次针对西顿的进攻，没有做出进一步解释。公元前5世纪的希腊历史学家希罗多德听说过《塞普里亚》中这个版本的描述，因为他提到了这段话，而且还引用了上面给出的这几行话作为证据，指出荷马对此也略有耳闻。由于荷马根本没有暗示这次停留是出于敌对，因此他的论点不是很令人信服。但是，希罗多德还详尽地叙述了该故事的另一种版本。在这个版本中，亚历山大/帕里斯和海伦被大风吹得偏航了，他们登陆的目的地是埃及而不是黎巴嫩（《历史》II：113—118）。有关这一点的情节有些扑朔迷离，因为接着就发生了希腊剧作家欧里庇得斯所写的类似的故事情节。欧里庇得斯在他的戏剧《海伦》（创作于公元前412年）中写道，真正的海伦被赫拉匆匆带走，并在埃及待了十年，取而代之的是一个与她相像的幽灵和亚历山大/帕里斯一起去了特洛伊。

根据《塞普里亚》的说法，在得知所发生的事情后，墨涅拉俄斯便回到家，并计划与其兄弟迈锡尼国王阿伽门农一起远征特洛伊，试图夺回海伦。然后，他环游希腊大陆，动员了皮洛斯国王涅斯托尔和奥德修斯。奥德修斯最初假装精神失常，后来才勉强同意参与这次行动。该摘要中没有提及其他希腊城邦领袖和同意参与的人，但《伊利亚特》中所谓的"船舶目录"（《伊利亚特》II：494—759）给出了完整的清单。这里列举了各位国王以及他们各自带来的舰船和士兵，克里斯托弗·马洛在《浮士德博士》一书中概述了他们的数量，关于海伦他如此写道：

是这张面孔发动了数千艘船，

烧毁了高不见顶的伊利昂塔吗？

甜美的海伦,一个吻让我永生。

　　根据《塞普里亚》的记载,来自迈锡尼的舰船及士兵聚集在希腊大陆维奥蒂亚东海岸的港口城市奥利斯,在那里向众神献祭,然后出发前往特洛伊。不幸的是,在其中一场无法预料的战争灾难中,他们在安纳托利亚大陆特洛伊城南部的一个名为铁乌特拉尼亚的地方登陆,将其误认为特洛伊,并摧毁了它。在他们纠正错误并攻击特洛伊之前,一场暴风雨袭击了他们,驱散了他们的船只。他们不得不在若干年——可能长达九年——之后才能在奥利斯重新组织起来,这是研究《史诗集成》片段的德国学者们提出的一个有趣的推测。这场为期九年的延误或许可以解释为什么整个特洛伊战争花了十年时间,但是《伊利亚特》只描述了发生在战争最后一年的一部分事情。

　　正当他们等待第二次从奥利斯起航时,一系列悲剧事件发生了,这些事件由于后来希腊剧作家们的记述而永久留存。女神阿尔忒弥斯刮起大风,阻止了舰队航行,她这样做的原因可能只有她自己最清楚。这让越来越不耐烦的阿伽门农采取了我们认为非常极端的措施。为了安抚女神,他计划用自己的女儿伊菲革涅亚献祭。然而,《塞普里亚》给这些事件塑造了一个美好的结局,里面写到,在最后一刻阿尔忒弥斯抢走了伊菲革涅亚,并在祭坛上伊菲革涅亚所在位置留下了一只雄鹿,这使她永垂不朽,就像《希伯来圣经》中《创世记》第二十二章记载的那样,亚伯拉罕原本打算用以撒献祭,后用一只羔羊代替了以撒。欧里庇得斯创作于公元前410年的戏剧《奥利斯的伊菲革涅亚》使用了同样的情节,在祭祀时用一只鹿代替了伊菲革涅亚。但是其他作家,比如稍早时期公元前5世纪的希腊剧作家埃斯库罗斯,在他创作于公元前458年的戏剧《阿伽门农》中,最后真让伊菲革涅亚充当了祭品。

不管怎样,这支远征军最终再次起航,首先到达特内多斯岛,其后再到达利姆诺斯岛,最后抵达了安纳托利亚海岸的特洛伊。这次他们袭击了正确的城市。但是攻击失败了,希腊人被特洛伊人击退。《塞普里亚》对这次战斗、其主要参与者以及后续发生的事情都有简要的描述,值得详细引述:

> 然后,希腊人试图在伊利厄姆登陆,但特洛伊人阻止了他们,普罗忒西拉奥斯被赫克托杀死。然后,阿喀琉斯杀死了波塞冬的儿子库克诺斯,并将特洛伊人击退。希腊人运回了他们战死疆场的人,并派遣特使前往特洛伊,要求交出海伦和她所带走的宝藏。特洛伊人拒绝了,希腊人首先袭击了这座城市,撤出后又蹂躏了周边的邦国及城市。此后,阿喀琉斯希望见到海伦,阿芙洛狄忒和西蒂斯设法促成了阿喀琉斯和海伦的会面。亚该亚人的下一个愿望是返乡,但被阿喀琉斯制止。随后,阿喀琉斯赶跑了埃涅阿斯的牛群,攻陷了吕耳涅索斯和佩达索斯以及许多邻近的城市,并杀死了特洛伊罗斯。帕特洛克罗斯抓走了吕卡翁,把他带到利姆诺斯岛当作奴隶卖掉了。在这些战利品当中,作为奖励,阿喀琉斯获得了布里塞伊斯,而阿伽门农获得了克律塞伊斯。之后,帕拉墨得斯去世,宙斯计划让阿喀琉斯脱离希腊同盟,从而为特洛伊解围。最后还有一份特洛伊联军的目录。

特洛伊战争

《塞普里亚》的内容摘要至此结束，这同时为荷马创作《伊利亚特》第一卷奠定了基础，也拉开了希腊英雄阿喀琉斯和国王阿伽门农之间战利品之争的序幕。正是因为这一点，《伊利亚特》才与众多史诗融为一体，共同构成了《史诗集成》。

《伊利亚特》

　　《伊利亚特》详细描述了特洛伊战争第十年（也是最后一年）发生的一些故事，故事情节终止于特洛伊城被占领和洗劫之前。阿喀琉斯与阿伽门农之争是第一卷的序幕，为其余部分故事情节奠定了基础。阿喀琉斯与阿伽门农之间之所以发生争执，是因为根据裁决，阿伽门农必须将战利品之一——来自特洛伊的俘虏、阿波罗祭司的女儿克律塞伊斯交还给她的父亲，而为了弥补自己的损失，阿伽门农夺走了阿喀琉斯从之前战斗中得到的战利品布里塞伊斯。反过来，阿喀琉斯发誓，在阿伽门农把布里塞伊斯归还给他并且向他道歉之前，他不会再参与战斗。阿伽门农拒绝这样做，结果希腊人失去了他们最优秀的战士阿喀琉斯的支持，虽然这只是暂时的，却造成了灾难性的后果。

　　这场战争持续了长达十年，但《伊利亚特》只讲述了其中不到五十天的故事。书中的信息详尽且令人印象深刻，但内容并不均衡。例如，第一卷讲述了约二十天的故事，而第二卷至第七卷只讲述了两天的故事，其中含有大量细节。第二卷中逐项列出了希腊部队和舰船的目录，还描述了一份相似但更简短的特洛伊部队目录。第三卷讲述了亚历山大/帕里斯和墨涅拉俄斯之间的一对一战斗，这场对决的赢家可以得到包括海伦在内的一切，目的是在不进一步战斗的情况下结束战争。但是，战争并非如此容易结束，因为在最后一刻阿芙洛狄忒解救了亚历山大/帕里斯。在这个故事里，墨涅拉俄斯几乎快要胜利了，当时他抓住亚历山大/帕里斯头盔上的头巾，正要把他拖出战场，这时阿芙洛狄忒设法让头巾断裂，从而在几乎必死无疑的情况下拯救了亚历山大/帕里斯，确保了战争将继续下去。第四卷至第七卷首先讲述了奥林匹斯山上诸神之间发生的事情，然后转向战场，描述了更多的战斗场面。

接下来第八卷至第十卷这三卷详述了一天中的战斗细节，包括亚历山大/帕里斯的哥哥赫克托与希腊巨人英雄埃阿斯之间一场漫长但未分出胜负的决斗。后来，埃阿斯自杀。第十一卷至第十八卷这八卷，占二十四卷本《伊利亚特》全部内容的三分之一，同样极为详细地介绍了一天中的战斗情况。部分原因是，第十六卷讲述了有关阿喀琉斯的同伴帕特洛克罗斯的一系列事件。帕特洛克罗斯借用了阿喀琉斯的盔甲，由于一整天内都在战斗而被误认为是阿喀琉斯，最后被赫克托杀死。第十七卷记述了在赫克托剥去阿喀琉斯的盔甲后，双方为了抢夺帕特洛克罗斯的尸体进行的战斗。

第十九卷至第二十二卷又记述了另一天的战斗。在第二十卷中，阿喀琉斯勇猛归来，参与到战斗当中。众神现在也加入了战斗，波塞冬制造了一场地震来影响战斗的结局。在第二十二卷中，阿喀琉斯杀死了赫克托，并且把赫克托的尸体拖回了希腊营地。第二十三卷至第二十四卷是《伊利亚特》的最后两卷，描述了接下来二十二天里发生的故事，或许是为了再现第一卷中所描述的那二十天里发生的事。在第二十三卷中，帕特洛克罗斯的遗体在一个巨大的火葬柴堆上进行火化，人们还举行了葬

礼活动。第二十四卷是《伊利亚特》的最后一卷,描述了阿喀琉
斯的愤怒与悲伤。尽管有疑虑,但他最终还是被说服了,把赫克
托的遗体交还给了国王普里阿摩斯。在停战的十二天期间,赫
克托的遗体又被火化于他自己的火葬柴堆,这作为最后一幕为
《伊利亚特》画上了句号。

其他并不完整的史诗讲述了特洛伊战争的剩余事件。这些
史诗包括《埃塞俄比斯》、《小伊利昂》和《伊利昂的毁灭》(意
为"特洛伊的毁灭"),据信这些史诗创作于公元前8世纪至公
元前7世纪。这些剩余事件在更晚一些的一部著作中也有记述,
这部著作创作于公元4世纪,作者是史诗诗人昆图斯·斯密尔
奈乌斯(士麦那的昆图斯)。昆图斯写了一首长诗,标题是《续
荷马史诗》,又名《特洛伊的陷落》,共有十四卷(章),涵盖了从
《伊利亚特》结局到特洛伊城陷落的这段时期。绝大多数现代
学者都认为,昆图斯可能使用了这些早期的史诗来撰写自己的
作品。

《埃塞俄比斯》

《埃塞俄比斯》从《伊利亚特》结束的地方写起,由米利都的
阿克提努斯创作,最早可能写于公元前8世纪,大概与荷马的著
作属于同一时期。《埃塞俄比斯》共包含五章或五卷。故事始于
阿喀琉斯先后杀死亚马孙女王彭忒西勒亚和埃塞俄比亚王子门
农。门农是普里阿摩斯的前任特洛伊国王拉俄墨冬的孙子,也
即普里阿摩斯的侄子、亚历山大/帕里斯和赫克托的堂兄弟。被
杀死的二人当时正带领军队支援特洛伊。

在阿波罗的协助下,亚历山大/帕里斯杀死了阿喀琉斯。由

于我们只有这部史诗的简短摘要，所以我们不知道阿喀琉斯是如何被杀死的。但是从后来其他的著作，比如奥维德的《变形记》（12：580—619）中得知，阿喀琉斯被箭射中了脚后跟，这是他身上唯一脆弱的地方。为了使阿喀琉斯刀枪不入，在他小的时候，他的母亲曾抓住他的脚后跟将他浸入冥河中。在为阿喀琉斯的尸体而战之后，希腊人将他带回了自己的船只，在火葬柴堆上将他火化，并为纪念他而举行了葬礼活动。影响这些事件的一件事是，奥德修斯和埃阿斯为了抢夺阿喀琉斯的盔甲而发生的争执阻碍了葬礼，但他们之间的争执要到《史诗集成》的下一部史诗《小伊利昂》才能解决。

《小伊利昂》

普罗克洛斯告诉我们，《小伊利昂》由米提林尼（莱斯沃斯岛上的一座城市）的莱切斯所创作，共有四章。通常认为他生活和创作于公元前7世纪。在这部史诗的开头，奥德修斯战胜了埃阿斯，并且赢得了阿喀琉斯的盔甲和武器。决出胜负之后，埃阿斯自杀，这个剧情后来成为索福克勒斯在公元前5世纪创作的一部戏剧的主题。在这之后又发生了多场战斗，双方都有大量人员战死，其中最重要的一个人就是亚历山大/帕里斯。亚历山大/帕里斯被一个名叫菲罗克忒忒斯的人所杀，后者后来成为索福克勒斯、埃斯库罗斯和欧里庇得斯所创作的戏剧中的主人公。亚历山大/帕里斯死后，一个本来名不见经传的名叫厄帕俄斯的人，按照雅典娜的指示建造了一匹木马。值得注意的是，这是《史诗集成》中第一次引入木马这个概念。

《小伊利昂》暗示这是厄帕俄斯的主意（"厄帕俄斯在雅典

娜的指示下建造了木马")。《奥德赛》（VIII：492—494；另参见XI：523—535）中多次把这个主意归功于厄帕俄斯，其中写道："但是现在，改变你的主题，为厄帕俄斯在雅典娜帮助下建造的木马歌唱吧，奥德修斯曾经奸诈地带着这匹木马攻入了城堡。"然而很久以后，昆图斯·斯密尔奈乌斯把这个主意归功于奥德修斯，只是将建造木马归功于厄帕俄斯：

> 唯一想到这个主意的聪明人，
>
> 就是拉厄尔忒斯的儿子（奥德修斯），
>
> 他在讲话中说道：
>
> "众神最为敬重的朋友，
>
> 如果这是命中注定，尚武的亚该亚人
>
> 会通过欺骗的方式攻陷普里阿摩斯的城池，
>
> 必须建造一匹装着领袖的木马，
>
> 我们将欢迎一场伏击的到来。"
>
> （昆图斯·斯密尔奈乌斯，《续荷马史诗》XII：23—29）

《小伊利昂》简要陈述了接下来发生的事情，其中写道："然后，在将最优秀的战士藏进木马并烧掉临时营房之后，希腊大军驶向特内多斯岛（紧邻海岸的一座岛屿）。特洛伊人以为自己的麻烦结束了，于是摧毁了一部分城墙，将木马推入城中，并盛宴庆祝，就好像他们已经征服了希腊人一样。"后来包括昆图斯·斯密尔奈乌斯（《续荷马史诗》VII：314—335）在内的希腊作家们，通常将木马内的人数定为三十人（有些传说将人数增加到四十人），并给出他们的名字，包括首领奥德修斯、小埃阿斯、狄俄墨得斯和墨涅拉俄斯自己。然而,《小伊利昂》的摘要很简短,甚至都没有给出这些人的名字,而是戛然而止。故事将在下一部史诗《伊利昂的毁灭》(又叫《特洛伊的毁灭》)中继续。

《伊利昂的毁灭》

《伊利昂的毁灭》(又叫《特洛伊的毁灭》)仅由两章组成,但情节丰富,使这一阶段的史诗传说进入了尾声。它的作者是米利都的阿克提努斯,此人也创作了《埃塞俄比斯》。在这部史诗中我们了解到,虽然特洛伊人将木马拉入了城中,但对此感到可疑,而且就下一步该怎样做进行了辩论。最终,他们决定将其献给雅典娜,并"相信战争已经结束,转而享受欢乐和盛宴"。然而,还有些人仍然持怀疑态度,在《埃涅阿斯纪》第二卷中,罗马诗人维吉尔让特洛伊的波塞冬祭司拉奥孔警告他的同胞们,他这样说道:"特洛伊人民,不要相信这匹木马。无论是什么,我都怕希腊人,甚至是那些带着礼物的希腊人。"从这里引申出我们熟知的一句谚语——"小心带着礼物的希腊人!"此外,由此也引申出了特洛伊木马作为计算机病毒的概念。这种病毒是现代技术的灾难,尤其是因为它让黑客能够通过秘密安装在计算机上的"后门"程序进入系统。

拉奥孔的警告很有先见之明,因为《特洛伊的毁灭》接下来就写道,希腊军队在夜幕掩护下从特内多斯岛返航,同时木马中的勇士"冲出来进攻敌人,杀死许多人并猛攻这座城市"。普里阿摩斯在宙斯的祭坛前被杀,赫克托的小儿子阿斯蒂阿纳克斯被敌人从城墙上扔了出去。

由于希腊人战胜了特洛伊人，墨涅拉俄斯重新得到了他的妻子海伦，并把她带到希腊的船只上，准备返家。在杀死更多人和分配完包括女俘虏在内的战利品之后，胜利的希腊人启程回家，并不认为雅典娜会计划在途中消灭他们。至此，《特洛伊的毁灭》的剧情就结束了。这部史诗讲述了特洛伊木马和希腊人征服特洛伊城的故事。它把战争结束后的故事留给了另外一部史诗《诺斯托伊》（又名《返乡》）。

《诺斯托伊》

根据普罗克洛斯的说法，共有五章的《返乡》由特洛伊西纳的阿基亚斯所撰写，其他资料认为这部史诗的创作时间可以追溯到公元前7世纪或公元前6世纪。特洛伊西纳是希腊大陆上的一个小镇，恰好也是传说中的英雄忒修斯的故乡。《返乡》讲述了除奥德修斯之外其他希腊英雄如何穿越爱琴海返回故乡和王国的故事。

在《返乡》中，皮洛斯国王涅斯托尔和赫拉克勒斯的侄子、阿尔戈斯国王狄俄墨得斯都毫发无伤地回到了家中。然而，曾与阿伽门农争论何时离开特洛伊的墨涅拉俄斯在航行返家过程中却被困在了暴风雨里。到达埃及时，他的船队只剩下了五艘船。《返乡》中没有告诉我们更多信息，但是荷马在《奥德赛》（III: 299—304）中充实了这部分内容，包括让墨涅拉俄斯后来告诉忒勒马科斯，他到埃及后在地中海以东地区游荡了八年，除了埃及之外还去了塞浦路斯、腓尼基、埃塞俄比亚和西顿。然后，他继续返回斯巴达的旅程。史诗中这样写道："我四处游荡，经历了很多苦难，在第八年的时候我才用船只把财富带回了家。

我游历过塞浦路斯、腓尼基和埃及,遇到过埃塞俄比亚人、西顿人和埃雷比人,然后我又去了利比亚,那里的羔羊从一出生就去掉了角。"(《奥德赛》IV:80—85)

另一方面,阿伽门农最初为了安抚雅典娜而留在了特洛伊,后来终于航行返家,却和同伴一起遭到他的妻子克吕泰墨斯特拉及其情夫埃癸斯托斯的谋杀。这个插曲以及随后关于他的两个孩子俄瑞斯忒斯和厄勒克特拉的事件,在后来的公元前5世纪希腊剧作家的作品中得到详细阐述。这些剧作家包括埃斯库罗斯、索福克勒斯和欧里庇得斯。这部史诗在结尾部分简单提到,墨涅拉俄斯在阿伽门农被谋杀后才最终返回了家,据推测海伦和他同行。

《奥德赛》

荷马所作的《奥德赛》是《史诗集成》中现存的另一部完整史诗,按照顺序排在《返乡》之后。《奥德赛》主要讲述了特洛伊战争结束后奥德修斯长达十年的归家旅途,以及旅途中所遭遇到的艰辛。《奥德赛》和《伊利亚特》一样,也包含二十四卷(章)。经过世世代代的口耳相传之后,这个故事已经广为人知。

奥德修斯的旅途与特洛伊战争的传说本质上并不相关,但这部史诗确实时不时地让奥德修斯或者他的某位战友有机会回顾一下战争年代,提供额外的细节,进而充实其他史诗概要中只是简短呈现的内容。经历了许多冒险之后,奥德修斯最终得以返回家中,并在儿子忒勒马科斯的帮助下,杀死了妻子珀涅罗珀身边成群结队的追求者。然后,他重新坐上了伊塔卡岛国王的宝座。

24

《泰列格尼》

在《奥德赛》之后，《史诗集成》中的最后一部作品《泰列格尼》问世。根据普罗克洛斯的说法，《泰列格尼》仅由两章组成，作者是昔兰尼的欧伽蒙。昔兰尼是希腊在公元前7世纪建立的殖民地，也即现在的利比亚。人们认为，欧伽蒙在稍后的公元前6世纪就创作了这部作品，基本上可以说是《奥德赛》的后记。《泰列格尼》始于珀涅罗珀追随者的葬礼，终于奥德修斯被杀。奥德修斯死于他的另一个儿子忒勒戈诺斯的手中，忒勒戈诺斯是奥德修斯在战后归国途中与女神瑟茜同居一年期间生下的儿子。

后期作家

后期的希腊剧作家，以及奥维德、李维和维吉尔等罗马作家，都在不断充实从《史诗集成》中发现的细节，尤其是战争后发生的事件。由于在时间上更接近特洛伊战争，因此早期史诗中发现的细节可能比后期作品中描述的细节更值得信赖。但是读者应该意识到，即使是这些早期的史诗，也是直到公元前8世纪，即最初战争后五百多年才由作家记录下来，并且可能是在两百年之后，即公元前6世纪才正式成文。因此，对于荷马时代的学者和青铜时代的爱琴海地区考古学家而言，这些细节的准确性值得关注。同样，荷马本人是否真实存在，以及他是不是《伊利亚特》和《奥德赛》的作者，也是一个疑问。

历史背景下的特洛伊战争：迈锡尼人、赫梯人、特洛伊人和海上民族

假如特洛伊战争确实发生了，那么古代和现代学者都会同意这样的观点：这场战争发生在青铜器时代晚期，接近公元前2千纪末期。在那个时期，希腊大陆的迈锡尼国和安纳托利亚的赫梯国是古代地中海地区两个最强大的国家，夹在这两个国家中间的是特洛伊和特洛阿德地区（安纳托利亚的比加半岛）。公元前1700年至公元前1200年，两大文明都在繁荣发展。假如特洛伊战争真的发生了，那么战争时间一定是在这两大集团灭亡之前。虽然特洛伊人只是由于安纳托利亚西北部希沙利克遗址的发掘才为人们所知，但迈锡尼人和赫梯人现在已经相当知名。另一个可能参与特洛伊战争的群体——不断迁徙的海上民族，虽然鲜为人知，但令世人充满好奇。

迈锡尼人

1876年，海因里希·施里曼开始发掘希腊大陆的迈锡尼古遗址，当时人们对青铜器时代晚期居住在该地区的文明知之甚

少。1870年，施里曼着手寻找普里阿摩斯的特洛伊城，并很快确定了它在土耳其西北部的位置，他决心找到阿伽门农的王宫。

他在迈锡尼的发掘工作给这个文明赋予了名字——迈锡尼文明。他在迈锡尼以及附近的梯林斯遗址的工作，很快得到了其他不同国籍的早期考古学家的补充。这些考古学家找到并且发掘了希腊大陆、克里特岛和基克拉泽斯群岛上的其他青铜器时代的遗址。不到二十年时间里，人们弄清楚了这样一个事实：在约公元前1700年至公元前1200年间，迈锡尼文明就已经在希腊大陆上建立起来了。有关这一主题的第一部权威著作——《迈锡尼时代：关于前荷马时期希腊遗迹和文化的研究》在1896年出版。

迈锡尼文明不仅可以从迈锡尼等遗址发掘过程中发现的物质遗迹中得到重现，还可以从希腊大陆甚至是克里特岛上的大多数主要迈锡尼遗址中发现的一系列泥板中再现。泥板上刻有一种如今被称为线形文字B的文字系统，它们是当黏土仍然湿润时就被刻在泥板表面的。线形文字B在1952年成功得到破译，它是希腊语的一种早期形式，主要由需要永久记录涉及人员和货物清单的库存以及商业往来的行政官僚机构使用。

20世纪30年代，美国辛辛那提大学考古学教授卡尔·布雷根在皮洛斯发现了最大规模的线形文字B泥板。传说皮洛斯是年老睿智的涅斯托尔国王的故乡。皮洛斯城位于希腊大陆西南部，在公元前1200年前后遭到毁坏。皮洛斯城的毁灭只是更大规模灾难的一部分，这场灾难终结了迈锡尼文明。火灾意外烘烤了泥板，将它们保存在掉落的地方，数千年后人们发现并且破译了它们。

28

刻在这些泥板上的文献不是文学杰作,而是简单的商业记录,主要包含一些普通的进出宫殿的物品清单,里面逐行记载着需要修理的战车车轮的数量、送回迈锡尼的布匹数量,以及需要喂养的奴隶的数量。在皮洛斯发掘的文献中列出的一些女性工人,通过解译,其种族名称起源于安纳托利亚西部。这些妇女来自土耳其西海岸的米利都、尼多斯和哈利卡纳苏斯。其他人则来自毗邻海岸的多德卡尼斯群岛。他们可能是特洛伊战争前几年被迈锡尼人购买或俘获的奴隶。

迈锡尼人的经济基于所谓的地中海三宝——葡萄、橄榄和谷物。这是一种主要以农业为基础的生活方式,耕作之外辅以少量渔业,至少对大多数人来说是这样。上层阶级能够享受更多的奢侈品,拥有黄金、白银、青铜、象牙和玻璃制成的商品和物品。诸如批发商、工匠和长途商贩之类的中产阶级维持并提供了上层阶级奢侈享受所需的东西。纺织业和香料业是利润最高的行业,橄榄油和葡萄酒的生产也是如此。

其中一些商品——尤其是纺织品、香料和橄榄油——不仅在希腊本土,而且远在埃及、迦南(今以色列、叙利亚和黎巴嫩)甚至美索不达米亚(今伊拉克)都很有市场。迈锡尼陶器在国内外也很热销,尽管人们并不总是清楚它的价值是来源于其本身还是有时它所装的内容物。在现代发掘过程中,人们发现了几千个迈锡尼的罐子、花瓶、高脚杯和其他器皿。从埃及延伸到安纳托利亚及包括特洛伊在内的其他地方,人们每年都能发现更多的物件。

为了与这片土地上至高权威的身份相称,迈锡尼国王的宫殿通常建在希腊每个地区最高的山丘上。它们戒备森严,城堡

特洛伊战争

入口处有厚厚的城墙和坚固的大门，比如迈锡尼所谓的狮门。然而，这些宫殿不仅仅是国王的住所，还用作储存地和分配中心，用于储存和分配来自国内外的商品和丰收时节收获的农产品，以备后用。在城堡围墙内，宫殿周围还建有国王的侍臣、行政人员及王族成员的住所，以及宫殿工匠们的作坊。

在希腊，几乎每个迈锡尼国王宫殿城堡下面的山坡上都散布着贫民区的房屋。这里和周围的小村庄里都居住着普通的农民、批发商、商贩和工匠，每个王国都要依赖这些人。这些人中的大多数，不管是男性还是女性，都不知道如何阅读或写作，可能只有不到1%的人识字。

迈锡尼文明在公元前1200年或之后不久走向终结，这是文明普遍崩溃的一个体现，当时影响了整个地中海地区。其走向终结的原因尚不完全清楚，但可能涉及多种因素，包括干旱、地震以及外部族群的入侵。

赫梯人

赫梯文明因《希伯来圣经》而得名，但直到公元19世纪被重新发现之前，这一文明实际上已经从现代世界的视野中消失。30《圣经》中多次提到赫梯人，主要是将其作为众多迦南部落中的一支，其他迦南部落还包括亚摩利人、希未人、比利洗人和耶布斯人。《圣经》中还具体提到了一些赫梯人，包括赫梯人埃夫龙，亚伯拉罕从他那里为自己的妻子萨拉买了一块墓地（《圣经·创世记》23：3—20）；以及赫梯人乌利亚，他是拔示巴的第一任丈夫（《圣经·撒母耳记下》11：2—27）。所罗门王的随从中也有"赫梯妇女"（《圣经·列王纪上》11：1）。

经过瑞士探险家约翰·路德维格·伯克哈特等先驱和英国亚述学家塞斯等学者的调查，最终真相大白，赫梯人的定居地点并不在迦南，而是在安纳托利亚。《圣经》中之所以写错位置，有可能是在《希伯来圣经》于公元前9世纪至公元前7世纪写作完成时，最初的赫梯人就已经消失了。然而，他们的后代——所谓的新赫梯人——当时已经在迦南北部地区稳固地定居下来。正是因为《圣经》的作者们很熟悉这些人，因此才会在提到他们时弄错时代。此外，很明显，"赫梯人"这个名字用词不当。由于《圣经》中提到了赫梯人，学者们就采纳了这个词，用于指代这个青铜器时代晚期的安纳托利亚王国。然而，赫梯人从不称自己为赫梯人，相反，他们称自己为"哈梯国的国民"。

到1906年，德国考古学家已经开始在赫梯国都城哈图沙进行挖掘。不到一年，他们就发现了泥板，这些泥板记录了日常生活的方方面面，此外还有一些官方档案记录和条约。这些记录是用几种不同的语言写成的，包括赫梯语、阿卡德语和卢维语，所有这些语言在很大程度上都已经被破译。所有的文献都可以追溯到青铜器时代晚期，原因在于赫梯文明同迈锡尼文明一样，其兴盛期也是在约公元前1700年到公元前1200年间。

我们从上述那些发掘以及在今土耳其国内许多其他地方的发掘中得知，在公元前17世纪中叶，赫梯国从一个面积较小、鲜为人知的王国发展成为一个初具规模的帝国，并把国都建在哈图沙（今博阿兹科伊，位于安卡拉以东一百二十五英里）。几十年后，他们已经强大到足以攻击巴比伦，推翻了由汉谟拉比创建的古巴比伦王国。此后，直到公元前12世纪赫梯文明崩溃之前，他们作为近东地区主要的超级大国与埃及相抗衡。

我们还从发现于现代埃及、叙利亚、伊拉克以及哈图沙的文献中了解到，在青铜器时代晚期，赫梯人即与其他大国之间开展了贸易、辩论以及其他方式的互动交流。上述大国包括埃及新王国、亚述王国、巴比伦王国，以及位于乌加里特和叙利亚北部、安纳托利亚等其他地方的较小王国，比如特洛伊（赫梯人称之为维鲁萨或维鲁西亚）。总体而言，虽然我们有文字证据表明赫梯人有时也会进口谷物，可能还有橄榄油和葡萄酒，但他们似乎已经相当自给自足。经过一个世纪的发掘和研究，学者们现在对于重现赫梯社会、宗教、外交、建筑和物质文化相当有信心。

　　赫梯国实力巅峰出现在公元前14世纪至公元前13世纪，特别是在国王苏彼鲁流玛一世和他之后的统治者统治期间，此时赫梯帝国的势力范围扩张至叙利亚北部，开始与埃及新王国频繁发生摩擦，偶尔还会爆发冲突。最后一位伟大的赫梯国国王图达里亚四世，其统治期为公元前1237年至公元前1209年，他声称征服了塞浦路斯岛，并带走了金银。在那之后不久，公元前1200年前后，赫梯帝国就土崩瓦解。根据埃及的文献资料，这可 32能是因为海上民族摧毁了"哈梯国"，或者是位于哈图沙北部的不友好邻国卡什卡消灭了它。

特洛伊人

　　从青铜器时代开始，特洛伊和特洛阿德地区就一直是主要的十字路口，控制着从南到北和从西到东的路线，包括连接地中海和黑海航道的达达尼尔海峡入口。因此，谁控制了特洛伊，谁也就有可能从经济和政治上控制整个地区。从特洛伊战争时代一直到第一次世界大战中的加里波利之战，为何这么多世纪以来会有如此多不同的民族都想占据这个地区，也就不难理解了。因此，我们或许不应该感到惊讶，迈锡尼人也会对特洛伊和安纳托利亚西海岸感兴趣，尤其是因为特洛伊不仅位于他们在爱琴海所控制地区的边缘，也位于赫梯帝国的边缘。

但是，人们对真正的特洛伊人知之甚少。迈锡尼人和赫梯人各自拥有多个可以找到他们物质文化和文献的地方，而特洛伊人只占据了一个地方，即特洛伊及其紧邻的周边区域。此外，正如学者们指出的那样，特洛伊人，照字面理解，就是指在某个特定时期碰巧生活在这座城市的任何人。由于这座城市在其历史上多次被摧毁和占领，至少有九座不同时期的城市遗址重叠在土耳其西北部希沙利克的土丘（此处被确定为古特洛伊城所在地）上，因此，将公元前3千纪的特洛伊人种族与一千年之后的公元前2千纪末期特洛伊战争时期相比，很可能已经发生变化；又过了一千年后，当希腊化时代的希腊人和罗马人占领这个地方的时候，特洛伊人的种族又会发生变化。

然而，如果我们专注于特洛伊战争时期，不仅可以从过去一个多世纪在希沙利克/特洛伊进行的四组发掘工作中收集到一些信息，而且还可以从同一时期其他文明所在地区发现的一些文献中获取信息。例如，我们在赫梯人的文献中发现了特洛伊，就可以认为我们将特洛伊等同于他们称为维鲁萨的城市是正确的。这些信息显示出一种持续数百年的关系，有时敌对，有时和平，其中特洛伊国王经常充当赫梯大帝的附庸国统治者的角色。

特洛伊人很可能也参与了标志着青铜器时代晚期世界进入国际化的国际贸易。在希沙利克的发掘过程中，考古学家们发现了许多与编织有关的纺锤，这表明当时出现了大规模的纺织品生产。荷马还将特洛伊人比作马的饲养者,马是青铜器时代军队双轮战车所必需的珍贵商品。然而,纺织品和马都是易腐材料,考古记录中几乎不会保留这些。因此,除了一种可能是特洛阿德地区生产的、已被确认为"特洛伊灰陶器"的特定类型陶器之外,我们很难确定此时可能出口到地中海其他地区以及迈锡尼的任何特洛伊商品。

海上民族

由于海上民族两次进攻埃及,一次在公元前1207年法老慕尼达统治期间,第二次在公元前1177年法老拉美西斯三世统治期间,所以我们对海上民族的了解主要来自埃及的记录。一直以来,它们都让古代地中海地区的历史学家和考古学家们感到困惑和迷惑,原因在于他们似乎是突然冒了出来,造成了广泛的破坏,与本地区一些最强大的国家较量一番之后,又突然从历史中消失了。埃及人在碑文中称他们为"海上民族",根据碑文中的描述,他们来自北方,来自海中的岛屿。拉美西斯三世具体说道:

> 异邦在他们的岛屿上策划了阴谋。各国疆土在战斗中一下子被毁灭和分散。在异邦人的武器面前,无一领土幸免,从哈特、库德、卡尔凯美什、阿尔萨瓦到阿拉西亚,这些国土瞬间就被切断。异邦在阿莫尔一地扎营,居民惨遭屠戮,此地仿佛从未存在。他们正向埃及走来,而圣火已经在他们面前准备好了。他们是由佩雷散特人、闸卡尔人、舍克利斯人、达奴那人和万舍斯人联合起来形成的联盟。他们

的铁骑踏遍地球，占领一切所到之处。他们坚信："我们的计划会成功！"

根据传统的解释，在青铜器时代晚期，即公元前1200年前后，海上民族终结了大部分文明世界，包括赫梯文明、迦南文明、迈锡尼文明和米诺斯文明，但随后海上民族自己又被埃及人所灭。在从西向东横渡地中海地区的劫掠浪潮中，海上民族所造成的破坏无法挽回。

然而，根据最近的解释，海上民族所进行的实际上可能更像是整个民族的迁徙运动，包括男人、女人、孩子和高高堆在牛车或其他役畜拉车上的财产，而非劫掠方。他们为什么开始迁徙是一个备受争议的问题；最有可能的原因是自然灾害，比如长期干旱，或者甚至是家乡发生了地震。他们可能本不应该像人们所想象的那样对青铜器时代末期可观察到的破坏负有责任，相反，他们只是导致地中海文明在那个时候终结的众多因素中的一个罢了。再者，尽管有人提出过相关设想，但目前尚不清楚他们是否袭击了特洛伊，或者与特洛伊战争有任何关联。

文学上的战争

青铜器时代晚期，生活并不总是太平，甚至贸易伙伴和邻近文明之间的关系也并非总是友好。尤其是在公元前1500年至公元前1200年期间，除了假定发生的特洛伊战争之外，还有许多重大战役，这些战役要么在当时的各个大国之间进行，要么在扩张时期由它们与较小的国家之间进行。例如，除了在公元前1207年和公元前1177年分别发生了对抗海上民族的战斗之外，埃及

35

人还在三个世纪前的公元前1479年，在位于现代以色列的美吉多（《圣经》中的哈米吉多顿）与迦南叛军的一支军队作战。这场战役以法老图特摩斯三世领导的埃及人取得决定性胜利而告终，其细节被妥善铭刻在位于埃及卢克索的卡纳克神庙的墙上，使其成为历史上第一次有记载的战役。

公元前1286年，埃及人在现代叙利亚的卡叠什遗址也进行了一场重大战役。这一次，法老拉美西斯二世率领的埃及军队与国王穆尔西里二世率领的赫梯军队对峙。他们开战是为争夺这一地区的土地控制权，该地区是赫梯帝国北部和埃及帝国南部之间存在争议的领土。这场战斗结束后，双方都声称自己取得了胜利，并签署了条约。该条约的副本可以在埃及和安纳托利亚的哈图沙找到。

这些战役的共同点是，虽然有文学证据提供支撑，而且没有理由怀疑其真实性，但目前还没有确实的考古证据能够证明它们发生过。可以说，特洛伊战争也是如此，我们也有文学证据，但没有明确的考古证据（尽管考古证据可能也在变化，但这取决于人们如何解释最近在希沙利克遗址的发现）。因此，在青铜器时代晚期，特洛伊战争并非独一无二，首先它的出现方式并不独特，其次如今将其呈现在我们面前的文学风格也不罕见。

第二部分

考察文学证据

第三章

荷马诸问题：荷马存在吗？《伊利亚特》中的记载是真的吗？

研究特洛伊战争希腊文学证据的现代学者们普遍关注所谓的"荷马诸问题"。这实际上由许多较小的问题组成，其中最相关的是："荷马存在吗？"以及"荷马的《伊利亚特》和《奥德赛》中的信息是否反映了青铜器时代（特洛伊战争时期）、铁器时代（荷马生活时期），或者这两个时代之间发生的事？"虽然这两个问题都很重要，但后者对于研究特洛伊战争、发掘特洛伊遗迹或者试图重现青铜器时代爱琴海和地中海东部地区生活的学者们来说，具有更为重要的意义。

荷　马

事实上，人们对荷马本人或他的生活知之甚少。古人将他视为最受尊敬的吟游诗人——一位吟唱过往时代英雄事迹的旅行吟游诗人。他仍然被认为是希腊最早出现的可能也是最伟大的史诗诗人。据说他的才华在于编纂、组合甚至最终写下了特洛伊战争的（或多个）故事。一位名叫巴里·鲍威尔的学者提 41

出了一个相当不寻常的推测，即发明希腊语字母就是为了记录史诗——它是"由一个人发明的……为了记录我们称之为荷马的诗人的希腊语六音步诗行"。还有人认为荷马可能创作了史诗，但原本只是想让这些史诗像早期史诗一样通过口头方式流传，而我们现在所知的《伊利亚特》和《奥德赛》被以文字记录，可能要到公元前6世纪甚至更晚。

假设荷马真实存在并且是史诗的作者（这两个问题还有待进一步讨论），那么他生活在什么时候，住在哪里？希罗多德认为荷马生活在他自己时代之前约四百年，他说："据我认为，荷马和赫西奥德……生活在我所处时代前四百年。"（《历史》II：53）由于希罗多德生活在约公元前450年，据此推测荷马应生活在公元前9世纪中叶，即约公元前850年。然而，经过几十年的讨论，学者们现在普遍将荷马生活的时代后推了大约一个世纪，即公元前750年，部分原因是他的一名学生——米利都的阿克提努斯（《埃塞俄比斯》和《伊利昂的毁灭》的作者）——据说出生于公元前744年（参见亚历山大城的克莱门特，《杂文集》1.131.6）。

古希腊学者、作家和诗人，其中包括亚里士多德和品达，就荷马的出身一直争论不休。有人认为荷马来自安纳托利亚西海岸的士麦那市（今土耳其伊兹密尔市），并在希俄斯岛工作多年；其他人则说他出生在希俄斯岛或伊奥斯岛上。简而言之，关于他的出身从未有过普遍共识。的确，许多学者坚持认为他从未存在过，至少不像人们普遍描述的那样。

另一方面，有人认为荷马不是单一的个体，而至少是两个人。事实上，长期以来德国学者（其中包括弗雷德里希·奥古斯特·沃尔夫在1795年的观点）尤为认定《伊利亚特》和《奥德赛》由不同的人写成。曾经由计算机对文献开展的文体分析似乎证实了这一结论，但尚未达成普遍共识。也有人认为荷马不是一名男性，而是一名女性。尽管人们最近对这一假设的情况进行了探索，但最初的假设可以追溯到一个多世纪以前，由塞缪尔·巴特勒于1897年写作时提出。

也许最有趣、最合理的说法是，"荷马"不是一个特定的人，而是一种职业。也就是说，没有一个名叫"荷马"的人，而是一个职业为"荷马"的以吟唱特洛伊战争史诗为生的旅行吟游诗人。如果是这样，那么当一种新的书写系统在公元前8世纪变得广泛可用时，这些职业吟游诗人可能已经写下了战争故事的口头版本。总体而言，有关荷马的推测和书籍并不缺乏。然而，一言以蔽之，我们实际上对他几乎一无所知，最重要的是，他是否真的写了那两部人们普遍认为应归功于他的著作——《伊利亚特》和《奥德赛》。

青铜器时代还是铁器时代？

至于"荷马诸问题"的第二部分，我们很可能会问，《伊利亚特》和《奥德赛》中的信息是否反映了青铜器时代（公元前1700年至公元前1200年）、铁器时代（公元前1200年至公元前800年）或者这两个时代之间发生的事件。为了回答这个问题，我们必须使用从文献中收集到的信息，并将其与考古中获得的信息进行比较。

首先，我们测试一个前提，即《伊利亚特》、《奥德赛》以及《史诗集成》中其他史诗的描述准确反映了青铜器时代的希腊社会，并且在公元前1250年至公元前750年之间的五百年间，这些史诗一字不差地流传了下来,没有被吟游诗人们淡化。五个世纪以来,某个诗人或众多诗人能否准确地记忆并传承数万行诗句的信息?我们有什么证据或者例子可以表明情况可能就是这样?

运用民族志类比分析的现代学者,比如20世纪20年代的米尔曼·帕里,通过记录下南斯拉夫、土耳其和爱尔兰等国的现代诗人和吟游诗人背诵并且演唱史诗的事例,已经证明吟游诗人确实可以准确地口头传承数千行史诗。显然,准确传承这样的诗句不成问题,特别是如果许多诗句或者描述都比较陈腐刻板而且多次重复的话,比如"灰眼睛的雅典娜"、"脚步敏捷的阿喀琉斯"和"玫瑰色的黎明"等。

《伊利亚特》中的"船舶目录"(《伊利亚特》II: 494—759)总共提及了1 186艘船,许多学者认为这是对青铜器时代遗留物合理准确的记录。在长达五个世纪的进程中,该"船舶目录"由一代又一代的吟游诗人口头传承。考古调查表明,目录中列出的许多派遣人员和船只的城镇仅在青铜器时代有人居住,而在荷马时代早已废弃。在荷马有生之年,如果这些曾经至关重要的地方还存在的话,也只剩下废墟了。传说和故事可以解释某些人记忆中的事物,但不是所有人。唯一能够让这个目录如此准确的方法是,它是在青铜器时代晚期城市繁荣时期编写的,由一代又一代的吟游诗人传承,直到最后作为一部分内容写入《伊利亚特》第二卷。然而,它并不是一份对青铜器时代完美无瑕的传承,因为如果一切都严格属于青铜器时代的话,有些本不应该存在的城市出现了,而有些本应该存在的城市却没有出现。相反,它似乎是一种混合,随着故事由吟游诗人口头流传,几个世纪以来不断发生着变化。

总体而言，《伊利亚特》似乎是一部从青铜器时代到铁器时代整个时间跨度内的细节和数据的汇编。如果为了使其新鲜如初且与时俱进，从而在流传了几个世纪的过程中不断地对这部史诗进行修改和更新的话，那么这是意料之中的事。例如，据说帕特洛克罗斯和赫克托在战斗中阵亡后都是在火葬柴堆上火化的（分别参见《伊利亚特》XVIII：138—257和XXIV：784—804），史诗中这样记载："他们满脸泪水地抬着勇敢无畏的赫克托，把赫克托的遗体放置在高耸的柴堆上，然后点燃了柴堆。"虽然相较于土葬，火葬在铁器时代的希腊比青铜器时代的希腊更为普遍，但人们在特洛伊/希沙利克遗址上发掘出了公元前14世纪后期的一处火葬墓地，在这块墓地里，骨灰安葬在骨灰瓮中。

此外，荷马详细描述的野猪獠牙装饰的头盔在青铜器时代末期已经不再使用。人们在希腊大陆的梯林斯、克里特岛的克诺索斯和提洛岛等地发现了这种头盔上的野猪獠牙，以及有关头戴这种头盔的战士的叙述，但是这类头盔在荷马所处时代也不可能再为世人所见，尽管《伊利亚特》（X：260—265）中对此有过如下很详细的描述：

> 墨里奥涅斯给了奥德修斯一张弓、一个箭筒和一把剑。奥德修斯还把一顶皮革制成的头盔戴在头上，头盔内侧用皮革呈丁字形牢牢交叉拴系，外侧则用一头野猪白光光的獠牙逐个紧密缝制，头盔中心位置还垫了一个毛毡，工艺可谓精湛。

同样，荷马对埃阿斯和他所使用的"塔盾"进行了描述，后

人认为这个"塔盾"不仅属于青铜器时代,而且属于青铜器时代中早于特洛伊战争的一段时期:

> 现在埃阿斯走到他身边,像一堵墙一样扛着他的用青铜和七层牛皮制成的盾牌,这是提基奥斯费了很大力气才打造成的。提基奥斯在海尔德的所有皮革工人中最为优秀。他先将取自强壮公牛的牛皮缝制七层,然后在七层牛皮之上又用锤子钉了第八层青铜护罩,从而制成了这面闪闪发光的巨大盾牌。(《伊利亚特》VII: 219—223)

这类盾牌和野猪獠牙装饰的头盔,可以在希腊圣托里尼岛阿克罗蒂里的一所房子里画的所谓微型壁画中看到,这很可能可以追溯到公元前17世纪,比传说中的特洛伊战争早四百年。一些学者认为埃阿斯是更早期的一位英雄,原本是另一部史诗(现在已佚)中的主要角色,后来作为一个家喻户晓的人物被引入了《伊利亚特》。

在其中一个场景中,特洛伊英雄赫克托也挥舞着一面塔盾,他的盔甲不时碰撞他的脚踝和脖子(《伊利亚特》VI: 117—118)。根据描述,赫克托披挂着"全副青铜盔甲"(《伊利亚特》XI: 65)。与本书其他地方的类似描述一样,这一点现在被认为可以通过迈锡尼附近登德拉遗址的一次考古发现得到证实。考古人员在上述遗址中发现了一整套盔甲(全副甲胄),这让人想起荷马对盔甲的描述,但这套甲胄可以追溯到公元前1450年前后。这将使荷马的记述成为人们了解青铜器时代的另一个例子。

更为常见的盔甲,包括"小腿防护良好的亚该亚人"用于保护小腿的护胫甲，在《伊利亚特》中有过多次描述（例如，《伊利亚特》III：328—339，IV：132—138，XI：15—45，XVI：130—142，XIX：364—391）。这些盔甲反映的也是青铜器时代的物品，而不是荷马自己时代的物品。这些装备总是按照相同的顺序穿戴，依次是护胫甲、胸衣、剑、盾牌、头盔，然后是长矛：

> 帕特洛克罗斯披挂着青铜制成的光彩夺目的盔甲，全副武装。他先将精致的护胫甲靠在腿上，用银质系带将护胫甲固定在脚踝上。之后，他穿上闪闪发光的胸衣，就像脚步敏捷的阿喀琉斯一样。他的肩上挎着一把带有银钉的青铜剑，上面挂着那面巨大而沉重的盾牌。他将那顶带有马毛羽冠的时髦头盔套在他硕大的头上，羽毛不停地上下摆动，非常瘆人。他拿起两支刚好可以握在手中的锋利长矛。（《伊利亚特》XVI：130—140）

根据《伊利亚特》中的描述，帕特洛克罗斯曾三次攀登特洛伊城墙，但每次都被阿波罗击退。荷马确切的描述是这样的："帕特洛克罗斯三次试图爬上高耸城墙的墙角，但太阳神阿波罗用其不朽之手猛击帕特洛克罗斯的闪亮盾牌，三次将他击退。"（《伊利亚特》XVI：702—703）。这暗示城墙是可以攀爬的，的确，在海因里希·施里曼、威廉·德普费尔德和卡尔·布雷根等考古学家发掘希沙利克/特洛伊遗址时，他们发现特洛伊VI城堡的墙壁呈特定角度，并且砖石之间有足够大的间距，至少有一个地方可以轻松攀爬。在荷马写作的时候，这些城墙很可能已经深埋在地表之下，数百年来都不曾为人们所见。因此，荷马的描述很可能源自对青铜器时代某座城堡城墙的准确回忆，但这座城堡在荷马生活时代很久以前就已经埋于地下了。然而，荷马似乎是在描述特洛伊城的外墙，而不是内城的城墙，因此他的描述在一定程度上有些混乱。

或许最能反映真实情况的是荷马笔下的勇士几乎总是使用青铜制武器，然而实际情况是在他自己那个时代，这些武器都是铁制的。《伊利亚特》中几乎没有提到铁制的器物，这符合这样一个事实，即在青铜器时代铁器为人所知但稀有珍贵。事实上，青铜器时代已知的为数不多的一件铁制武器是霍华德·卡特在埃及国王图坦卡蒙墓中发现的一把匕首，其历史可以追溯到公元前14世纪，这可能与阿喀琉斯哀悼帕特洛克罗斯时所持的铁刀类似（《伊利亚特》XVIII：32—34）。

荷马提供的其他细节将青铜器时代的器物和做法与铁器时代的器物和做法混淆了。这些内容讲的主要是一些琐事，比如荷马笔下战士们所用战车的车轮上使用的辐条数量，以及牵引这些战车的战马数量。例如，考古学家在迈锡尼"竖井墓穴"的墓碑上以及迈锡尼和其他地方墓葬中的金戒指上发现了青铜器时代的描述，这些描述表明特洛伊战争时期的战车车轮上有四根辐条，由两匹战马牵引，用作战斗的移动平台。然而，根据荷马的描述，当时的战车车轮上有八根辐条（《伊利亚特》V：720—723），通常由四匹战马牵引，并被用作"战斗运兵车"将战士运往前线，之后他们下马徒步作战——所有这些都是铁器时代战车和战斗战术的已知特征，可以追溯到特洛伊战争发生很久之后的年代。

同样，荷马笔下的战士通常携带两支长矛，用于投掷（《伊利亚特》III：16—20，VII：244—248）。这是铁器时代一种常见的战术，而在青铜器时代战士们更多地使用单支长矛，用于近距离刺向对手而不是远距离投掷。荷马很少描述这种长矛。然而，他确实提到了赫克托（《伊利亚特》VI：318—320）挥舞的十一腕尺长的长矛和属于阿喀琉斯（《伊利亚特》XXII：273）的一支长矛。荷马还经常描述主要敌对英雄之间的一对一战斗或决斗，旨在强调单个勇士的荣耀事迹，例如，埃阿斯和赫克托（《伊利亚特》VII：224—232）之间的决斗，阿喀琉斯和赫克托之间的决斗（《伊利亚特》XX）。荷马还描述了以紧密队形行进的步兵（《伊利亚特》III：1—9）。这些个人决斗和行军方式似乎都是铁器时代的战斗方法，而不是青铜器时代的方法。

此外，荷马经常谈到铁器时代后期以及具有迈锡尼时期特征的武器和其他器物。在他的描述中，迈锡尼人使用的武器有"镶银剑"（《伊利亚特》XI：29—31），即剑柄上铆有银钉或金钉的剑，就像在公元前16世纪至公元前15世纪的迈锡尼的"竖井墓穴"中发现的一样，以及一种镶嵌着金钉的权杖（《伊利亚特》I：245—246）。他还描述了阿喀琉斯的新盾牌（《伊利亚特》XVIII：474—607），其制作方式类似于在迈锡尼和其他地方的"竖井墓穴"中发现的镶嵌饰品的匕首（使用金、银和一种称为黑金的黑色黏质材料，嵌入青铜质基面）。所有这些都是名副其实的青铜器时代手工艺品。但荷马也描述了阿喀琉斯原有的盾牌（在帕特洛克罗斯阵亡时丢失），根据他的描述，盾牌上面有一张蛇发女怪的脸："阿喀琉斯拿起那面由很多人合力精心制作的盾牌，这是一件光彩夺目的宝物……盾牌正中是蛇发女怪毫无表情的脸，她的眼睛凝视前方，这眼神令人毛骨悚然。盾牌上还刻着'恐惧'和'恐怖'。"(《伊利亚特》XI：32—37)。带有这种纹章的盾牌直到铁器时代才开始普遍使用，并且在公元前7世纪的希腊重装步兵方阵战争中，其用途达到顶峰。

总而言之，荷马根据记忆对特洛伊战争的描述，以及关于那些战士、装备和战斗的微小细节，就像我们看到的《伊利亚特》版本中描绘的那样，是青铜器时代和铁器时代实践的一种结合。这种结合可能反映出原始故事在流传五个世纪之后所引入的变化。因此，包括考古学家和古代历史学家在内的学者们在试图重建爱琴海地区的青铜器时代时，对于使用荷马提供的细节资料都非常谨慎。事实上，之所以早期古典学者会对特洛伊战争是否真正发生过持怀疑态度，部分原因正是这种将不同时期混为一谈的时间组合。

然而，人们显然可以提出相反的论点。荷马的论述包含许多只有在青铜器时代才使用的器物和地点的细节，而这些内容直到现代考古学家在20世纪初开始发掘后才被重新发现。因此，如果荷马史诗确实反映了青铜器时代末期发生的真实事件，即使他的描述中包含一些不准确的内容或细节，人们也不应对此感到惊奇，原因在于这些内容或细节是几个世纪以来由吟游诗人们口头流传下来的。

新分析

然而，还有一点需要考虑，那就是一些学者的评估，他们认为《伊利亚特》、《奥德赛》和《史诗集成》不仅涉及铁器时代后期的器物，而且涉及可以追溯到青铜器时代较早期（即公元前13世纪之前，当时特洛伊战争据信已经发生）的人、地点和事件。这些学者共同组成了一个名为德国新分析学派的非正式团体，他们认为可以找到（吟游诗人）后期添加到荷马史诗中的较早期史诗的点滴内容。

例如，根据《塞普里亚》的记载，第一次被派往特洛伊拯救海伦的亚该亚人远征队遭遇厄运，据称结果是在真正的特洛伊战争马上就要开始前，阿喀琉斯和其他亚该亚勇士在铁乌特拉尼亚发生激烈战斗。铁乌特拉尼亚是位于特洛伊以南、安纳托利亚西北部的一个地区。古代学者和现代学者估计，每两次远征之间的间隔时间通常从几周到九年不等。新分析学者把对这次远征的描述视为前荷马时期一个很好的例子，这最可能指的是较早期的"特洛伊战争"。他们还认为，手持塔盾的埃阿斯属于前一个时代，是更早期史诗中的一个人物形象。同样的情况还出现在伊多墨纽斯、墨里奥涅斯甚至奥德修斯等人物身上。

新分析学者和其他学者还指出，《伊利亚特》本身就提到，希腊英雄赫拉克勒斯在普里阿摩斯的父亲拉俄墨冬时代仅用六艘船就攻陷了特洛伊（《伊利亚特》V：638—642），其中写道："人们说，是强大的赫拉克勒斯，在战斗中坚定不移，雄心勃勃。由于拉俄墨冬的母马，他只带了六艘船和一支人数不多的军队来到特洛伊，但洗劫了伊利昂（即特洛伊），并破坏了城中街道。"（位于阿提卡海岸边，距离雅典不远的埃伊纳岛阿帕亚神庙东边的三角楣上描绘了这次对特洛伊的远征。）如果每艘船的载量为五十人，那就只有三百人，这是一支相当小的战斗力量。然而，后来的希腊作家阿波罗多罗斯和狄奥多罗斯提到的另一种传说认为，在赫拉克勒斯袭击特洛伊时，他指挥的是十八艘船，而不是六艘船，这意味着当时他手下有九百人，这是一支相当强大的军队。

显然,希腊有一种传说,甚至在《伊利亚特》和《史诗集成》中也有提到,即在真正的特洛伊战争之前,迈锡尼勇士已经在安纳托利亚西海岸进行了几十年也许上百年的战斗和探险,而特洛伊本身可能在阿伽门农接替普里阿摩斯之前将近一个世纪就遭到了迈锡尼人的攻击。古代历史学家摩西·芬利在他的著作《奥德修斯的世界》(1956)中提出,青铜器时代发生过许多次"特洛伊战争"。

结　语

这给我们留下了一些重要的常识性问题。《伊利亚特》和《史诗集成》中讲述的事件和情节可信吗?荷马和其他史诗诗人所描述的事件真实发生过吗?如果发生过,是以他们所说的方式发生的吗?整个国家(或其在古代对等的叫法)真的会为了一个人而开战吗?阿伽门农真的是那个召集众人索回其兄弟之妻的"万王之王"吗?青铜器时代晚期的迈锡尼社会真的可以以这种形式组织起来吗?此外,人们真的能制造出特洛伊木马这样的机器,并成功用此结束战争吗?

以上所有问题的答案都是肯定的。例如,即便那些军队、武器和战术来自很长的时间跨度,反映了几个世纪以来口头流传的故事,但荷马对于个体活动、旅行、战斗和其他细节的描述都是真实的,《伊利亚特》中描述的事件也是可信的。此外,青铜器时代的希腊确实分裂成了许多本质上是城邦的国家,每个国王统治着一个大城市,比如梯林斯、皮洛斯、迈锡尼及其周边地区。当然,迈锡尼似乎比当时的其他城市更强大,与其他城市的联系也更紧密，特别是考古学家们发现了当时迈锡尼进口的外国商品，这些都可以表明其国际地位。

尽管海伦遭绑架可能提供了一个方便的借口，但发动战争的真正原因不太可能是这一点。同古代世界的大多数战争一样，这场战争真正的动机可能是政治和商业利益，为了获得土地并控制利润丰厚的贸易路线。然而，后来也出现了一些历史事例，其中个体的活动被用作发起战争的借口和催化剂。最经典的例子当然是引发第一次世界大战的斐迪南大公遇刺事件。无论如何，这场战争可能注定要发生，但暗杀事件成了导火索。第二个例子来自赫梯人的世界，公元前14世纪，国王苏彼鲁流玛一世的儿子扎南扎王子在与一位不知姓名的埃及女王结婚的途中被不明身份的袭击者杀害。他的父亲以其遇害为借口，发起了一场赫梯人和埃及人之间的战争——这场战争可能无论如何最终都会打响，但同样是出于领土原因，与他儿子的死无关。

特洛伊木马是传说中最不可信的内容之一，但它的存在依然可以得到解释。坦率地讲，希腊人不太可能建造这样一匹马并将士兵藏匿其中。特洛伊人更不可能会愚蠢到将它带进他们的城市。然而，荷马和其他吟游诗人都是诗人，因此，他们可能使用了诗的破格。特洛伊木马可能代表了某种攻城器械，比如说巨大的攻城槌，就像罗马人在公元74年用来摧毁马萨达（位于今以色列国内）周围城墙时用的一样；或者是一座塔楼，里面的勇士们可以出来参与战斗，就像辛那赫里布在他位于尼尼微的宫殿门板上描绘的公元前701年对耶路撒冷南部拉吉的围攻一样。由于波塞冬是希腊地震之神，其象征物是一匹马，因此也有人认为，特洛伊木马是对那场摧毁城市的地震的隐喻。

最后一个问题有关荷马描述的究竟是一场特洛伊战争还是数场特洛伊战争。根据希腊史诗的记载，在青铜器时代晚期，迈锡尼人对特洛伊和特洛阿德地区至少发起过三次攻击：第一次发生在赫拉克勒斯和拉俄墨冬时代，当时特洛伊被攻陷；第二次是阿伽门农和他的手下对铁乌特拉尼亚的错误进攻；最后是《伊利亚特》中描述的特洛伊之战。这些战争中哪一个是荷马笔下的特洛伊战争？抑或它们全部都是？荷马是否将这些战争浓缩成了一部伟大的史诗，用诗意的语言象征性地表现了几百年来在安纳托利亚西部海岸发生的无数次小冲突？事实上，包括考古发现和文字记载在内的其他迹象表明，早在公元前17世纪之前，希腊勇士就已经在安纳托利亚的西北部海岸（具体来说也许就是特洛伊）战斗过了。

特洛伊战争

赫梯文献：阿苏瓦、阿希亚瓦和维鲁萨的阿拉克山杜

希腊人记录了特洛伊战争，但位于安纳托利亚中部的赫梯人同样也记录了这场战争。在青铜器时代晚期，从公元前1700年至公元前1200年，赫梯人控制了该地区的大部分土地，赫梯王国的国土从特洛伊所在的西海岸一直延伸到这个王国的东部——如今土耳其与叙利亚交界处。德国考古学家在赫梯王国都城哈图沙（位于今安卡拉以东200千米处）发现了刻有赫梯语、阿卡德语和同时期其他语言文字的泥板。

维鲁萨

在这些泥板当中，有一些提到了一个城市或地区，赫梯人称之为维鲁萨。维鲁萨与赫梯统治者之间的密切联系至少保持了三百年的时间，其中一些时期，维鲁萨国王在赫梯人的授意下施行统治，有时只能作为傀儡国王。根据大多数现代学者的说法，维鲁萨城似乎与荷马和史诗诗人们所称的伊利昂（即特洛伊）是同一个地方。赫梯档案中记录了青铜器时代晚期在这座城市 54

进行的至少四场战争的详细信息。我们甚至知道相关国王的名字，其中一位名叫阿拉克山杜，他曾被卷入公元前 13 世纪初的一场冲突；另一位名叫瓦尔姆，几十年后他被敌军赶下了台。这两个事件都与荷马笔下的特洛伊战争发生在同一时期，并且其中一个或者两个可能都与特洛伊战争有关。

从 1911 年开始一直持续到今天，许多学者认为阿拉克山杜很可能是希腊名字亚历山大的赫梯语版本。如果这个假设正确，人们可以暂时将赫梯人称为维鲁萨的阿拉克山杜的那个人，与希腊人称为伊利昂/特洛伊的亚历山大/帕里斯的那个人等同起来。如果这两者不是同一个人，那就意味着有两个名字非常相似的统治者几乎同时在安纳托利亚西北部统治着两个名字非常相似的城市。这种巧合似乎不太可能，因此人们可以合理地认为，这两者即为同一人。

有趣的是，我们还有一份条约文献。在维鲁萨/特洛伊打了一仗之后，维鲁萨国王阿拉克山杜和赫梯国王穆瓦塔利二世于公元前 13 世纪初签订了这份条约。我们不知道这份文件中提到的是在特洛伊进行的许多战争中的哪一场，因此我们不能肯定地说这份文件是支持还是反对这样一种观点，即同一人在两种文化的文学中发挥了作用。因此，我们必须回到公元前 13 世纪那场战争之前的时代，然后在时间上往前推，从而确定赫梯条约中描述的那场战争是否就是荷马和希腊诗人描述的特洛伊战争。虽然刚开始我们不熟悉这些名字，但现在我们要扎根于赫梯历史当中，研究大量可供参考的细节。

阿希亚瓦

我们必须首先考虑在哈图沙发现的大约两打文献，其中提到了一个叫作阿希亚瓦的强国和民族。自从一位名叫埃米尔·弗雷尔的瑞士学者提出阿希亚瓦指的就是青铜器时代的迈锡尼人（即荷马称为亚该亚人的民族）之后，关于阿希亚瓦的身份认定及其可能与特洛伊战争相关的学术争论已经持续了一个多世纪。弗雷尔进行了更加深入的研究，确定了赫梯文献中所提到的具体人物的身份，并将他们与荷马笔下的勇士们联系起来。例如，在他看来，荷马提到的阿特柔斯和厄忒俄克勒斯就是赫梯文献中的阿塔里希亚和塔瓦伽拉瓦。

其他人很快也加入了讨论，包括德国学者费迪南德·萨默，他在1932年出版了一部包含当时已知的所有阿希亚瓦文献的鸿篇巨制，其主要目的是反驳弗雷尔的提议。从那以后，争论不休。现在大多数知识渊博的权威都承认，弗雷尔将阿希亚瓦人认定为亚该亚人（迈锡尼人）是正确的，这些人很可能来自希腊大陆。56

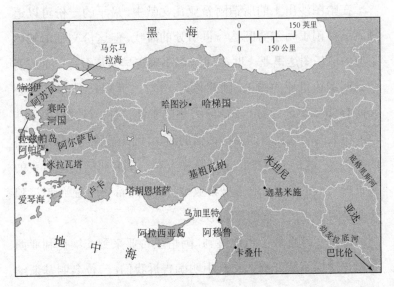

图3 约公元前1500年至公元前1200年，安纳托利亚地区的赫梯王国

如果是这样，我们可以说我们有文献证据表明，迈锡尼人早在公元前15世纪就卷入了安纳托利亚西海岸的战斗和冲突当中。

然而，如果弗雷尔的观点有误，也即阿希亚瓦人不是迈锡尼人，那么我们就没有任何赫梯语文献证据能够证明，生活在爱琴海两岸的两个最强大的群体之间曾建立过联系，或他们自己和迈锡尼人之间曾有过接触。然而，这似乎不太可能，因为如果是这样的话，我们将拥有一个赫梯文献中没有提到过的青铜器时代晚期的重要文化（迈锡尼文化），同时拥有一个得到重要文献证明，却没有留下任何考古遗迹的青铜器时代晚期的城邦或王国（阿希亚瓦）。正如大多数学者现在认可的那样，简单地将两者等同起来更能说得通。

马杜瓦塔和阿塔里希亚

在哈图沙出土的所谓阿希亚瓦文献中，最早的一份可以追溯到赫梯国王阿尔努旺达一世所处的时代，但这份文献却叙述了他的前任图达里亚一世／二世（尚不确定早期是否有一个或两个名叫图达里亚的国王，因此称为一世／二世）统治期间（约公元前1450年至公元前1420年）发生的事件。有一份文献由于涉及一位名为马杜瓦塔的赫梯诸侯的活动，因此被称为《马杜瓦塔的控诉》。这份文献中记录了赫梯人和一个名叫阿塔里希亚的人直接交战的细节，阿塔里希亚被称为"阿希亚的统治者"（阿希亚是阿希亚瓦一词的早期形式）。

这份文献直截了当地讲到，阿塔里希亚来到安纳托利亚西海岸与赫梯军队开战。文献中明确告诉我们，一位名叫基斯纳比利的赫梯军官率领数千名步兵和一百辆战车对抗阿希亚瓦统治者的军队。尽管文献中没有提到步兵或战车遭受的损失，但我们后续进一步了解到双方各有一名军官战死。这场战争应该比荷马所描述的特洛伊战争早了将近两百年。如果人们相信这些数字，那么对阵双方都实力雄厚，并且进行了一场真正的战争。由于在那个时代一百辆战车是一支庞大的战斗力量，因此这不是一场小规模冲突。

阿苏瓦叛乱

此外，在哈图沙考古学家发现的文献中，可能有六篇提到了在一处被称为阿苏瓦的地区（该地区唯一可能的位置在安纳托利亚西北部）发生的叛乱。这是一个由22个城邦组成的联盟，其名称最终演变为我们现代的地理名称"亚洲"。该联盟在赫梯记录中出现过，主要出现在同一个赫梯国王图达里亚一世／二世统治时期，即公元前15世纪下半叶。

当时，阿苏瓦和它的国王发动叛乱，反对赫梯人较早前建立起的对该地区的霸权。在阿苏瓦联盟的22个已知成员中，维鲁西亚是维鲁萨的别名（即特洛伊／伊利昂）。还有一个叫作塔鲁伊萨的地方，它还在另一个赫梯文献中出现过一次，但在此处紧接着维鲁西亚。曾经也有人提出塔鲁伊萨就是特洛伊，或者更有可能是特洛阿德地区。如果真是这样的话，那么在同样的特洛阿德地区就出现了这几个明显可相互替代的名称——维鲁萨／维鲁西亚和塔鲁伊萨，这与希腊人对同一地区也有可替代名称（比如伊利昂和特洛伊）的情况如出一辙。

根据赫梯人的记录，特别是人们所熟知的《图达里亚编年史》的记录，当图达里亚一世／二世正从对阿尔萨瓦、哈帕拉和赛

哈河国等位于西海岸或紧邻内陆地区的西安纳托利亚国家的战
58 斗中返回时,阿苏瓦联盟开始发动叛乱。图达里亚亲自率领军
队对抗阿苏瓦联盟并且击败了他们。上述年代史中这样记载:
一万名阿苏瓦士兵、六百匹战马和它们拉着的阿苏瓦战车,以及
大部分民众还有他们的牲畜和财产,都作为俘虏和战利品被带
回了都城哈图沙。其中包括阿苏瓦国王皮雅玛-库伦塔、他的儿
子库库里以及其他一些皇室成员。

　　这些事件实际发生的顺序尚不完全清楚,但图达里亚随后
显然任命库库里接替其父亲做了阿苏瓦国王,并允许联盟在作
为赫梯王国附属国的前提下重新建立。库库里本人随后又发动
了叛乱,但第二次反抗也以失败告终。最终,库库里被处死,阿
苏瓦联盟也被摧毁。因此,由于图达里亚一世/二世的干预,这
一联盟显然很快就消亡了,它似乎主要存在于公元前15世纪。

　　还有两点与此密切相关。首先,当一名推土机操作员于
1991年在一条通往都城哈图沙古遗址的道路上进行道路维护
时,意外发现了一把青铜剑。这把剑上刻有一行文字,是用当时
的通用语言阿卡德语写的,翻译过来就是:"当图达里亚大帝击
溃了阿苏瓦国时,他把这些剑献给了他的主人风暴之神。"

　　显然,由于这样的铭文只有在战争胜利后才会被刻在剑刃
上,因此这把剑是图达里亚在他战胜阿苏瓦后缴获并献给风暴
之神的。另外,由于我们从记录中得知图达里亚敬献了"这些
59 剑",因此也很明显,最初敬献的剑不止一把。然而最重要的是,
这不是当时安纳托利亚民众平常使用的剑,它似乎是一种仅在
公元前15世纪后期才由希腊大陆的迈锡尼人专门制作并使用的
剑。在阿苏瓦联盟叛乱期间,这把剑被人使用并缴获的事实表

明，要么迈锡尼人自己也参与了这场反对赫梯人的冲突，要么他们曾向阿苏瓦联盟提供武器并以其他方式对阿苏瓦联盟提供了支持。这提供了不同于文献证据的独特物证实例，表明迈锡尼人参与了在特洛伊周围地区发生的一场冲突，这比荷马笔下的特洛伊战争早了整整两个世纪。

维鲁萨和阿希亚瓦

此外，联盟中至少有一个城邦，具体来讲就是维鲁萨/维鲁西亚，在那场叛乱之后又继续存在了两个世纪。由于在28篇提及阿希亚瓦或者阿希亚瓦人的已知赫梯文献中，有几篇专门描述了他们与维鲁萨之间的相关活动，因此在那段时间里，维鲁萨不仅与赫梯人互动交流，而且明显与名为阿希亚瓦的政治实体以及该实体中的特定个体联系密切。如果像绝大多数学者认同的那样，把阿希亚瓦人确定为迈锡尼人是正确的，那么我们就有文献证据证明，从公元前15世纪到公元前13世纪，迈锡尼人代表维鲁萨（特洛伊）城邦参与了上述战事。

例如，在阿苏瓦叛乱中迈锡尼与维鲁萨之间的牵连可能还体现在更晚的阿希亚瓦文献中，该文献是阿希亚瓦国王在公元前13世纪初寄给赫梯国王（可能是穆瓦塔利二世）的一封信的赫梯语译本。我们知道，穆瓦塔利的统治期大约在公元前1295年至公元前1272年。这封信的部分内容与更早些的事件有关，直到不久前人们都认为是由穆瓦塔利寄给阿希亚瓦国王的，但现在已经证明这封信的邮寄路线其实正相反，这其实是阿希亚瓦国王寄给赫梯国王的极少数信件之一。

信中讨论的主要话题是安纳托利亚爱琴海沿岸的一组岛屿

60

的所有权，这些岛屿以前属于阿希亚瓦国王，但显然已被赫梯人占领。我们从这封信中可以得知，一位名叫图达里亚的赫梯国王曾在过去的某个时间打败了阿苏瓦国王并征服了他。这与较早的《图达里亚编年史》中的记载相符，毫无疑问讲述的就是阿苏瓦叛乱，所以我们知道这封信里讲的是通信前大约一百五十年所发生的事件。

这封信已经破损，内容也不完整，但现在根据新的译本来看，在阿苏瓦联盟发动叛乱之前，时任阿希亚瓦国王的曾祖父和一位阿苏瓦公主之间已经有了外交联姻，而且阿苏瓦国王还把这些岛屿作为嫁妆的一部分转让给了阿希亚瓦国王。赫梯人声称，在叛乱期间图达里亚战胜了阿苏瓦，从而使他们获得了阿苏瓦沿岸领土的所有权，但根据这封书信的作者——时任阿希亚瓦国王的说法，他们是在这些领土已经交给阿希亚瓦之后才赢得的胜利。一个半世纪后，阿希亚瓦国王寻求通过外交手段重申他对这些岛屿的权利。

这封书信的新译本表明，在公元前15世纪中叶，阿希亚瓦人和阿苏瓦人之间保持着良好的关系，而且最有趣的是，他们之间显然存在王朝联姻。如果我们的鉴定是正确的话，即阿希亚瓦人就是迈锡尼人，特洛伊人（维鲁萨人）是阿苏瓦联盟的一部分，那么这份文献就很好地说明了这两个地区之间的关系，无论是联姻还是其他关系，都比亚历山大/帕里斯和海伦之间发生不正当恋情的推测时间早了几个世纪。然而，这封信并没有明确表明迈锡尼人确实被卷入了阿苏瓦叛乱，正如之前的译本所暗示的那样，但在哈图沙发现的刻有铭文的青铜剑确实暗示了（迈锡尼人的）某种参与，以及迈锡尼和特洛伊盟军遭遇到的失败。

特洛伊战争

在安纳托利亚西海岸发现的其他阿希亚瓦文献以及陶器和手工艺品表明，在整个公元前14世纪，迈锡尼人一直与该地区保持着联系。此外，与维鲁萨明确相关的一系列文献可以追溯到公元前13世纪初期和中叶，与荷马笔下的特洛伊战争差不多属于同一时期。

《阿拉克山杜条约》和其他赫梯文献

在这些文献中，第一个文献是赛哈河国国王玛纳帕-塔胡恩塔写给赫梯国王（可能是穆瓦塔利二世）的。赛哈河国位于安纳托利亚西部，紧邻特洛阿德地区南部。这封信主要讲的是一群技术娴熟的赫梯工匠叛逃的事，但其中特别提到了赫梯人对维鲁萨的一次进攻行动："[如是说]玛纳帕-塔胡恩塔，您的仆人：对[陛下，我的主人]说：[此刻][国土上]一切都很好。[卡苏]来到（这里），带来了赫梯军队。[当]他们返回来进攻维鲁萨时，[我]病倒了。"

我们不知道穆瓦塔利和赫梯人为什么会在公元前13世纪初这个时候进攻维鲁萨。但是，随后穆瓦塔利起草并与维鲁萨的阿拉克山杜签署的这份条约大体上可追溯到公元前1280年。这份条约清楚地表明，赫梯人声称对这座城市拥有控制权，之后不久便声称对该地区拥有控制权，就和他们在扫平阿苏瓦叛乱之后所做的一样。

所谓的《阿拉克山杜条约》概述了维鲁萨人和赫梯人之间的防守联盟。穆瓦塔利在其中写道："您，阿拉克山杜，仁慈地保护着我。此后您也将保护我的儿子和我的孙子，到第一代和第二代。而我，陛下，因为您父亲的话，也将诚心诚意地保护您，阿拉克山杜,帮助您,为您消灭您的敌人,以后我的子子孙孙也一定会替您保护您的后代,到第一代和第二代。如果有敌人反对您,我不会抛弃您,就像我现在没有抛弃您一样。我会为您消灭您的敌人。"

这是条约中最令人感兴趣的部分,因为穆瓦塔利本人告诉我们,他在位(公元前1295年至公元前1272年)早期的某个时候,曾帮助阿拉克山杜消灭了他的敌人。由于穆瓦塔利没有理由说错或者记错双方都知道的这一通用信息,因此我们可以得出结论,这条信息可能是准确的。然而,问题在于阿拉克山杜的敌人是什么身份。遗憾的是,我们不知道其姓名或国籍,同时也不知道有关此事件详情的任何细节。相反,穆瓦塔利则继续重申了他们已经制定的共同防御条约。

简而言之,我们从赫梯文献中找到了证据,能够证明就在公元前1280年之前紧邻的某个时间点,维鲁萨国王阿拉克山杜至少参与了两场冲突。在其中一场冲突中,阿拉克山杜对阵一个不知姓名的敌人,且最后取得了胜利,但这只是因为穆瓦塔利和赫梯军队帮助了他。尽管这场战争与荷马所描述的特洛伊战争大体上处于同一时代,但我们不能肯定迈锡尼人就是这场冲突中的敌方。在另一场冲突中,阿拉克山杜对阵赫梯人,他被击败并被迫签署条约。这两个事件都与《伊利亚特》或《史诗集成》中告诉我们的故事不一致。因此,无论把维鲁萨的阿拉克山杜与伊利昂/特洛伊的亚历山大/帕里斯等同为一人的猜想多么有吸引力,除非我们认定荷马描述的细节有误,否则我们都没有确凿的证据能够将这些冲突和这份条约与荷马所说的特洛伊战争联系起来。

塔瓦伽拉瓦的书信

在与维鲁萨有一定关系的另外两篇阿希亚瓦文献中，所谓的塔瓦伽拉瓦书信引起了人们的极大兴趣。人们认为它是一位赫梯国王写的，可能是哈图西里三世，其统治期为公元前1267年至公元前1237年，但也可能是稍早前的统治者穆瓦塔利二世所为。我们只有这封信的第三个也可能是最后一个碑片，其内容讲述了皮亚马拉都斯的活动。皮亚马拉都斯是一个"赫梯叛徒"，与阿希亚瓦互动积极。这封信没有给出阿希亚瓦国王的名字，但确实给出了他的兄弟的名字——塔瓦伽拉瓦。塔瓦伽拉瓦显然亲自到过安纳托利亚西部，协助将当地叛军运送到阿希亚瓦领土。从弗雷尔开始，许多学者认为塔瓦伽拉瓦可能是希腊名字厄忒俄克勒斯（Eteokles，迈锡尼语拼作 E-te-wo-ke-le-we）的赫梯语表述。

在这封信中，赫梯国王试图让阿希亚瓦讲出这番话（或者刻在碑片上），要求他与某人（可能是皮亚马拉都斯）交流特定的话题。赫梯国王非常明确地说道："哦，我的兄弟，如果没有（其他事）的话，请给他写信讲这样一件事：'关于维鲁萨国土一事，赫梯国王已经说服了我，之前赫梯国王和我就此事发生了冲突，但现在我们已经讲和。现在（？）我们之间不适宜发生敌对行动。'［把这封信］发给他。"隔了几行之后，他又说道："考虑到引起我们之间发生冲突的维鲁萨问题，［因为我们已经讲和，］下一步怎么办？"

这是迄今为止破译的所有赫梯文献中仅有的一个实例，也是自图达里亚一世/二世所处时代以来的第一个实例，具体讲到

了赫梯和阿希亚瓦之间的冲突。即使在《阿拉克山杜条约》中，

阿拉克山杜的敌人也没有具体名姓，他们可能不是阿希亚瓦人。此外，我们不知道塔瓦伽拉瓦书信中所描述的那场冲突的规模。昆士兰大学的特雷沃·布莱斯指出，这篇文献中使用的那个赫梯语词汇可以翻译为"全面战争、一两次小规模冲突，或者仅仅是通过外交渠道进行的一场口水仗"。尽管如此，这可能证明在《伊利亚特》中描述的那些事件发生的前后，赫梯人和阿希亚瓦人（即迈锡尼人）之间发生了另一次冲突。

维鲁萨国王瓦尔姆

最后，与该主题相关的最后一篇参考文献是一封书信，可能是公元前13世纪后期由最后一位赫梯国王图达里亚四世（统治期为约公元前1237年至公元前1209年）所写。这封信被称为"米拉瓦塔的书信"，原因在于它主要讲述了米拉瓦塔城（米利都城）以及皮亚马拉都斯一直以来进行的活动（见表1）。

那位赫梯国王在这封信中指出，一位之前被不知名敌军驱逐出国土的名叫瓦尔姆的维鲁萨国王将被复职，但可能成为一名军事封臣。他如是写道："现在，我的儿子，只要你照顾好陛下的福祉，我，将信任您的善意。把瓦尔姆交给我，我的儿子，这样我就可以让他重新成为维鲁萨土地上的国王。现在［他将］是维鲁萨土地上的国王，就像他以前一样。他现在将成为我们的军事封臣，就像他以前一样。"由于赫梯人发誓要帮助他的后代至第一代和第二代，显然（穆瓦塔利）与阿拉克山杜签订的那个条约仍然有效。在这场最后的冲突中，叛军的袭击导致维鲁萨

国王失去了王位，而赫梯人却将王位归还给他，因此人们可能会

特洛伊战争

表 1　赫梯文献中记载的已知的特洛伊（维鲁萨）战争

事　件	维鲁萨统治者	赫梯国王	大致时间	结　局
阿苏瓦叛乱，两个阶段	皮雅玛－库伦塔和他的儿子库库里	图达里亚一世/二世	公元前 1430 年至公元前 1420 年	父亲被流放到哈图沙，儿子被处死
第一次遭敌人袭击，第二次遭赫梯人袭击	阿拉克山杜	穆瓦塔利二世	公元前 1280 年	第一次受到赫梯人的帮助，第二次被赫梯人打败
赫梯人和阿希亚瓦人在维鲁萨问题上发生冲突	未知	哈图西里三世	公元前 1267 年至公元前 1237 年	问题得到解决
遭到敌军袭击	瓦尔姆	图达里亚四世	公元前 1237 年至公元前 1209 年	被敌人废黜，但后来赫梯人将其复职

推测，这场冲突也许促成了荷马后来理解特洛伊人已经输掉战争这件事。

有这样一部《维鲁西阿德》吗？

讲到荷马和赫梯人，哈佛大学的卡尔弗特·沃特金斯于1984年在布林莫尔学院举行的关于特洛伊和特洛伊战争的会议上首次提出：某些其他赫梯文献中可能包含《维鲁西阿德》的剩余部分。他认为，这将是另一部关于特洛伊战争的史诗，但它不是从希腊人的视角写成的，而是从特洛伊人或者赫梯人的视角写成的。

《维鲁西阿德》是用卢维语写成的，这是当时安纳托利亚通用的一种语言或方言，但我们只剩下其中两行诗了。其中一行诗非常简单，它作为引语插入在赫梯典礼文献中，具体内容是："[他们歌唱：]当他们来自陡峭的维鲁萨。"这种语言风格让人想起荷马，他在《伊利亚特》中将特洛伊称为"陡峭的伊利昂"的情况不少于六次。第二行诗出现在另一部赫梯文献中，重新组织语言后可以读作："当这个人从陡峭的[维鲁萨……]走来。"

遗憾的是，目前我们除了有这两行诗外别无其他。但这种情况可能会改变，因为欧洲和美国的藏品中还有更多尚未破译的赫梯碑文正等着学者翻译。

推　测

前文所述的许多提议都是基于学术上的推测，例如将维鲁萨等同于伊利昂/特洛伊，将阿希亚瓦人等同于亚该亚人/迈锡尼人，将阿拉克山杜等同于亚历山大/帕里斯等。所有这些提议或多或少都有道理，因而其中一些提议已经被学者们争论了一个多世纪。没有一个提议全无可能，有些的可能性甚至还很高，很明显，如果一切最终被证明是错误的，我们将没有任何实质性的东西可以依仗，这当然也是一种可能。然而，目前大多数学者支持上述部分或者全部等同，尤其是阿希亚瓦人与亚该亚人之间的相关性，这使我们能够利用赫梯文献作为暗指可能存在几次特洛伊战争的文献证据。

那么在赫梯文献记载的这四场或者更多冲突中，哪一场是荷马所讲述的特洛伊战争？任何一场都是吗？从某种意义上讲，这些战争中至少有两场，也可能是全部，似乎与迈锡尼人（阿希亚瓦人）有关。然而，目前尚不确定这些冲突中的哪一场（如果有的话）是荷马和史诗诗人们所记录的特洛伊战争，或者希腊诗歌是否作为将无数事件浓缩成一系列关于这场"终结一切战争之战争"的史诗，反映了赫梯人和阿希亚瓦人（迈锡尼人）之间时断时续历时几百年的冲突。

由于仍未达成定论，我们必须求助于考古证据，这些证据表明青铜器时代曾发生过数次战争，导致被认定为古特洛伊城的希沙利克城被毁。有九座不同时期的城市遗址重叠在这个古老的土丘上，因此我们也必须思考，究竟是哪座城市（如果存在的话）由于荷马在其描述爱情与战争的宏大史诗《伊利亚特》中的记载而变得不朽。

第三部分

研究考古学证据

早期发掘者：海因里希·施里曼和威廉·德普费尔德

寻找特洛伊的故事与19世纪商人海因里希·施里曼的故事密不可分。尽管并不准确，但施里曼经常被人称为"迈锡尼考古学之父"。施里曼是一位来自德国白手起家的百万富翁，他是有史以来考古发掘中最幸运的人之一。他的一生中充满了成功的故事，因为作为一名自学成才的"业余"考古学家，他是第一个在现在大多数学者都认为可能是古代特洛伊城的遗址上进行全面发掘的人。他突破重重困难不顾一切地这样做，也违背了当时学术界的普遍看法，他们中的大多数人都坚信特洛伊战争从未发生过，因此不存在像古代特洛伊城这样的地方。施里曼还在希腊大陆的迈锡尼和梯林斯遗址成功进行了发掘，以寻找阿伽门农和他的军队。

但是，根据最近的研究，施里曼显然也是一个伪造发掘日志的无赖。无论是对特洛伊战争的专业视角还是私人生活细节方面，他都不一定可信。例如，在他的考古发掘中，他没有把功劳归于将他带到希沙利克古代特洛伊城遗址的弗兰克·卡尔弗

71

特。此外，施里曼可能完全编造了他找到"普里阿摩斯宝藏"的说法，原因在于这些发掘物既不属于普里阿摩斯，本身也不是宝藏，而是一批生产年代早于特洛伊战争一千年的珍贵工艺品。

施里曼的寻找

施里曼在四十五岁左右以百万富翁的身份从商业企业退休后，开始寻找特洛伊。他声称从七岁开始就一直等待着开始他的寻找之旅，并决心证明特洛伊战争确实发生过。他在《伊利昂：特洛伊人的城池与国家》（1881）一书的序言中详细叙述了这样一件事：1829年，他的父亲送给他一本书作为圣诞节礼物，在这本书中，他看到一幅木刻画，上面画着埃涅阿斯从熊熊燃烧的特洛伊城出逃，背着年迈的父亲，手拉着年幼的儿子。

施里曼告诉他的父亲，（木刻画上的）故事一定发生过，特洛伊一定存在，否则艺术家不可能知道如何雕刻这幅画。（这就是一个七岁孩子的逻辑和推理。）然后他告诉父亲，长大后他将找到特洛伊。这是一个精彩的自传故事，而且在提到施里曼时人们仍然经常讲述这个故事。遗憾的是，这个故事可能从未发生过。在最终发现特洛伊并向全世界宣布特洛伊战争确实发生之前，这个故事从未在施里曼的任何著作中出现过，包括他的私人日记和为其他书籍所写的序言。现在学术界普遍认为，施里曼晚年时编造了这个故事，原因只有他自己知道。

施里曼是一名成功的商人，他在克里米亚靠卖靛蓝、茶、咖啡和糖赚了一大笔钱，在1851年至1852年的加利福尼亚淘金热期间又赚了一大笔钱。正是在加利福尼亚州，他在萨克拉门托充当银行家/中间人，从矿工那里购买金粉，然后通过罗斯柴尔德家族银行在旧金山的业务代表卖给罗斯柴尔德家族银行。他低买高卖，据传还对交易进行了一些违规操作，最后从中获得了可能高达200万美元的利润。在这期间他也因为运送的金粉数量过多而受到指控，但他很可能在受到法律制裁前提早一步离开了加利福尼亚。

施里曼一生都在记日记，1851年至1852年他在美国时也不例外。遗憾的是，施里曼在这一时期记下的一些日记表明，即使是他自己随意记录的内容也不可信。例如，施里曼写道，他在1851年6月目睹了旧金山的一场大火，这一点高度可疑，原因在于这场大火实际上发生在一个月前的5月份，而当时施里曼在萨克拉门托，并没有在旧金山。加州大学戴维斯分校教授戴维·特雷尔对此进行了一番探查后表明，施里曼只是将《萨克拉门托每日联盟报》头版的一条报道逐字复制到他的日记中，再通过把自己加入其中稍微改变了一下故事内容。

伊利诺伊大学的威廉·考尔德将类似的事件统称为"编造的经历"。其他"编造的经历"可能包括1851年2月的一篇日记，施里曼在其中写道，他当时在华盛顿特区一场奢侈的接待会上与米勒德·菲尔莫尔总统聊了一个半小时。正如考尔德和特雷尔所指出的那样，尽管这并非完全办不到，但即便施里曼英语流利，总统似乎也不太可能去会见一位名不见经传的二十八岁的德国人。与那场记录旧金山火灾的日记一样，这篇日记也可能是从一篇报纸文章中摘选出来的，而施里曼把他自己加到了文章内容中。

施里曼1851年生活在萨克拉门托期间提交了一份意向声明，申请获得美国公民身份，但直到将近二十年后，即他在1869年3月下旬抵达纽约市的时候，这份申请才获批。然而，为了得到美国公民身份，施里曼不得不说服一位名叫约翰·博兰的人，让他发誓：施里曼此前在美国已经连续生活了五年，而且已经在纽约州生活了一年以上（即使这两者都不是真实的）。博兰不得不做伪证，但它奏效了。施里曼在抵达纽约仅两天后就获得了公民身份。

几天后，也就是1869年4月上旬，施里曼搬到了印第安纳州，那里当时拥有美国所有州中最宽松的离婚法。在那里，他申请与他的第一任妻子凯塔琳娜离婚，凯塔琳娜后来回到了德国。施里曼与凯塔琳娜生了三个孩子，其中有两个在童年时期幸存了下来。到6月底，他在印第安纳州已经生活了三个月，虽然按照要求需在该州住满一年才能批准离婚，但他还是收到了离婚令。最有可能的情况是，就像他在纽约州的所作所为一样，为了达到目的，他又找了一个人为他做证。

与此同时，施里曼已经开始全心致力于寻找古特洛伊城遗址，并力图证明特洛伊战争发生过。一年前的1868年，施里曼先后到访了希腊的伊塔卡和迈锡尼，然后继续前往土耳其。在那里，他考察了许多其他考古学家认为是特洛伊遗址所在地的几个古老土丘，包括名为"布纳尔巴西"和"巴利达格"的遗址，一无所获，后来施里曼与美国驻土耳其副领事弗兰克·卡尔弗特成为朋友。卡尔弗特认为他自己已经发现了特洛伊。事实上，他已经买下了古遗址的一部分——一个叫作希沙利克的土丘——并且已经挖好了几条试验坑道。卡尔弗特绝不是第一个认为希沙利克可能包含青铜器时代特洛伊遗址的人。苏格兰记者查尔斯·麦克拉伦是数个学术性地理协会的会员，他于1822年，也就是施里曼出生那年，在其出版的一本书中首次提出了这

74

个推测。卡尔弗特主动提出与施里曼联手，施里曼欣然接受了他的提议，原因在于他有钱但没有场地，而卡尔弗特有场地但没有钱。这注定是一次非常有价值的合作。

　　施里曼于1869年9月从美国回来后，即他通过不正规甚至可能是非法的方式获得美国公民身份并离婚后几个月，便与索菲亚·恩加斯特罗梅诺斯在雅典成婚。此时，他四十七岁，而她十六岁。他们有两个孩子，分别取名为安德洛玛刻和阿伽门农，这部分内容会在后面讲到。

　　1870年4月，施里曼无视他尚未获得土耳其当局的发掘许可这一事实，开始在希沙利克进行发掘。1871年，他再次在希沙利克发掘，但直到1872年，他才开始对这个土丘进行最大胆的发掘。他在这个古老土丘的正中间挖出一条大约四十五英尺深的巨大坑道，并让他的工人们尽可能快速、尽可能深入地发掘，因为他相信一座有着三千年历史的城市会被埋在地下很深的地方。他和他的搭档凿出了一层又一层的古老定居点，先是一座，然后是两座，再然后是三座城市，还有更多。最终，在他于十年后聘用的建筑师威廉·德普费尔德的帮助下，施里曼从重叠起来的众多城市中发现了遗迹。他认为这里曾有过六座城市，也可能是七座。经过一个多世纪的遗址发掘之后，人们现在很清楚地知道这里实际上总共有过九座城市，每座城市都经历了很多个阶段的建设和后期改造。当时，施里曼和德普费尔德都没有意识到会有这么多层。

特洛伊II和"普里阿摩斯宝藏"

　　施里曼确信，他所说的"焚毁之城"就是普里阿摩斯治下的特洛伊。起初他并不清楚这是在该遗址建造的第二座城市——现在所知的特洛伊 II——还是第三座城市。施里曼最初认为这是第二座城市，但在包括卡尔弗特在内的其他人的说服下，他在他的书《伊利昂》（1881）中错误地将其确定为第三座城市。仅仅一年后，即在1882年，德普费尔德便向施里曼证明他最初的想法是正确的，这确实是第二座城市，而不是第三座。不管是第几座城市，施里曼都认为这就是迈锡尼人用木马计谋花了十年时间才攻下的城市。1873年，施里曼在发掘时发现了"普里阿摩斯宝藏"，这让他更加确信他的鉴定是正确的。

　　施里曼记录了自己发现"普里阿摩斯宝藏"时的过程：5月底的一天早上，他在发掘现场周围徘徊，眼睛注视着所有工人，突然他注意到一名工人正在挖出一个巨大的铜制物体，铜制物体背后可以看到一丝金光。尽管这时还远未到早餐时间，但施里曼迅速向工人们宣布早餐时间到了。在工人们吃饭的时候，他把他的妻子叫来，"用一把大刀挖出了宝藏"（见图4）。

　　施里曼自称他和索菲亚挖出了这些器物，包括青铜器、银器以及金制器皿、珠宝和其他工艺品。根据施里曼的说法，他们这样做冒了极大的风险，因为在他们头顶上方有一个很高的土堆，随时都有可能坍塌下来砸在他们身上。索菲亚用围裙或披巾将较小的器物聚集在一起，然后把它们带进屋子，施里曼则拿着较

大的器物跟在后面。

　　进屋之后，他们快速清点了物品，发现这批宝藏包括一个铜制盾牌和一个花瓶；各种金制、银制或金银合金器皿；十三个矛头；十四把战斧；几把匕首、一把剑和其他铜制或青铜制品；以及许多金器，包括两个王冠、一个头带、六十个耳环和将近九千

特洛伊战争

图4 海因里希·施里曼展出了发现自特洛伊的"普里阿摩斯宝藏"中的
工艺品。这些工艺品最终被证明源自青铜器时代早期,而不是青铜器时代
晚期,比普里阿摩斯生活的年代早了一千年,因此不可能属于普里阿摩斯

个更小的装饰品。然后，他们把所有东西都打包装入几个大木箱，并做好安排将它们偷偷运出土耳其，穿过爱琴海运到他们在雅典的家中。当他们和宝藏都安全到达希腊后，施里曼给妻子戴上黄金首饰并拍下她的照片，然后向全世界宣布他找到了"普里阿摩斯宝藏"（见图5）。

施里曼在个人生活上的不可靠发出了一个危险信号，即我们也不太能相信他对职业生涯的记录，尤其是他在挖掘日记中记录的那些细节。现在人们已经明白，施里曼关于发现宝藏的描述中存在很多问题，首先也是最重要的，就是在施里曼发现宝藏的那天，索菲亚甚至根本不在特洛伊。根据他自己日记中的记录，索菲亚当时在雅典。后来他也承认了这一点，说他就是太想让她参与到他的生活中了，才把她写进了故事里，认为这会让她对他终生挚爱的事业更感兴趣。

最近，这份宝藏成为众多学术研究的焦点。很明显，它不可能是"普里阿摩斯宝藏"，因为施里曼确定它的发现地点位于"焚毁之城"，即特洛伊 II，而我们现在知道特洛伊 II 可以追溯到公元前2300年左右。事实上，这份宝藏中的物品与从位于东部的美索不达米亚（今伊拉克）的所谓"乌尔死亡坑"到位于西部的爱琴海利姆诺斯岛上的波利奥克尼遗址这片地区所发现的珠宝饰品十分相似。这些物品都可以追溯到大约相同的时期，就在公元前3千纪中叶之后，比特洛伊战争早了一千多年，因此不可能属于普里阿摩斯、海伦或任何与特洛伊战争有关的人。

此外，许多学者都确信施里曼编造了发现宝藏的整个故事——他不仅把本不在场的索菲亚置于现场，而且从最开始就编造了宝藏的存在。尽管人们并不怀疑施里曼确实在特洛伊找

特洛伊战争

图5　索菲亚·施里曼在雅典佩戴着"普里阿摩斯宝藏"中的珠宝进行展
示,然而这些珠宝的年代实际上比普里阿摩斯所处时代和特洛伊战争早了
一千多年

到了所有这些物品，但很有可能他不是一下子全部找到的。相反，许多人认为他可能在整个发掘时期在整个遗址上获得了一系列较小的发现，但一直推迟宣布这些发现，直到最后他积累了足够多的东西，并将它们组合成一个巨大的"宝藏"，他认为这样一经宣布必将让世界震惊。讽刺的是，如果施里曼没有错误地将这些物品标记为"普里阿摩斯宝藏"，它们就不会像今天这样具有价值，也不会像今天这样引起人们如此大的兴趣。但施里曼是个善于引起公众注意的人，他知道一旦给这些物品贴上这个标签，无论准确与否，都会将全世界的注意力吸引到他的发掘现场，以及他关于发现特洛伊城的声明上，结果证明确实如此。

最终，施里曼将"普里阿摩斯宝藏"运到了德国，并将它们在柏林博物馆进行展出，一直到第二次世界大战结束前夕。后来它们突然消失了近五十年。20世纪90年代初，俄罗斯政府才承认这些珍宝已于1945年作为战争赔款的一部分被带到了莫斯科。这些珍宝现在在普希金博物馆展出。

由于施里曼认为普里阿摩斯治下的特洛伊就是"焚毁之城"，即他在遗址上发现的九座城市中的第二座，因此他和他的工人们草率地发掘了位于上层的城市，尤其是在19世纪70年代初的时候。在1879年以及19世纪80年代的后期发掘行动中，他则更加谨慎，并经常听取学者们的建议，但仍然有很多来自这些上层以及后期城市的材料直接被丢弃。事实证明，这非常令人惋惜，因为在他生命将要结束时，德普费尔德以及他本人在希腊大陆迈锡尼和梯林斯的发现（更别提还有其他学者的观点）都让施里曼最终承认他弄错了。特洛伊II确实比他曾认定的早了一千年，特洛伊VI或特洛伊VII，即第六座或第七座城市，更有可能属于特洛伊战争时期。

施里曼最终明白了这一点，因为他在迈锡尼和梯林斯发现了与他之前在特洛伊VI和特洛伊VII发现的相同类型的迈锡尼陶器，这意味着这些地层可以追溯到青铜器时代晚期的大致同一时期。多年以来，包括弗兰克·卡尔弗特在内的其他人一直在向他和其他愿意倾听的人指明这一点。遗憾的是，为时已晚。施里曼的工人们已经摧毁或者舍弃了他一直以来在寻找的许多建筑物和物品。他没有意识到，后来的希腊人和罗马人为了建造他们自己城市的寺庙和其他建筑，已经把土丘最高的部分削平了。因此，普里阿摩斯治下的特洛伊——由于希腊化时代的希腊人和罗马人的掘土运土行动——比施里曼所猜想的更接近现代地表。

施里曼开始准备在遗址上进行新的发掘行动，但在真正开始之前，他于1890年圣诞节那天在那不勒斯一条繁忙的城市街道上昏倒，第二天便去世了。他的遗体被送往雅典，安葬在第一公墓，这是一处荣耀之所。他的坟墓上有一座希腊小神庙样式的纪念碑，上面刻有与特洛伊战争以及他在特洛伊、迈锡尼、梯林斯和其他地方发掘行动有关的各种场面，最后还附了一张施里曼手持《伊利亚特》的照片。

德普费尔德与特洛伊VI

施里曼去世后，他的建筑师威廉·德普费尔德接手了他的工作，负责希沙利克的发掘，部分资金由索菲亚·施里曼提供。他分别在1893年和1894年进行了两次发掘，这次重点是特洛伊第六座城的废墟。特洛伊VI首次建于公元前1700年前后，其后经历了多次整修和至少八个子阶段,后来被考古学家发现并以字母"a"至"h"标注,直到几百年后最终被摧毁。

虽然施里曼在希沙利克发掘了城堡的大部分核心区域,但他并未触及城堡外缘,而德普费尔德正是把绝大部分时间、金钱和精力都花在了寻找外缘上。当他在特洛伊Ⅵ城堡周围发现了一堵巨大的防御墙时,他的付出得到了回报。这堵防御墙由精心打造的石灰岩制成,与荷马英雄史诗里的描述很相配。

德普费尔德发掘出了三百码长的墙体、入口大门和一座仍然矗立的二十五英尺高的瞭望塔。今天,人们在参观希沙利克/特洛伊城遗址的时候,可以看到这些防御工事的遗迹(见图6)。虽然荷马可能混淆了城堡内墙和城市外墙,但他在《伊利亚特》中对这些防御工事做了相对准确的描述,包括在描写帕特洛克罗斯试图爬上城墙时提及的"夹角"或"斜坡"(《伊利亚特》XVI:702—703)。

这座城市的最终版本特洛伊Ⅵh最令人印象深刻,城堡周围不仅有高墙和石塔,大型房屋和宫殿也为内城增光添彩了不少。这是一座富裕的城市,一处兵家必争之地,它控制着连接爱琴海和黑海的通道——达达尼尔海峡,并且通过贸易和税收变得更加富有。在此期间的某些特定阶段,尽管可能无法与迈锡尼本身相媲美,但它的财富和对外交往程度可能已经能媲美较大的迈锡尼王室。达达尼尔海峡的风向和水流经常给希望航行到黑海的船只带来不利条件,因此这些船只可能会被迫在此停留,有时会连续停留数周,直到天气变得有利于航行为止。特洛伊城及附近位于比斯克山丘的港口设施将接待这些船只的船员

和乘客,不管他们是商人、外交官还是战士。

特洛伊战争

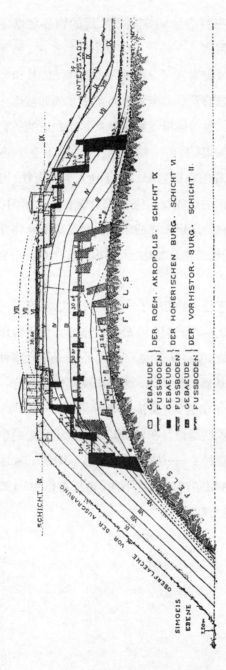

图 6 这是一张特洛伊城的断面示意图，根据威廉·德普费尔德的说法，它展示了层叠起来的九座主要城市。土丘顶部的虚线显示了希腊化时代的希腊人和罗马人把土丘顶部削去的部分，这清除了一些青铜器时代的材料，从而导致施里曼错误地估计了普里阿摩斯阿冶下特洛伊所处的地层

考古学家们在特洛伊 VI 废墟中发现的物品足以证明这座城市曾经拥有的财富。在施里曼去世后的数年里，德普费尔德经过认真的考古发掘发现了从美索不达米亚、埃及和塞浦路斯进口的物品。后来的发掘者卡尔·布雷根和曼弗雷德·考夫曼也对此有所发现。包括施里曼和德普费尔德在内的所有发掘者都发现了迈锡尼陶器，其中尤以德普费尔德发现的为多。在特洛伊 VI 中发现这样的迈锡尼物品似乎让人感到奇怪，因为阿伽门农和他的战士们对这座城市进行了可能长达十年的围攻，但事实是迈锡尼人和特洛伊人在战争之前曾是贸易伙伴并且关系友好，甚至荷马的说法也是如此，人们想到这一点就不会觉得奇怪了。

德普费尔德发现，在经历了一系列时期以及数百年来持续不断的人类居住之后，特洛伊 VI 最终被摧毁。他相信迈锡尼人已经占领了这座城市，将其夷为了平地，而正是这一事件构成了荷马史诗传说的基础。他认为，这一发现将结束争论。德普费尔德在他于 1902 年出版的《特洛伊和伊利昂》一书中写道："长期以来关于特洛伊城是否存在以及其遗址位于何处的争论已经结束。特洛伊人胜利了……施里曼已经被证明是正确的。"

然而，与德普费尔德的观点不同，造成特洛伊 VI 毁灭的可能不是人类，而是大自然。

重返希沙利克：卡尔·布雷根和曼弗雷德·考夫曼

1932年，卡尔·布雷根代表辛辛那提大学开始在希沙利克启动发掘工作，此时距离德普费尔德发表关于"长期争论已终结"的言论已经过去了三十年。在此期间，没有人在这座山丘进行过发掘。这种空档期在全世界的著名考古发掘场地都不罕见，因为持续发掘需要大量的投入、资金和准备。此外，为从有关部门获得必要的许可，通常还需要进行数月或数年的谈判，尤其是对于人们认为特别重要的考古场地，这些部门不会轻易授予此类许可。

布雷根不同意德普费尔德将特洛伊VI认定为普里阿摩斯治下的特洛伊。他相信有无可争辩的证据表明，最后阶段的特洛伊VI不是被人类而是被大自然所摧毁，其原因具体而言就是一场地震。布雷根倾向于认为，特洛伊VI之后的一座城市特洛伊VIIa才是普里阿摩斯治下的特洛伊。

布雷根出版了一本半通俗的书《特洛伊与特洛伊人》（1963），其中描述了他的发掘团队在重新调查特洛伊VI各个时期时在发掘现场发现的情况。尽管这座山丘的整个顶部在希腊化时代和罗马时代因为修建雅典娜神庙而被削平，并且幸存下来的很少一部分器物后来也被施里曼清除，但沿着边缘，他们发现未被移动的沉积物仍然存在，有十五到十八英尺（五到六米）深，就在防御墙内。在这个他所谓的"硕大堆积物"中，是从特洛伊VIa到VIh的八个连续地层（见图7）。

布雷根发现这八个地层包含了特洛伊VI的整个历史，其中没有文化断裂的痕迹，这意味着当地居民在几个世纪里没有受到外来干扰的情况下，重新组织并改造了他们的城市。虽然陶器就像建筑物一样会随着时间的推移而改变，但总体而言，很明显一代又一代的特洛伊人曾在这座城市里生活过。虽然这里也曾遭到一些轻微的破坏和干扰，比如考古人员在公元前15世纪

图7　特洛伊 I 至 IX 的平面图，展示了埋在古老的希沙利克的山丘下各座城市所处的不同地层。为了展示得更清楚，图中将特洛伊 VI 单独放大了

特洛伊战争

末或公元前14世纪初的VIf时期发现了那时火灾的遗迹，但总体来说，文化连续性贯穿特洛伊VI的整个时期，这意味着当时没有出现新居民或侵略者的大规模介入。

虽然这座城市历史的下一个时期被考古学家们称为特洛伊VIIa，但它也与前一座城市显示出了类似的文化连续性。事实上，德普费尔德和布雷根都认为，这并不是一座真正意义上的新城市——它只是修复城墙和房屋之后的特洛伊VIh的重建版。1932年至1938年布雷根在现场发掘期间，德普费尔德还于1935年提议，特洛伊VIIa实际上应该称作特洛伊VIi，它是这座城市的第九个时期，而不是一座新城市的第一个时期。然而，正如布雷根所说，虽然这"肯定与观察到的事实相符……但我们还是保留了既定的术语，以免让那些早已熟悉它的人感到困惑"。在布雷根发掘行动的五十年后，曼弗雷德·考夫曼再次到现场进行发掘，他发表了类似的评论："应该注意到，德普费尔德已经指出了这一点，由于与前一时期存在高度相似性，因此VIIa时期确实应该作为特洛伊VIi划分到特洛伊VI……基于最近的发现，我们也更倾向于这种划分。"

地震的证据

在很多情况下，布雷根都与德普费尔德观点相同，包括该遗址是在特洛伊VIh末期被摧毁的，因为他的发掘也提供了大规模火灾和破坏的证据。但他在这座城市如何被摧毁以及为何被摧毁这个问题上持不同观点。根据布雷根的说法，这里没有入侵者的迹象，没有出现新类型的陶器，也没有发生可能表明这座城市已被迈锡尼人或其他任何人摧毁的重大变故。

在特洛伊VIIa中甚至还发现了迈锡尼陶器,其中大部分是由特洛伊人或当地迈锡尼人制作的仿制品,这无法证明迈锡尼人在特洛伊VI末期是否已经彻底摧毁了这座城市并将其付之一炬,就像荷马所描述的那样。相反,似乎当时迈锡尼人仍在与特洛伊人进行贸易,或者至少在特洛伊VIIa时期的很长一段时间(持续超过一个世纪)里,迈锡尼人与特洛伊人仍然保持着联系。所有这一切都向布雷根表明,当地居民——特洛伊VI时期最后一座城市被摧毁之后的幸存者——只是重建了这座城市并继续生活了下去,开启了这座长寿第六城的下一个时期。四百多年来,人们建成了这座城市,并且在一系列不同的历史时期不断地对它进行重建。

因此,虽然德普费尔德认为迈锡尼人已经占领了特洛伊VIh并将其焚毁,而且正是这一事件构成了荷马史诗传说的基础,但由于注意到了特洛伊VIh和特洛伊VIIa之间的连续性,布雷根礼貌地表达了不同意见。他认为特洛伊VIh是被地震摧毁的,而非人类。如果是这样的话,这将不是第一次(地震),因为有证据表明较早期的城市——特洛伊III、特洛伊IV和特洛伊V——也都遭遇过地震破坏。此外,众所周知,希沙利克遗址就坐落于北安纳托利亚大断层线附近。20世纪90年代后期出现的摧毁该地区的大地震表明,这个区域的地震活动目前依然活跃。

布雷根提供的证据能够支持他关于特洛伊VIh被地震摧毁的假设——发掘现场可见被震得凹凸不平的墙壁以及倒塌的巨大塔楼,到处都是受过巨大外力和剧变的迹象(见图8)。正如他在发掘队发布的最终报告中指出的那样:"我们确信可以将这场灾难归咎于一场严重的地震……关于城墙的倒塌,强烈的地

图8 这是20世纪30年代卡尔·布雷根在发掘特洛伊VI期间拍摄的一张照片，其中倒塌的石块和受损的墙壁表明此处可能受过地震破坏

震冲击比任何可能的人类行为都更有说服力。"一位受人尊敬的地质考古学家后来进行了重新调查，他同意布雷根的结论，认为"辛辛那提挖掘人员提供的证据……似乎无懈可击"。

88

一些学者争辩说，迈锡尼人可能利用了袭击特洛伊的这次地震，并且他们可能通过突遭毁坏而倒塌的城墙进入了城内。这反过来又引起了鉴定上的问题，因为虽然特洛伊VI在许多方面都符合荷马的描述——它的城墙足够高大，它的房屋足够宏伟，它的街道足够宽阔，它足够富有——但荷马却丝毫没有提到过地震。

下面再来讨论特洛伊木马。尽管有不少学者认为特洛伊木马实际上是攻城槌或其他某种战争机器，但德国院士弗里茨·沙赫迈尔提出，特洛伊木马不是战争机器，而是地震的诗意隐喻。他的推理很简单：波塞冬是希腊地震之神，而波塞冬的象征物通常是一匹马（就像雅典娜的象征物是猫头鹰一样）。根据古希腊人的说法，在拉着坐在战车上的波塞冬的时候，马蹄踏地的声响不仅产生了海浪的撞击声，而且产生了与地震如影相随的巨响。因此，特洛伊木马可能是荷马描绘波塞冬为夷平特

洛伊城墙而引起地震的方式。从字面上理解，特洛伊木马指的就是地震，但这只是比喻性的说法。这是一个巧妙的提议，但可能有点牵强。但如果我们把自己放在荷马的位置上，这是在不完全改变这座城市真正历史结局的情况下结束故事的唯一方法。此外，如果人们希望特洛伊VI成为普里阿摩斯治下的特洛伊，那么没有其他方法可以解释，为什么这座城市除了其毁灭方式之外在各方面都符合荷马的描述。

重新定代和再次利用

近期，对在特洛伊VIh地层中发现的进口及本地迈锡尼陶器进行的重新调查，重新确定了这座城市的毁灭年代。布雷根起初将这些陶器所处的年代确定为公元前1275年前后，但后来的学者对这个时间界定争论不休，有些人甚至认为它最晚可能追溯到公元前1130年至公元前1100年。这项新研究由佩内洛普·芒乔伊在20世纪90年代完成。佩内洛普·芒乔伊是一位备受尊敬的学者、多部有关迈锡尼陶器的权威著作的作者，同时也是几十年来首位有能力处理和重新调查布雷根发现的所有陶片的人。她在她内容详细的论文中得出这样的结论：特洛伊VIh被摧毁的时间最可能在公元前1300年前后。她还与布雷根持相同的观点，即特洛伊VIh的命运可能因地震而终结，而与阿伽门农或迈锡尼人无关。

布雷根注意到，特洛伊VIh城堡内存在许多大型富丽房屋的废墟，其中有一部分被立即重建并在特洛伊VIIa中重新使用，但现在有许多隔断墙把这些房屋的内部进一步细分，就好像许多家庭生活在此前单一家庭居住的地方；另一部分被再次利用，当地居民借助被毁坏的精美房屋的墙柱，在原址上建造起破烂不堪的茅舍和房屋。同时还有其他线索也让他认为这座防御严密的城堡的人口突然之间增长了许多倍。在他看来，这次人口爆炸的一个主要迹象是许多储物罐，也即用于存放酒、油和粮食的大口陶瓷坛——不仅存在于房屋内，有的还埋在地面以下，因此只能看到和触及它们的顶部。通过埋藏这些罐子，当地居民能够在不具备冷藏条件的时代让一些易腐烂变质的物品保存在低温环境中，与此同时，他们还能够将谷物、葡萄酒、橄榄油和其他生活必需品的整体存储容量增加至原来的两倍甚至三倍。

特洛伊VIIa的毁灭

布雷根确信他正在发掘一座曾经被围困的城市。当时，面对不断迫近的敌军，来自贫民区以及周围村庄的居民像潮水一样涌入了这座富裕的城镇要塞。他认为他的怀疑得到了证实，因为他在城堡内的街道上发现了人体骨骼或未埋葬的部分尸体，他还发现了箭头，确切说来是爱琴海地区制造的箭头，以及火灾和房屋被焚毁的证据，这些都让他相信特洛伊VIIa是被战争摧毁的。他和他的发掘队同事在最终报告中写道，特洛伊VIIa的废墟上"到处都有被焚毁的痕迹"，"在VIIa定居点被火烧过的废墟中发现的散落的人体骨骼残骸无疑可以表明，它的毁坏过程中伴随着暴力（见图9）。几乎不需要

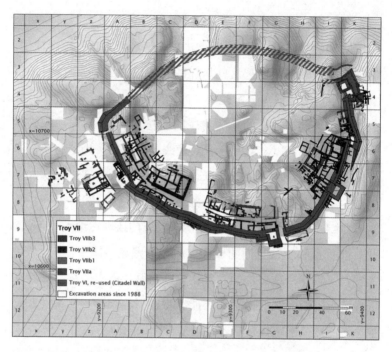

图9　这是一张特洛伊VIIa的平面图。曼弗雷德·考夫曼1988年至2005年间在该遗址牵头开展发掘的情况显示，特洛伊VIIa重复利用了特洛伊VI的城墙

　想象力就能明白这里反映出的信息，一座古老城镇惨遭死敌占领和洗劫的命运"。

　　布雷根说，很明显，迈锡尼人付之一炬的是特洛伊VIIa，而不是特洛伊VIh。基于他对陶器的年代测定，以及希望将这一地层与特洛伊战争联系起来的愿望，他把这座城市的毁灭年代确定为大约公元前1260年至公元前1240年。他知道，如果迈锡尼人像荷马所描述的那样卷入了特洛伊战争，他们就必须在自己的文明受到攻击，自己在希腊大陆上的宫殿遭摧毁之前参与其中。在某些地方，这开始于公元前1225年。在他1963年出版的

《特洛伊与特洛伊人》一书中，布雷根总结道："被火烧黑的定居点废墟生动地描绘了一个被死敌围攻、占领和劫掠的城镇经常遭受的残酷命运，就像荷马史诗中对四处劫掠的远征军所描述的那样。"

在确信特洛伊VIIa就是普里阿摩斯治下的特洛伊之后，布雷根又着重强调了下一座城市，这座城市直接建在灰烬和废墟上，此前的考古发掘人员已经将其标记为特洛伊VIIb。布雷根能够将其细分为两个独立的时期——VIIb$_1$和VIIb$_2$。这两个子时期中的第一个——特洛伊VIIb$_1$，与特洛伊VIIa相似度很高，因此布雷根断定，这可以证明"以某种方式逃脱了那场将特洛伊VIIa城堡付之一炬的幸存者们，马上又再次占领了这座城堡"。事实上，他一度再次写道："假如我们可以完全随心所欲地修改德普费尔德对遗址上地层的编号，我们应当认识到特洛伊VIIa和特洛伊VIIb$_1$之间的文化联系，从而将其分别命名为特洛伊VIi和特洛伊VIj，这才更为恰当。"根据布雷根的说法，这个子时期持续了大约一代人的时间，但他不清楚是什么导致它在公元前1150年走向终结，因为他没有发现任何暴力迹象，没有火灾，没有劫掠，VIIb$_1$城也没有陷落。布雷根将其视为未解之谜，没有继续研究。

这两个子时期中的第二个——特洛伊VIIb$_2$，与之前发生的一切完全不同。由于它是如此与众不同，所以如果可以的话，布雷根宁愿将其称为特洛伊VIII。特洛伊VIIb$_2$不只是同一座城市的第二个时期那么简单，因为在这个时期，城市的规划完全改变了，房屋结构与以前不同，陶器也焕然一新。特洛伊VIIb$_2$的居民也与此前全然不同，就好像特洛伊VIIb$_1$的先前居住者全部消

92

失了一样。这个子时期持续了两到三代人的时间，然后这座城市在公元前1100年前后再次被摧毁，原因可能是敌人的攻击或另一场地震。在这之后，特洛伊废弃了几个世纪，最终从公元前700年前后的铁器时代开始才又有人居住，然后一直持续到罗马时期以及之后。

有关布雷根解读的一些问题

那么，布雷根最终解开了这个谜团并且确定了发生特洛伊战争的那座城市吗？特洛伊战争真的发生在特洛伊VIIa吗？他的鉴定存在几个问题。一方面，特洛伊VIIa不符合荷马的描述——在荷马笔下，这是一座富裕的城市，拥有高耸的城门、高大的城墙、宽阔的街道、大房子和宏伟的宫殿。而布雷根发掘出的是一座经过重建的贫穷城市，大型房屋被隔断墙分割，地下还埋有储物罐。布雷根认为这是一座被围困的城市；佩内洛普·芒乔伊最近则表示，这只是一座试图从毁灭性的地震中逐步恢复的城市，（人们）在废墟中匆忙建造了用于临时居住的房屋。无论如何，这都不是一座需要花费十年时间才能攻克的城市，更不是一座值得书写史诗的城市。事实上，特洛伊VIIa与荷马史诗唯一相匹配的地方就是它被摧毁的方式——一场蓄意制造的战争。也许荷马在书写宏伟的特洛伊VI城的同时，也在书写特洛伊VIIa城的毁灭——换言之，借助诗人的自由发挥，把历史事件压缩，从而创造一部宏大的史诗传说。但这只是一种可能的情况。

此外，在过去的半个世纪里，布雷根对特洛伊VIIa被毁年代的认定多次受到质疑，这些质疑总是基于考古发掘人员在定

93

居点发现的陶器。一些学者据此认为，特洛伊VIIa被毁的年代至晚可以确定为公元前1050年。最近，芒乔伊基于她自己对那些陶器的重新分析，将上述年代重新确定为公元前13世纪的最后几十年到公元前12世纪的头几十年，大约在公元前1230年至公元前1190/1180年之间。除非希腊大陆上迈锡尼人的宫殿正是因为他们所有的战士都在特洛伊参加战斗而遭到袭击并被摧毁，否则可能很难解释为何迈锡尼人应对这座城市的毁灭负责。事实上，芒乔伊认为，不是迈锡尼人摧毁了特洛伊VIIa，而是海上民族摧毁了它。她认为，迈锡尼人摧毁的城市是更晚期的特洛伊VIIb$_2$城，这场战争发生在约公元前1100年。不过，由于后一种说法在时间上过于靠后，因此不太可能。

为了造成更大规模的破坏，海上民族选择在这个时候进攻和摧毁特洛伊VIIa城当然合适。有些人推断，这座遭受重创的城市的幸存者在随后的行动中加入了海上民族的行列。然而，尚不清楚海上民族是否真的袭击了特洛伊，因此特洛伊VIIa的破坏者的身份仍然是一个悬而未决的问题，对于特洛伊VIIb$_1$和特洛伊VIIb$_2$而言也是如此。

考夫曼在特洛伊的发掘

布雷根在特洛伊的发掘工作结束整整五十年后，下一个发掘小组在1988年启动了工作。该小组由德国图宾根大学的曼弗雷德·考夫曼领导，他对调查该遗址的青铜器时代地层十分有兴趣。通过与考夫曼协作，对遗址后青铜器时代地层（希腊化时代和罗马时代的遗迹）的调查也重获启动，第一位负责人是布林莫尔学院的斯特拉·米勒，之后是辛辛那提大学的布莱恩·罗斯。

考夫曼和他的青铜器时代团队首先对山丘中心的早期青铜器时代遗迹重新进行了彻底的调查，并首次在发掘现场收集了所有时期的放射性碳样本。后来，他们主要关心的是重新调查特洛伊VI和特洛伊VII这两座城市，希望确定这两座城市的规模，青铜器时代晚期那里的生活是什么样的，以及这两座城市究竟发生了什么，以至于它们其中一个遭遇了戏剧性的结局。

考夫曼坚称他不是在调查特洛伊战争，也根本没有兴趣证明或反驳这个传说，而是在调查一座非常有意思的青铜器时代晚期城市。这个城邦与其他国家有着广泛联系，并且在公元前2千纪末期是该地区的一个强国。然而，到2001年，考夫曼确信他正在发掘的城市（他用德语称之为特罗亚）无疑就是赫梯人称为维鲁萨的那座城市。从那时起，他的发掘报告就把该遗址称作特罗亚/维鲁萨，这一认定已为许多其他学者所接受。

考夫曼和他的团队借助出色的发掘技术和高科技设备获得95 了许多发现。一方面，他们发现并确定了另一个子时期——特洛伊VIIb$_3$，它持续了近一个世纪，并在该遗址被废弃数百年之前的公元前1000年左右走向终结，原因尚不明确。

他们还在该遗址发现了第一份手写笔迹材料——一枚在两侧都刻有铭文的双凸型青铜印章。这枚印章于1995年在VIIb$_2$地层发现，年代可追溯至约公元前1100年，其中一面刻着男人的名字，另一面刻着女人的名字，并有迹象表明该男子可能是一名抄写员。

贫民区

迄今为止，他们最重要的当然也是最大的发现，是在1988年项目开始后不久获得的。几年之内，考夫曼和他的团队确信他们通过遥感设备已经查明这里存在一个规模宏大的贫民区，从实际的希沙利克的山丘向南延伸超过一千三百英尺（四百米）。这一发现使特洛伊城的规模和人口比之前猜测的增加了十到十五倍。它还清楚地表明，青铜器时代晚期的特洛伊确实是一座富裕繁荣的城市，占地面积五十到七十五英亩（二十万到三十万平方米），居民人口约四千人到一万人。此次调查持续了十几年的时间，一直到2005年，考古学家才得以确认希沙利克的山丘周围几乎所有的土地都覆盖在整个贫民区之上，包括可追溯到特洛伊VI和特洛伊VIIa时期的地层，以及后来位于这些地层之上，按照既定的南北/东西方网格布局的希腊化时代和罗马时代的废墟。事实上，后期的遗迹完全覆盖了青铜器时代贫民区的遗迹。它们"保存不善"，并且"挖掘起来很困难，只能一小块一小块地挖"，一位考察队员如是说。

考夫曼团队使用了几种不同类型的磁力计，这是一种很受欢迎的遥感设备，因为它能让考古学家在开始发掘之前就观察

表2　希沙利克/特洛伊地层年表（约公元前1300年至公元前1000年）

遗址地层	大概的结束日期	可能的毁灭原因	结　局
特洛伊 VIh	公元前1300年	地震	延续/重建
特洛伊 VIIa	公元前1230年至公元前1190/1180年	敌人袭击	延续/重建
特洛伊 VIIb₁	公元前1150年	不明	引入新文化
特洛伊 VIIb₂	公元前1100年	地震或敌人袭击	延续/重建
特洛伊 VIIb₃	公元前1000年	不明	废弃了数个世纪

到地下的情况。通过在特定点测量预定发掘区域内的局部磁场强度，该团队能够创建地下图像：根据局部磁场的变化确定地下是墙、沟渠或者什么都没有。随后开展的实际发掘旨在核实最初遥感设备发现的东西。

很明显，施里曼、德普费尔德和布雷根一直在发掘宫殿所在的城堡或这座城市的富人区，其规模仅为656英尺乘656英尺（200米乘200米）。回想起来，特洛伊有一处贫民区不足为奇，因为当代迈锡尼的大部分宫殿遗址都有一个城堡和一个贫民区。但是，考夫曼和他的团队是用现代科学设备和一些有根据的猜测找到的特洛伊的贫民区。

这项技术，或者至少是对它的解读，并不绝对可靠，考夫曼和他的团队就曾被引入歧途。1993年2月，他们大张旗鼓地宣布，他们的遥感设备已经表明地下深处存在某种东西，它是环绕着距离城堡一千多英尺远的贫民区。该团队将他们的发现解读为一堵巨大的防御墙。当时，这成为世界各地的头条新闻。然而，在那年夏天进行发掘时，人们发现它根本不是防御墙，而是一条大型防御壕。这条防御壕的年代可追溯到特洛伊 VI 时期，它切入基岩，深度在三到六英尺（一到二米），宽度达十三英尺（四米）。几千年来，这条壕沟内已经填满了泥土和垃圾，因此在他们的扫描仪中显示为一个固体块状物，他们最初将其误解为一堵墙。

在发现这条防御壕之后的头两年（1993年和1994年）中，该团队探测出这条沟渠的长度达一千多英尺，后来发现了一个三十英尺（十米）宽的大门。他们还发现有两条这样的防御壕，其中一条距离城堡更远，使用时间也更晚，这显然是在特洛伊 VI

后期人口向外扩张的结果。每个防御壕后面可能还有一个木栅栏或者高篱笆，但早已瓦解。考古学家们还能够追踪到城堡周围巨大的特洛伊VI石墙的遗迹，这是由德普费尔德首次发现，暴露出的部分比之前发掘人员发现的还要多。

1997年至2001年间，考夫曼团队还完整发掘了所谓的"泉洞"——一套由相互连接的人造隧道、竖井和水平巷道共同组成的刻入原生岩石中的给水系统。它位于城堡的城墙外，贫民区的西南部。主隧道在重新发掘期间就已经被发现，但由于在隧道入口和入口附近处有鱼塘和其他建筑的遗迹，因此人们认为它可以追溯到罗马时代。前面的这些遗迹确实可以追溯到罗马时代，但到2001年，考夫曼和他的团队已经能够将隧道系统的建造年代追溯到公元前3千纪的青铜器时代早期，并表明它已经使用差不多有两千年了。这对考夫曼来说极为重要，尤其是从把希沙利克/特洛伊与赫梯文献记录中已知的维鲁萨城联系起来这个角度看，因为这可能就是《阿拉克山杜条约》中提到的"维鲁萨国中的地下河道"。

考夫曼和特洛伊VIIa

同之前的布雷根和德普费尔德一样，考夫曼竭力说明特洛伊VIh和特洛伊VIIa之间不存在文化断裂。考夫曼与先行者的不同之处在于，他认为特洛伊VIIa（或特洛伊VIi）已经持续存在了一个多世纪。考夫曼援引佩内洛普·芒乔伊和她对迈锡尼陶器的重新调查，宣称特洛伊VIIa肇始于约公元前1300年，并在经过了几个建造时期后"由于受到战争的破坏"而终结于约公元前1180年。

早在 1995 年，考夫曼就在贫民区发现了表明特洛伊 VIIa 时期已经在火灾和战争中终结的证据，这是他最引人注目的发现之一。正如他在一份初步报告中所指出的那样，他们的发掘表明，城堡山丘西南部有一处年代可以追溯到特洛伊 VIIa 末期的被烧毁的地层，他们认为这是由"一场军事行动"所致。后来，他在大众杂志《考古学》中指出，他们在该地区发现了一些骨架和"成堆的投石器投掷的石弹"，最终显示其中包含一座带有储藏室的大型庭院式住宅的遗迹。有趣的是，在这座特洛伊 VIIa 时期庭院式住宅的正下方是一座特洛伊 VIh 时期的建筑，这座建筑在考夫曼看来也因地震而被完全烧毁。因此，在这样一个单独的小区域内，考夫曼就发现了一处被敌人行动摧毁的特洛伊 VIIa 时期建筑层叠在一处被地震摧毁的特洛伊 VIh 时期建筑上的证据。

多年来，考夫曼团队在贫民区发现了青铜箭头，至少一具未掩埋的年轻女孩尸体的骨架，以及几堆供防御者即时使用的投石器石弹（见图 10）。他的一名团队成员将这种场景描述为一场输掉的战争，事实上，至少对考夫曼来说，所有这些都是城市遭到敌军进攻的明确证据。他曾经在 2004 年播出的一部英国广播公司纪录片中宣布："现有证据显示（那座城市）遭遇了一场火灾，那里有很多人体骨架，比如说我们发现了一个十六七岁女孩的尸体骨架半埋在土中，她的脚被火烧伤了。令人感到奇怪的是，这次快速掩埋竟然发生在城市内的公共空间……我们还发现了成堆的投石器石弹……这是一座被围攻的城市，同时城中也在进行防御抵抗。他们输掉了战争，显然他们被打败了。"然而，考夫曼没有具体说明他认为破坏是由谁造成的，也没有对

99

特洛伊战争

图10 在特洛伊贫民区的特洛伊VIIa地层中发现的箭头表明，该城市在战斗中被敌军摧毁

迈锡尼文明当时处于强势阶段这一事实做出评论。　　　　　　100

　　事实上，人们完全不清楚到底是谁摧毁了贫民区。迈锡尼人可能使用这种青铜箭头，但是海上民族或其他人也完全有可能使用这种青铜箭头。如果像考夫曼所指出的那样，导致这座城市被毁的事件最晚可以追溯到公元前1180年，那么这次毁灭既有可能与迈锡尼人有关，也很可能与拉美西斯三世时期海上民族的第二次入侵有关。不过，这种年代测定是基于芒乔伊分析迈锡尼陶器得出的最新可能日期,因此根据同一项研究,这次袭击很可能早在几十年前就发生了。如果真是这样,那么这次被毁可能与赫梯泥板中记录的维鲁萨国王瓦尔姆最初被推翻有关,并且终究可能牵扯到迈锡尼人。然而,这个假设很大程度上是基于推测。

一场新的特洛伊战争

尽管尚不清楚特洛伊VIIa是被迈锡尼人还是被其他人摧毁的,但考夫曼的新发现可能最终会为特洛伊战争这个问题找到答案。他的数据同大多数考古学家的数据一样,仍然需要解释。在这一方面,考夫曼的工作已经受到了抨击,质疑者出人意料,正是他在图宾根大学的同事——弗兰克·库伯。

从2001年夏天开始,一场有关特洛伊的大型展览在斯图加特开幕,然后巡回到不伦瑞克,最后到了波恩。在这场大型展览期间,库伯指责考夫曼在特洛伊发掘过程中夸大其词,做出误导性声明并开展劣质学术研究。库伯声称特洛伊没有贫民区,贫民区和在基岩上凿出的防御壕都是考夫曼凭空想象出来的,旨在欺骗公众。

这种争论越来越激烈,最终导致该大学在2002年2月举行了一场为期两天的会议——这近乎一次模拟审判。每天有八百多人参加会议,第二天的三小时一般性讨论通过广播向德国大部分地区的热情观众进行现场直播。六十多名记者报道了整个过程。据其中一位记者称,这场会议最终以考夫曼和库伯之间的斗殴结束,这位记者将其称作"一场不合时宜的互殴",但最终裁决支持考夫曼和他对特洛伊的解释。此后不久,一些参加会议的青铜器时代专家撰写了一篇篇幅很长的重新评估报告，对考夫曼及其对特洛伊的解释提供了支持。然而，库伯并没有放弃抗争，这场争论在学术期刊上还在继续。

2005年8月，考夫曼突然去世。随着他的去世，特洛伊、图宾根、谢菲尔德及其他地方的考夫曼的同行接过了他未竟的事业。图宾根大学一直继续着在特洛伊进行的青铜器时代发掘工作，在2005年夏天首先由考夫曼能力十足的副手彼得·雅布隆卡负责，此后由考夫曼的多年同事恩斯特·佩尼卡负责。

后 记

　　最后，关于特洛伊战争，我们知道什么，我们又相信什么？荷马所描述的是发生在青铜器时代末期的一次真实历史事件，还是迈锡尼人在他们自己的文明崩溃前，在安纳托利亚海岸发动的最后一场冲突？在遥远的过去以及最近，人们已经创作了很多关于特洛伊和特洛伊战争的文章。有人声称特洛伊位于英格兰、斯堪的纳维亚半岛甚至是土耳其的奇里乞亚，也有人声称这个传说实际上是亚特兰蒂斯传说的混乱版本，甚至在最近几年有些人竟然把不着边际的奇特想法写成了书籍出版。学者们自己仍在争论荷马和特洛伊战争的历史真实性，有人说荷马史诗应该被视作纯粹的幻想作品，但也有人说"特洛伊战争主题……可能是公元前8世纪凭空捏造出来的"，这种说法令人难以置信。

　　有两个问题仍然至关重要。安纳托利亚西北部是否真的发生过一场战争，而后荷马据此写成了《伊利亚特》？我们是否已经发掘过普里阿摩斯治下的特洛伊城曾经矗立的地方？撇开老

103

爱唱反调的人不说，大多数学者都会同意这两个问题的答案都是肯定的，但这只是在一定程度上的肯定。提供明确答案所面临的难题不在于我们拥有的数据太少，而在于我们拥有的数据太多。古希腊史诗、赫梯语记录、卢维语诗歌和考古遗迹提供的证据表明，特洛伊战争不止发生过一次，而是多次，这些战争发生在我们称为特洛伊和特洛阿德的地区。因此，有关荷马笔下特洛伊战争的证据既令人向往又模棱两可。在这方面，没有"确凿的证据"。

到底有多少场战争？

根据希腊文献证据，至少发生了两场特洛伊战争（一场由赫拉克勒斯发起，另一场由阿伽门农发起），而不是一场。事实上，如果算上阿伽门农早些时候对铁乌特拉尼亚进行的那次未遂的攻击，一共发生了三场战争。然而，根据赫梯文献证据，从公元前15世纪后期的阿苏瓦叛乱到公元前13世纪后期维鲁萨国王瓦尔姆被推翻，这期间至少发生了四场特洛伊战争。此外，根据考古证据，在公元前1300年到公元前1000年之间，特洛伊/希沙利克的三次毁灭中至少有两次是由人为引起。其中一些情况人们早已知晓，而其余内容直到最近才为人们所知。

遗憾的是，这些单个事件中没有一个可以确定地说与另一个事件相关联。例如，人们会认为，在相关赫梯记录中看到的瓦尔姆被推翻事件会在特洛伊VIIa的毁灭中有所反映，但我们不能完全自信地说这两者肯定有联系。

然而，这却是这类早期阶段的考古中经常遇到的一个难题——即使从考古学上可以证实某个遗址遭到了破坏，而且有书面文献记载这座城市曾遭到了攻占和/或破坏，通常也很难把这两者联系起来。与此有关的最好例子是以色列的美吉多，我们从书面记录中得知，埃及法老图特摩斯三世在公元前1479年左右占领了这座城市。我们在该地点也发现了几个考古地层，可以表明此地遭到了破坏。然而，迄今为止我们还无法将书面文本与考古证据关联起来。

还有一点必须明确，任何从历史和考古学上确定特洛伊战争发生地点的尝试必然都基于一种间接论据，该论据会援引一系列假设和观察结果，从而产生看似合理但仍然是假设条件下的重现。这些假设包括以下内容，人们可以利用其中的部分或者全部：

- 维鲁萨可能是伊利昂（特洛伊）。
- 维鲁萨国王阿拉克山杜可能是伊利昂/特洛伊的亚历山大/帕里斯。
- 维鲁萨国王瓦尔姆在公元前13世纪后期被敌军废黜。
- 阿希亚瓦人可能是希腊大陆的迈锡尼人。
- 特洛伊 VIh 可能是被地震摧毁，而非被人类摧毁。
- 特洛伊 VIIa 是在战争中被人类摧毁的。

荷马与历史

有人可能会争辩说，荷马为了创作一部以十年斗争为主题的引人入胜的史诗，借助文学特权将人和事件以及几个世纪断断续续的战争浓缩在了一起，这是非常可信的。他的诗歌并不注定成为一本历史书，而注定是一部涉及爱情和荣誉等普遍主题的弘扬民族自豪感的史诗。

在荷马可能采用的素材中,除了他对青铜器时代爱琴海地区勇士和武器的理解之外,还包括阿苏瓦叛乱和在公元前1420年图达里亚一世/二世时期迈锡尼可能参与阿苏瓦叛乱的故事,以及他对公元前1300年前后被地震摧毁的富裕城市特洛伊VIh的了解。口头文学可能也讲述了重建的特洛伊VIIa城,以及公元前13世纪中叶哈图西里三世时期赫梯人和阿希亚瓦人在维鲁萨问题上积累的仇恨。特洛伊VIIa城首先在约公元前1280年穆瓦塔利二世时期由阿拉克山杜统治,然后在约公元前1225年或图达里亚四世后期由瓦尔姆统治。荷马可能也听说过在公元前1230年至公元前1180年间一场战争中毁灭的特洛伊VIIa城,甚至可能还听说过后来于公元前1100年前后毁灭的特洛伊VIIb$_2$城。

因此,荷马在《伊利亚特》中对特洛伊的描述可能取材于他对特洛伊VIh的了解,而对其毁灭的描述则可能取材于他对那场终结了特洛伊VIIa的火灾的认识。如果是这样,人们可以认为荷马所描述的特洛伊战争是一个过程而非一个事件,它融合了青铜器时代晚期数百年间人物、地点和事件的细节,更不用说随后在特洛伊战争和荷马所处时代之间五百年中所发生的一切了。荷马可以将旧史诗中的素材编入他自己的材料,为了更好适应自己所处时代的需要,他将野猪獠牙装饰的头盔、塔盾和埃阿斯等更早期的人物包括在内,并且更新了某些情况下使用的装备和战术。此外,他还用亲切友好却令人生畏的特洛伊VI城代替了瓦尔姆治下更加摇摇欲坠的重建之城特洛伊VIIa。

荷马可能还没有完全弄清楚事实真相,可能也并不在乎。毕竟,自中世纪以来,一些最伟大的史诗诗人和诗歌在我们了解历史真相之前就已经改变了它，有时一部伟大的英雄传说是围绕着一个事件写成的，这个事件意义不大或者已被歪曲得再也无法辨认。只需看下《罗兰之歌》和《尼伯龙人之歌》，这两部史诗都改变了实际历史事件的细节。因此，即便对其中一些细节可能还有疑问，但在认识到特洛伊战争传说的基本要素可以得到确认之后，我们应该感到满足，因为我们了解的东西比某些人可能意识到的还要多得多。

自施里曼时代以来，即便我们还没有证明阿伽门农是否曾经存在过，但我们已经确认了迈锡尼人及其文明的存在。即便我们还没有最终确定发掘现场中的哪个地层属于普里阿摩斯生活的年代，甚至还没有证明普里阿摩斯是否也真正存在过，但我们已经确认特洛伊城确实存在过。虽然不能具体确定阿喀琉斯和帕特洛克罗斯是否曾存在过，但我们已经证实，或者至少可以非常自信地推测，在青铜器时代后期三个多世纪的时间里，迈锡尼的勇士们在安纳托利亚西北部海岸上断断续续地参加过很多场战斗，确切地说就是在特洛伊地区。此外，即便我们无法明确地说在公元前13世纪早期与阿拉克山杜打仗的人，或者在公元前13世纪后期废黜了瓦尔姆的人就是阿伽门农，但我们现在知道，赫梯的记录表明同一时期发生了很多场战争或冲突，有些发生在特洛伊，有些是因特洛伊而起。换言之，无论亚历山大和海伦、阿伽门农和普里阿摩斯、阿喀琉斯和赫克托是否真的存在过，荷马所写传说的基本轮廓是真实的。

但是，特洛伊战争的原因会是对一位女性的爱吗？一场为期十年的战争会因为一个人遭绑架而引发吗？答案当然是肯定的，就像公元前13世纪一位赫梯王子的死引发了埃及与赫梯之间的战争，而第一次世界大战的爆发则是源自斐迪南大公遇刺。但正如人们所说，第一次世界大战可能无论如何都会发生，其他某个事件或许只是诱因。所以人们也可以认为，无论有没有海伦，特洛伊战争都会不可避免地发生。为了控制土地、贸易、利润和黑海通道，这场战争注定会发生，而假设条件下的海伦遭到绑架一事仅仅是一种借口罢了。

这样一场战争会持续十年之久吗？这看起来当然不太可能，其中也许还有其他因素在起作用。或许像一些人推测的那样，最初对铁乌特拉尼亚的突袭和最终对特洛伊的袭击之间有九年的间隔。或许就像康奈尔大学古典学教授巴里·施特劳斯所说，十年只是近东的一种表达方式——"有九必十"，意思就是很长一段时间。或者它真的持续了十年。我们可能永远无法知晓。

此外，特洛伊战争的真正原因也可能与特洛伊人本身无关。特洛伊位于迈锡尼帝国和赫梯帝国的边缘，夹在古代地中海世界的两个大国之间，可以称之为"有争议的外围地区"。双方都认为他们应该占有特洛伊，并且双方都愿意为争夺这座城市的控制权而开战。特洛伊人自己想要什么无关紧要，或者至少产生不了什么影响。因此，明显会有这种可能性存在，即特洛伊战争实际上是在迈锡尼人和赫梯人之间进行的，而特洛伊人只是被裹挟在中间的不幸民族（但荷马和赫梯人的记录都认为他们站在赫梯人一边反对迈锡尼人/阿希亚瓦人）。

影响多个时代的一场战争

当然，从艺术和文学上对特洛伊战争及其知名参与者（包括奥德修斯）的命运的重新诠释已经演绎了数百年,直至今日还在继续。因此,我们不仅有后来的希腊剧作家和罗马诗人,还有乔叟的《特洛伊罗斯与克丽西达》、莎士比亚的《特洛伊罗斯与克瑞西达》、卡米尔·圣桑的歌剧《海伦娜》(1904)、詹姆斯·乔伊斯的《尤利西斯》,以及银幕上对史诗的各种不同演绎——自20世纪初以来,出现了许多以特洛伊战争、海伦、阿喀琉斯、奥德修斯和/或特洛伊木马为主题的电影。

　　在这些后期作品中,有一些作品的部分细节或情节可能被认为是不准确的,或者不忠实于荷马的描述——例如,在2004年的好莱坞大片中,没有出现男神或女神;布拉德·皮特把硬币放在死去的帕特洛克罗斯闭上的眼睛上,这显得不合时宜,因为这种货币在大约五百年后的公元前7世纪才在吕底亚被发明出来;阿伽门农和墨涅拉俄斯都在特洛伊被杀,而帕里斯/亚历山大却没有,从而改变了人们所熟知的荷马/《史诗集成》版本中的内容——但这是一个由来已久的传统,可以追溯到希腊剧作家时期,他们在继承荷马的同时,也自认为可以自由地改变其中的一些细节。更重要的是,每个人都在以自己的方式重新诠释这个传说,其中的某些变化和细微差别通常反映出那个特定时代的焦虑和欲望,例如中世纪的基督教之于乔叟,伊丽莎白时代的世界观之于莎士比亚,以及伊拉克战争之于电影《特洛伊》的导演沃尔夫冈·彼得森。

　　对各个时代而言,战争的重要性显而易见,也许最能说明这一点的是帕特里克·肖-斯图尔特的一首无题诗。帕特里克·肖-斯图尔特是一位来自牛津的古典文化学者,他在第一次世界大战中曾参加过加里波利之战,而加里波利与特洛伊之间

> 哦，船只和城市见鬼去吧，
> 像我这样的人见鬼去吧，
> 支持海伦令人丧命，
> 我为什么必须追随你？

> 阿喀琉斯来到了特洛伊，
> 而我来到了克尔索涅斯半岛，
> 他带着愤怒走向战场，
> 而我却刚经历了三天的和平。

> 有那么难吗，阿喀琉斯
> 那么难以丧命吗？
> 你最知晓，而我则不知
> 而我也更开心。

　　1964年，著名历史学家摩西·芬利提议，在找到更多证据之前，我们应该将特洛伊战争的叙述从历史领域转移到神话和诗歌领域。许多人会争辩说，我们现在有了额外的证据，特别是论述阿希亚瓦和维鲁萨的赫梯文献以及来自特洛伊的新考古数据。然而，我们已经看到，不存在人们可以最终确定的"特洛伊战争"，至少不像荷马在《伊利亚特》和《奥德赛》中所描述的那样。相反，我们已经在特洛伊发现了几座城市，而且发现这里发生了几场这样的特洛伊战争，这足以让人们得出结论，所有故事背后都存在某种历史真相的内核。

　　特别是在宙斯、赫拉和其他众神卷入战争时，现实与幻想之间的界限可能会变得模糊。我们可能会在一些细节上争论不休，但总体而言，特洛伊和特洛伊战争就在它们该在的地方，它们存在于安纳托利亚西北部，并被镌刻在青铜器时代晚期的世界里，就像我们现在从考古发掘和赫梯记录中所知道的那样，而且我们还在荷马和《史诗集成》中发现了与此相关的古希腊文学证据。此外，爱情、荣誉、战争、亲情和责任等经久不衰的主题引起了后来希腊人和罗马人的共鸣，然后从埃斯库罗斯、索福克勒斯和欧里庇得斯到维吉尔、奥维德和李维，再到乔叟、莎士比亚和后来的作家，这些主题持续影响着各个时代，因此，即使到了今天——在最初的那些事件或者某些由此演变的事件发生三千多年之后，这个传说仍然具有广泛的吸引力。

词汇表：人物和地名

阿喀琉斯（Achilles）：希腊英雄。

埃斯库罗斯（Aeschylus）：公元前5世纪古希腊剧作家。

《埃塞俄比斯》（*Aethiopis*）：《史诗集成》的一部分。

阿伽门农（Agamemnon）：斯巴达国王墨涅拉俄斯的哥哥；希腊大陆迈锡尼国王。

阿基亚斯（Agias），来自特洛伊西纳（Troezen）：可能是《返乡》的作者。

阿希亚瓦（Ahhiyawa）：可能是迈锡尼语中"希腊"的赫梯语名称。

埃阿斯（Ajax）：可能出自更早希腊神话中的希腊英雄。

阿卡德语（Akkadian）：公元前2千纪古近东地区使用的口头和书写语言；当时的外交通用语。

阿拉克山杜（Alaksandu）：维鲁萨国王，统治期约为公元前1280年前后。

阿拉克山杜条约（Alaksandu Treaty）：维鲁萨的阿拉克山

杜与赫梯国王穆瓦塔利二世于公元前1280年签署的冗长条约。

亚历山大（Alexander）：特洛伊王子帕里斯的别名；普里阿摩斯的儿子；海伦的情人。

阿芙洛狄忒（Aphrodite）：象征爱与美的希腊女神。

阿克提努斯（Arctinus），来自米利都（Miletus）：可能是《埃塞俄比斯》和《特洛伊的毁灭》的作者。

阿尔努旺达一世（Arnuwanda）：赫梯国王，图达里亚一世/二世的继任者；统治期约为公元前1420年前后。

阿苏瓦（Assuwa）：约公元前1420年前后，安纳托利亚西部22个城邦组成的联盟。

雅典娜（Athena）：集智慧、勇气和其他特质于一身的希腊女神。

阿塔里希亚（Attarissiya）：阿希亚瓦统治者。

克吕泰墨斯特拉（Clytemnestra）：阿伽门农的妻子。

111 **《塞普里亚》（*Cypria*）**：《史诗集成》的一部分。

塞普里亚斯（Cyprias），来自哈利卡纳苏斯（Halicarnassus）：可能是《塞普里亚》的作者。

厄帕俄斯（Epeius）：希腊勇士，建造了特洛伊木马。

《史诗集成》（*Epic Cycle*）：关于特洛伊战争的史诗故事的零散收集。

欧里庇得斯（Euripides）：古希腊剧作家，生活在公元前5世纪。

哈图西里三世（Hattusili III）：赫梯国王（统治期约为公元前1267年至公元前1237年）。

赫克托（Hector）：特洛伊英雄。

特洛伊战争

赫克犹巴（Hecuba）： 特洛伊国王普里阿摩斯的妻子。

赫格西亚斯（Hegesias），来自萨拉米斯（Salamis）： 可能是《塞普里亚》的作者。

海伦（Helen）： 墨涅拉俄斯的妻子；迈锡尼斯巴达的王后；亚历山大/帕里斯的情人。

赫拉（Hera）： 宙斯的妻子。

赫拉克勒斯（Heracles）： 希腊英雄；曾作为特洛伊战争之前的一代人袭击特洛伊。

希罗多德（Herodotus）： 古希腊历史学家，生活在公元前5世纪。

希沙利克（Hisarlik）： 最可能包含特洛伊古城遗址的山丘。

赫梯语（Hittite）： 公元前2千纪安纳托利亚（今土耳其）地区使用的口头和书写语言。

赫梯国（Hittites）： 安纳托利亚地区（今土耳其）的主要国家，存在于公元前1700年至公元前1200年。

荷马（Homer）： 据说是《伊利亚特》和《奥德赛》的作者，生活在公元前750年前后。

《伊利亚特》（*Iliad*）： 一部描述特洛伊战争末期情况的荷马史诗。

伊利昂（Ilios）： 特洛伊的另一个名称，原写作"Wilios"。

《伊利昂的毁灭》（《特洛伊的毁灭》）（*Iliupersis*）：《史诗集成》的一部分。

伊菲革涅亚（Iphigenia）： 阿伽门农的女儿；为了让迈锡尼舰队在奥利斯获得有利风势，阿伽门农同意将其献祭。

库库里（Kukkulli）： 阿苏瓦国王（统治期为公元前1420年

前后），皮雅玛-库伦塔（Piyama-Kurunta）之子。

拉俄墨冬（Laomedon）： 赫拉克勒斯袭击时的特洛伊国王，普里阿摩斯前任。

米提林尼的莱切斯（Lesches of Mitylene）： 可能是《小伊利昂》的作者。

《小伊利昂》（*Little Iliad*）： 《史诗集成》的一部分。

卢维语（Luwian）： 公元前2千纪安纳托利亚（今土耳其）地区使用的口头和书写语言。

马杜瓦塔（Madduwatta）： 在阿希亚瓦书信往来中经常提及的一位赫梯附属国国王。

玛纳帕-塔胡恩塔（Manapa-Tarhunta）： 特洛阿德以南赛哈河国的国王（统治期为公元前13世纪）。

墨涅拉俄斯（Menelaus）： 海伦的丈夫；阿伽门农的弟弟；迈锡尼斯巴达国王。

112 **米拉瓦塔（Milawata）：** 米利都城的赫梯语名称，位于小亚细亚/安纳托利亚海岸地区。

米拉瓦塔的书信（Milawata Letter）： 可能为公元前13世纪后期赫梯国王图达里亚四世（统治期约为公元前1237年至公元前1209年）书写和发出的书信；与米拉瓦塔（即米利都）以及一位参与阿希亚瓦战事的"变节的赫梯将军"皮亚马拉都斯持续开展的行动有关。

米诺斯人（Minoans）： 青铜时代爱琴海地区克里特岛上的居民。

穆瓦塔利二世（Muwattalli II）： 赫梯国王（统治期为公元前1295年至公元前1272年）。

迈锡尼（Mycenae）：公元前1700年至公元前1100年间，希腊大陆伯罗奔尼撒半岛地区迈锡尼人的主要城市；施里曼在19世纪70年代首次发掘出该城。

迈锡尼人（Mycenaeans）：亚该亚人（Achaeans）；公元前1700年至公元前1200年期间的希腊大陆定居者。

涅斯托尔（Nestor）：希腊大陆皮洛斯（Pylos）国王。

奥德修斯（Odysseus）：希腊英雄。

《奥德赛》（*Odyssey*）：荷马史诗，讲述特洛伊战争之后奥德修斯的归家旅途。

奥维德（Ovid）：古罗马诗人，生活在公元前1世纪至公元1世纪。

帕里斯（Paris）：特洛伊王子亚历山大的别名；普里阿摩斯之子；海伦的情人。

帕特洛克罗斯（Patroclus）：阿喀琉斯忠诚的朋友；身穿阿喀琉斯的盔甲参战时被杀。

菲罗克忒忒斯（Philoctetes）：用箭射中阿喀琉斯脚后跟杀死了他。

皮雅玛–库伦塔（Piyama-Kurunta）：公元前1420年前的阿苏瓦联盟领袖。

皮亚马拉都斯（Piyamaradu）：公元前13世纪，一位参与阿希亚瓦战事的"变节的赫梯将军"。

普里阿摩斯（Priam）：特洛伊战争时期特洛伊国王。

普罗克洛斯（Proclus）：《史诗集成》的编纂者，生活在公元2世纪或5世纪。

昆图斯·斯密尔奈乌斯（Quintus Smyrnaeus）：公元4世纪

119

的史诗诗人。

《返乡》(*Returns*)：《史诗集成》的一部分。

海上民族(Sea Peoples)：公元前1207年至公元前1177年间两次穿越地中海地区的漂泊/迁徙族群；可能为终结该地区青铜时代晚期做出过贡献。

索福克勒斯(Sophocles)：古希腊剧作家，生活在公元前5世纪。

塞浦路斯的斯达西努斯(Stasinus)：可能是《塞普里亚》的作者。

苏彼鲁流玛一世(Suppiluliuma I)：一位伟大的赫梯国王（统治期为公元前1350年至公元前1322年）。

塔瓦伽拉瓦(Tawagalawa)：名字以赫梯语字母书写，阿希亚瓦国王的兄弟，生活在公元前13世纪中期。

塔瓦伽拉瓦的书信(Tawagalawa Letter)：可能由赫梯国王哈图西里三世（统治期为公元前1267年至公元前1237年）书写；书信与一位参与阿希亚瓦（可能是迈锡尼人）战事的"变节的赫梯将军"皮亚马拉都斯开展的行动有关。

忒勒马科斯(Telemachus)：奥德修斯之子。

铁乌特拉尼亚(Teuthrania)：遭到阿喀琉斯和其他迈锡尼人错误袭击的特洛伊以南地区。

特洛伊人(Trojans)：古特洛伊的居民。

特洛伊(Troy)：伊利昂；普里阿摩斯、亚历山大/帕里斯以及赫克托的故乡；特洛伊战争发生地；可能与如今土耳其境内的希沙利克有关。

图达里亚一世/二世(Tudhaliya I/II)：赫梯国王（统治期

特洛伊战争

为约公元前1450年至公元前1420年），镇压了阿苏瓦叛乱。

图达里亚四世：赫梯国王（统治期为约公元前1237年至公元前1209年）。

维吉尔（Virgil）：古罗马史诗诗人，生活在公元前1世纪。

瓦尔姆（Walmu）：维鲁萨国王，统治期为公元前13世纪晚期。

维鲁萨（Wilusa）：可能是特洛伊（伊利昂）的赫梯语名称。

扎南扎（Zannanza）：赫梯王子，苏彼鲁流玛一世之子；公元前14世纪中期在前往古埃及途中被杀。

宙斯（Zeus）：古希腊敬奉的众神之首。

114

索 引

（条目后的数字为原书页码，
见本书边码）

特洛伊战争

索引

特洛伊战争

Eric H. Cline

THE TROJAN WAR

A Very Short Introduction

Dedicated to the memory of my mother,
for introducing me to the wonders of the Trojan War
when I was seven years old.

Contents

The Trojan War

List of illustrations

Acknowledgments

This book is a very short introduction to the Trojan War and the discovery and excavation of Troy/Hisarlik, written along the lines of the seminar course that I have taught several times at George Washington University. I have written previously about the Trojan War, including various scholarly articles, a book for young adults co-authored with Jill Rubalcaba (*Digging for Troy: From Homer to Hisarlik*; Charlesbridge, 2010), and a course guide that accompanied my audio lectures (*Archaeology and the Iliad: The Trojan War in Homer and History*; The Modern Scholar/Recorded Books, 2006). The present text represents an update in every instance, including recent re-examinations and interpretations of this much-studied subject.

I would like to thank my editor, Nancy Toff, for her marvelous efforts, as usual, and her assistant, Sonia Tycko; my wife, Diane Harris Cline; my father, Martin J. Cline; and two anonymous readers for OUP, for all reading through the entire manuscript and making editorial changes and suggestions. I would also like to thank Ed White at The Modern Scholar/Recorded Books for permission to use and rework the material originally published in conjunction with my audio course; Eric Shanower, Christoph Haußner, Trevor Bryce, Carol Hershenson and the Classics Department at the University of Cincinnati, and Peter Jablonka and the Troia Project at the University of Tübingen for illustrations; Carol Bell, John Bennet, Joshua W. Cannon, Erwin F. Cook, Oliver Dickinson, Peter Jablonka, Susan Sherratt, Rik A. Vaessen, and Erik van Dongen for bibliographic references and pdfs of articles; my students at GWU for their patience as I tried out new material on them over the course of the past several years; and, as always, my family for their usual forbearance.

1. The Late Bronze Age Aegean and Western Anatolia, ca. 1250 BCE, including the major sites on mainland Greece, Crete, the Cycladic Islands, and the western coast of Turkey (Anatolia).

Introduction

Was there a conflict sometime back in antiquity that gave rise
to the legend of the Trojan War? Did the battles of that war take
place near the site that we now call Troy? The ancient Greeks
and Romans certainly thought that such a war had taken place,
and they thought they knew the site of its battles, in northwest
Anatolia (modern Turkey). Later, they built their own cities,
Hellenistic Ilion and Roman Ilium, respectively, at the same
location. It is said that Alexander the Great even slept with a
copy of the *Iliad* annotated by Aristotle under his pillow and
visited the presumed site of Troy during his Asian campaign in
334 BCE.

The Greeks and Romans believed that the Trojan War was both
a real event and a pivotal point in world history; Herodotus and
Thucydides discussed the Trojan War briefly in the opening pages
of their respective books, written during the fifth century BCE.
However, none of the later Greco-Roman scholars and authors
was quite certain when it had actually happened. Estimates for the
date of the war, including those by Herodotus, ranged from 1334
BCE to 1135 BCE, but those estimates were usually based on little
substantive evidence; dates were put forth as "a thousand years
before Alexander the Great's visit" or "eight hundred years before
the time of Herodotus." Eventually, the third-century BCE Greek
geographer Eratosthenes's estimated date of 1184 BCE ("407 years

before the first Olympiad") became the most favored, although it too was based mostly on guesswork.

Classical scholars during the Middle Ages and into the early modern era were more dubious and frequently minimized the importance of the Trojan War, or even dismissed it entirely as a piece of fiction. Only when Heinrich Schliemann, the so-called father of Mycenaean archaeology, claimed to have again located the site of Troy in the 1870s was attention seriously paid to the possibility that the story may have had a basis in historical reality, with interest focused on his newly excavated remains at the site of Hisarlik (Turkish *Hisarlık*, "Place of Fortresses"). Since then, scholarly discussion has continued unabated, with academic debate focused on several areas, including the literary evidence and the archaeological data for the existence of—and specific details concerning—Homer, Bronze Age Greece, Troy, and the Trojan War itself (see fig. 2).

The tale of the war, as related by Homer in the eighth century BCE, and by other Greek poets and playwrights in the centuries following, contains themes that have resonated down through the ages. The basic story, a timeless epic of love and war, rivalry and greed, heroes and cowards, is easily told. It revolves around a few central characters and a host of supporting actors. Those immediately central to the story include, on the one side, Helen, the wife of the Mycenaean Greek king of Sparta, Menelaus; Menelaus's brother Agamemnon, king of Mycenae; Achilles, a Mycenaean warrior from Thessaly who is almost without equal in battle; and Odysseus, the Mycenaean king of Ithaca. On the other side are, among others, Paris, the son of King Priam of Troy; Priam himself; and Hector, an older son of Priam.

The story of the Trojan War has fascinated humans for centuries and has given rise to countless scholarly articles and books, extensive archaeological excavations, epic movies, television documentaries, stage plays, art and sculpture, souvenirs and

**2. After retiring from a successful business career, the wealthy
Heinrich Schliemann devoted the rest of his life to finding and
excavating Troy.**

collectibles. In the United States there are thirty-three states
with cities or towns named Troy and ten four-year colleges and
universities, besides the University of Southern California, whose
sports teams are called the Trojans. Particularly captivating is
the account of the Trojan Horse, the daring plan that brought the
Trojan War to an end and that has also entered modern parlance
by giving rise to the saying "Beware of Greeks bearing gifts" and

serving as a metaphor for hackers intent on wreaking havoc by inserting a "Trojan horse" into computer systems.

But, is Homer's story convincing? Certainly the heroes, from Achilles to Hector, are portrayed so credibly that it is easy to believe the story. But is it truly an account based on real events, and were the main characters actually real people? Would the ancient world's equivalent of the entire nation of Greece really have gone to war over a single woman, however beautiful, and for ten long years at that? Could Agamemnon really have been a king of kings able to muster so many men for such an expedition? And, even if one believes that there once was an actual Trojan War, does that mean that the specific events, actions, and descriptions in Homer's *Iliad* and *Odyssey*, supplemented by additional fragments and commentary in the *Epic Cycle*, are historically accurate and can be taken at face value? Is it plausible that what Homer describes actually took place and in the way that he says it did?

In short, the bigger picture involves the investigation of several major questions: What evidence do we have that the Trojan War actually took place? If it did, then where and when was it fought? What was its cause and who were the principal protagonists? What is the historical context into which the tale should be placed? Is there a kernel of truth at the center of the stories about the legendary deeds and actions of the Mycenaeans and Trojans, and do we need to bring other groups, contemporary to the Late Bronze Age, such as the Hittites of central Anatolia, into the equation?

The continuing mysteries, and the ongoing search for answers to these questions, keeps the modern investigation of the Trojan War lively and intriguing today, more than three thousand years after it presumably took place. Therefore, despite the beautiful simplicity of the tale, a book about the Trojan War is not as simple as it might at first appear. It will by necessity be far more detail-oriented and complex than one might expect, for the retelling of Homer's story is just the tip of the proverbial iceberg. Both Greek and Hittite sources document more than one Trojan War, so that one has to decide which is Homer's war, if any. Furthermore, since there are nine cities, built one on top of another, at the site of Hisarlik (ancient Troy), one has to decide which one was Priam's, if any. But before proceeding to these discussions, it is imperative to go through the story itself and ascertain what we know about the Trojan War from the Greek sources.

Part I
The Trojan War

Chapter 1
The story according to the
Iliad, the *Odyssey*, and the
Epic Cycle

The story of the Trojan War is well known, especially to those who were assigned to read the *Iliad* or the *Odyssey* in high school or college, or who have read one or more of the numerous translations that have appeared in recent years or seen the Hollywood movie *Troy*. Surprisingly, despite their length and detail, neither the *Iliad* nor the *Odyssey* emphasize many of the events with which the modern reader is familiar, including a fateful encounter on a hillside in ancient Turkey, the capture of Troy using the stratagem of a hollow wooden horse, and the subsequent journeys of the Greek warriors, apart from Odysseus, back to their homes across the sea. The Trojan Horse, for example, is mentioned only once in the *Odyssey*, within Book IV, when Menelaus is describing his travels and travails. It is not mentioned at all in the *Iliad*.

For the full story of the Trojan War and its aftermath, we must turn to the group of twelve epic narratives now known collectively as the *Epic Cycle*, which most likely date to the eighth to sixth centuries BCE, the approximate time of Homer and shortly thereafter. The *Iliad* and the *Odyssey* are the only complete works remaining from this group. The rest of these early epic poems were mostly lost over the course of time, and only portions remain, quoted or summarized by later authors. These literary fragments were gathered together by an individual who identified himself as Proclus—now thought by some scholars to be Eutychius Proclus, a grammarian and tutor of the Roman emperor Marcus Aurelius who lived during the second century CE. Alternatively, some attribute the collection to an individual named Proclus who was versed in the philosophy of Plato (a "Neoplatonist") and who lived three hundred years later, during the fifth century CE.

In any event, one or the other Proclus published these brief summaries and snippets of quotations from the various epics in a book called the *Chrestomatheia Grammatiki*. Its title derives from the Greek words meaning "useful to learning" and from which comes our modern word "chrestomathy," frequently defined as "a selection of choice literary passages from one or more authors." In uniting these fragmentary epics, Proclus created what now appears to be a seamless tale out of what were once disparate stories.

The literary fragments of the other epics expand on the sometimes-sparse details given by Homer. When gathered together, they provide information on the origins of the Trojan War. They also describe a first failed attempt by the Greeks to take Troy, and they give a complete account of the Trojan Horse. Later treatments of the story by the playwrights of Classical Greece in the fifth century BCE, as well as alternative versions, expansions, and continuations of the saga by much later writers including Virgil, Ovid, Livy, and Quintus Smyrnaeus, add still more details and flesh out the story into the form that we now know today. Not surprisingly, these later additions frequently contradict the original storyline, including details such as whether Helen was actually at Troy during the war.

The *Cypria*

The *Epic Cycle* begins with the *Cypria*, which was initially eleven books (or chapters) long and covered both the events leading up to the Trojan War and the first nine years of the war. Only a lengthy, but useful, summary of the *Cypria* still survives. Proclus tells us that the original author was not Homer but either a man named Hegesias, reportedly from the island of Salamis, or one named Stasinus, supposedly from Cyprus. A different tradition holds that the epic was actually written by Cyprias of Halicarnassus (on the western coast of Turkey) and that the title derives from his name. All three possible authors of the text probably lived during the sixth century BCE.

At the outset of the *Cypria*, we are told that Zeus—for reasons that are not specified—plotted to begin the Trojan War. To this end, he sent the goddess of Strife, Eris, to the wedding of Peleus, a war-hero and royal prince from the island of Aegina, and Thetis, a sea nymph. They would later become the parents of the as-yet-unborn hero Achilles.

At their wedding, Eris induced an argument between Hera (wife of Zeus), Athena (goddess of wisdom and war), and Aphrodite (goddess of love and beauty), as to which one of them was the most beautiful. Later sources elaborate upon this story, stating that Eris deliberately started the quarrel by throwing a golden apple, inscribed "for the most beautiful," into the crowd of guests. Hera, Athena, and Aphrodite, each one believing that it was meant for herself, could not settle the dispute by themselves. Therefore, Zeus ordered the messenger god Hermes to lead the three goddesses to Mount Ida, in what is now western Turkey (ancient Anatolia), where they came upon a young man.

The text identifies the young man as Alexander, while a note made by a later commentator in the margin of one of the earliest extant editions indicates that this Alexander, who appears here in the

Epic Cycle for the first time, is specifically to be equated with Paris. Although Homer and the early Greek poets refer to him far more often as Alexander, modern audiences know him better as Paris, perhaps to avoid confusion with the later Alexander the Great, who was not yet alive at the time that Homer was writing. Here Alexander/Paris is described as the "fairest of mortals," who agrees to decide among the three goddesses, in what is now known as the "Judgment of Paris." The painting by that name by Peter Paul Rubens provides a striking visual image of what is said to have happened on Mount Ida.

Although Alexander/Paris was the son of Priam, king of Troy, he had been banished from the royal court as a new-born infant. Apparently, Priam had a dream in which his wife Hecuba gave birth not to a son but to a torch of flaming snakes. Sparks from the torch lit the tall grass surrounding the city of Troy on fire and burned the city to the ground. When Priam summoned the dream interpreters, they declared that the unborn child would be a curse upon the city and to his father. They recommended that he be left in the forest to die, so that the prophecy might not come to pass.

As soon as he was born, the child was given to Priam's herdsman, who took the infant to Mount Ida and left him out in the open to die. He was saved, however, by a bear, which nurtured him until the herdsman returned and found the boy still alive. The herdsman then took the boy home and raised him as his own son.

When making his great decision as to who was the most beautiful of the three goddesses, Alexander/Paris was unaware that he himself was of royal birth. It was only later that he went to Troy, discovered his true identity, and was reunited with his father, mother, and entire family. It may be for this reason that he has two names: the one given to him either at birth or after rejoining his family and the one given to him by the herdsman. There are, of course, numerous other possible explanations for his two names, including that one was used by the Trojans and the other by the Greeks or that we are seeing here the conflation of two myths or legends that were originally separate, one featuring someone named Paris and the other Alexander.

This latter suggestion—that what we are seeing here is the result of the merging of similar stories—seems perhaps most likely, for it has been pointed out that there are numerous instances of duplicate, and even triplicate, names found in these epics; not only two names for Alexander/Paris but also two names for the major river near Troy (Skamandros and Xanthos) and fully three names for the Mycenaeans (Achaeans, Danaans, and Argives). We may note the duplication readily in his case, since, for example, he is called both Alexander (Ἀλέξανδρος) and Paris (Πάριος and Πάρις) even within Book III of the *Iliad* (compare lines 16 and 30 with lines 325 and 437). Overall, within the *Iliad*, he is called Paris in seven books and Alexander in five books; he is also referred to by both names in the *Epic Cycle*.

As for the city itself, it also has two names. Although Homer and all other authors always called the inhabitants Trojans, the city in which they live is called Troy (Τροίη) once and Ilios (Ἴλιον or Ἰλίου) six times in the *Epic Cycle*. Homer also uses the two terms interchangeably; in the *Iliad*, for instance, he calls the city both Ilios and Troy already within Book I (compare lines 71 and 129). Scholars have long known that the name Ilios was originally written with an initial digamma in Greek, meaning that it was spelled and meant to be pronounced with a "W" at the beginning, thus "(W)ilios" rather than simply "Ilios." Over time, the initial digamma was lost, leaving the name of the city simply as Ilios.

In any event, this rather unbelievable story is known as a "foundation myth," commonly used in antiquity to describe and explain the rise of someone unexpected to the throne of a country or the leadership of a people. The best-known examples from elsewhere in the ancient world, including both legendary and historical figures, are Sargon the Great of Akkad in Mesopotamia during the twenty-third century BCE; Moses in Egypt during the thirteenth century BCE; Romulus and Remus in Italy during the eighth century BCE; and particularly Cyrus the Great of Persia during the sixth century BCE. Each of these stories resembles that of Alexander/Paris to a certain degree.

According to the *Cypria*, and as repeated in other ancient Greek myths and writings, Alexander/Paris chose Aphrodite as the winner of the beauty contest between the three goddesses after she promised him that he would win the love of, and marry, Helen—described elsewhere as the most beautiful woman in the world. The bribes offered by the other two goddesses, wisdom from Athena, and wealth and power from Hera, were apparently not as appealing as the prospect of marrying the beautiful Helen.

The *Cypria* then skips over the reuniting of Alexander/Paris with his family and his move back to Troy, and resumes with his voyage across the Aegean to the Greek mainland. There he is entertained by the Mycenaean king of Sparta, Menelaus, and his beautiful wife, Helen.

Menelaus was either very trusting or not very bright, for he left for Crete soon after Alexander/Paris's arrival. It is not made clear in the *Cypria* why he departed, despite the fact that he was still entertaining Alexander/Paris and his entourage. And why did he not take Helen with him to Crete? The summary merely says—very discreetly—that while Menelaus was gone, "Aphrodite brings Helen and Alexandrus [Alexander/Paris] together, and they, after their union, put very great treasures on board and sail away by night." Of course, the Greeks claimed that she had been kidnapped, whereas the Trojans claimed that she had left willingly with Alexander/Paris. In any event, Menelaus had every right to sue for "alienation of affection"; either that, or go to war with the Greeks and win her back.

This may not have been the first time that Helen was "kidnapped." A later Greek author, Athenaeus of Naucratis, who lived and wrote ca. 300 CE, reports that she had earlier also been kidnapped, as a young girl, by the hero Theseus, who is perhaps better known for having made off with Ariadne, daughter of King Minos, after killing the minotaur (half man/half bull) on Crete.

Interestingly, the *Cypria* does not say that Alexander/Paris and Helen went straight to Troy but rather that Hera, still miffed by her rejection, stirred up a storm against them, so that their ship was carried to Sidon, in what is now Lebanon. Instead of simply disembarking, Alexander/Paris interrupted his dalliance with Helen long enough to attack and capture the city. Only then did the two lovebirds continue on and return to Troy. Homer agrees, in the *Iliad*, that they stopped off at Sidon before reaching Troy, saying:

> There lay the elaborately wrought robes, the work of Sidonian
> women, whom Alexandros [Alexander/Paris] himself, the godlike,
> had brought home from the land of Sidon, crossing the wide sea, on
> that journey when he brought back also gloriously descended Helen.
> (*Il.* VI.289–92)

In any event, the *Cypria*'s brief mention of the attack against Sidon is not further explained. Herodotus, the fifth century BCE Greek historian, knew of the version presented in the *Cypria*, for he makes reference to it and notes that Homer knew of it as well, quoting as proof the lines given above. His argument is not very convincing, since Homer gives no indication that the visit was at all hostile. However, Herodotus also relates at length an alternative version of the story, in which Alexander/Paris and Helen were blown off course and landed in Egypt rather than Lebanon (*Histories* II.113–18). At this point, the plot gets a bit murky, since a similar story line was followed by the Greek playwright Euripides. He says in his play *Helen*, produced in 412 BCE, that the real Helen was whisked away by Hera and spent ten years in

Egypt, having been replaced by a phantom look-alike who went with Alexander/Paris to Troy.

According to the *Cypria*, when Menelaus heard what had happened, he returned home and planned an expedition to Troy with his brother, Agamemnon, the king of Mycenae, in order to regain Helen. He then traveled around the Greek mainland, recruiting Nestor, the king of Pylos, and Odysseus, who pretended at first to be insane and only later reluctantly agreed to take part in the mission. No mention is given in the summary of the other Greek leaders and men who also agreed to participate, but a full list is given in the so-called Catalogue of Ships in the *Iliad* (*Il.* II. 494–759). Here the various Mycenaean kings and the ships and men that they each brought are enumerated; Christopher Marlowe summarized their numbers well in *Doctor Faustus*, when he wrote of Helen:

> Was this the face that launch'd a thousand ships
> And burnt the topless towers of Ilium?
> Sweet Helen, make me immortal with a kiss.

According to the account in the *Cypria*, the Mycenaean ships, and the men upon them, then gathered together at Aulis, a port city on the eastern coast of Boeotia in mainland Greece, where they made sacrifices to the gods and then set out for Troy. Unfortunately, in one of those unpredictable misfortunes of war, they instead landed at a place called Teuthrania, located to the south of Troy on the Anatolian mainland, mistook it for Troy, and destroyed it. Before they could rectify their error and attack Troy itself, a storm hit and scattered their ships. They had to regroup at Aulis an unspecified time later—perhaps as much as nine years later, according to an interesting suggestion made by German scholars studying these *Epic Cycle* fragments. A nine-year delay would explain why the entire Trojan War took ten years, but only a portion of the last year of fighting is described in the *Iliad*.

It is while they were waiting to set sail from Aulis for the second time that a tragic series of events, immortalized by the later Greek playwrights, took place. Because the goddess Artemis, for reasons best known to herself, had sent winds that prevented the fleet from sailing, the increasingly impatient Agamemnon took measures that we would regard as rather extreme. He planned to sacrifice his own daughter Iphigenia in order to placate the goddess. The *Cypria*, however, puts a pleasant spin on these events, stating that Artemis snatched Iphigenia away at the last minute, making her immortal, and left a stag on the altar in her place, much as Isaac was replaced by a ram during the intended sacrifice by Abraham, as related in Genesis 22 of the Hebrew Bible. Euripides's play, *Iphigenia at Aulis*, produced around 410 BCE, follows the same scenario in replacing Iphigenia with a deer. But other authors, such as the slightly earlier fifth-century BCE Greek playwright Aeschylus, have her actually sacrificed, as seen in his play *Agamemnon*, produced in 458 BCE.

In any event, the expedition eventually set sail again, first to the island of Tenedos, then to the island of Lemnos, and finally reached Troy on the Anatolian coast. This time they attacked the correct city. But the attack failed and the Greeks were driven back by the Trojans. This event, its protagonists, and what follows is described succinctly in the *Cypria*; it is worth quoting in detail:

> Then the Greeks tried to land at Ilium, but the Trojans prevent
> them, and Protesilaus is killed by Hector. Achilles then kills Cycnus,
> the son of Poseidon, and drives the Trojans back. The Greeks
> take up their dead and send envoys to the Trojans demanding the
> surrender of Helen and the treasure with her. The Trojans refusing,
> they first assault the city, and then go out and lay waste the country
> and cities round about. After this, Achilles desires to see Helen,
> and Aphrodite and Thetis contrive a meeting between them. The
> Achaeans next desire to return home, but are restrained by Achilles,

who afterwards drives off the cattle of Aeneas, and sacks Lyrnessus and Pedasus and many of the neighbouring cities, and kills Troilus. Patroclus carries away Lycaon to Lemnos and sells him as a slave, and out of the spoils Achilles receives Briseis as a prize, and Agamemnon Chryseis. Then follows the death of Palamedes, the plan of Zeus to relieve the Trojans by detaching Achilles from the Hellenic confederacy, and a catalogue of the Trojan allies.

Thus ends the summary of the contents of the *Cypria*, setting the stage for the first book of Homer's *Iliad* and a quarrel between the Greek hero Achilles and King Agamemnon over their prizes of war. It is at this point that the *Iliad* fits into the series of poems that make up the *Epic Cycle*.

The *Iliad*

The *Iliad*, which describes in detail some of the action that takes place in the tenth, and final, year of the Trojan War, ends before the actual capture and sacking of Troy. The quarrel between Achilles and Agamemnon is the opening act in Book I and sets the scene for the rest of the story line. The quarrel arises because it is decreed that one of Agamemnon's war prizes, the Trojan captive Chryseis, daughter of a priest of Apollo, must be returned to her father. In order to make up for his loss, Agamemnon then takes Briseis, Achilles's prize from the earlier battle. Achilles, in turn, swears that he will not fight again until Briseis is returned to him and Agamemnon has apologized. Agamemnon refuses to do so, with the result that the Greeks lose the services of Achilles, their best fighter, albeit temporarily, but with disastrous results.

The story of the *Iliad* covers no more than fifty days during the course of the ten-year-long war. The information in the account is detailed and impressive, but uneven. For instance, Book I covers approximately twenty days, while Books II–VII cover only two days in a wealth of detail. In Book II, we are given an itemized description of the Greek forces—the Catalogue of Ships—followed by a similar but shorter description of the Trojan forces. Book III describes a one-on-one battle between Alexander/Paris and Menelaus, a duel with the winner taking all, including Helen, in a bid to end the war without further fighting. The war was not to be ended so easily, however, for Aphrodite rescued Alexander/Paris at the last minute. In the story, with Menelaus nearly victorious and dragging Alexander/Paris off the field of battle by the chinstrap of his helmet, Aphrodite causes the chinstrap to break, thereby saving him from certain death and ensuring that the war would continue. Books IV–VII are concerned first with events among the gods on Mount Olympus and then shift to the battlefield, with scenes of more fighting.

The next three books, VIII–X, are taken up with details of fighting during the course of a single day, including a long but inconclusive duel between Hector, Alexander/Paris's older brother, and Ajax, a giant Greek hero who would later take his own life. Eight books, XI–XVIII, making up one-third of the entire contents of the twenty-four-book *Iliad*, also consist of an account of a single day's fighting, presented in great detail. In part this is because Book XVI contains the events surrounding the death of Patroclus, Achilles's companion. Patroclus had borrowed Achilles's armor and was mistaken for Achilles as he fought throughout the day, only to be killed by Hector in the end. Book XVII describes the fighting over Patroclus's body, after Hector has stripped it of Achilles's armor.

The events of still another day take up Books XIX–XXII. By Book XX, Achilles has returned ferociously to the fight. The gods have now entered the fray as well, and Poseidon sends an earthquake to influence the outcome of the battles. In Book XXII, Hector is killed by Achilles, who then drags the corpse back to the Greek camp. Books XXIII–XXIV, the final two books in the *Iliad*, describe the actions that take place over the next twenty-two days, perhaps to mirror the twenty days of events covered in Book I. In Book XXIII, Patroclus's body is cremated on a huge funeral pyre and funeral games are held. Book XXIV, the final book of the

Iliad, describes Achilles's anger and grief. Despite misgivings, he is eventually persuaded to give Hector's body back to King Priam. Hector's body is then cremated in turn on his own funeral pyre, during a twelve-day armistice. And, with that final scene, the *Iliad* comes to an end.

The remaining events of the war are told in additional, but fragmentary, epics: the *Aethiopis*, the *Little Iliad*, and the *Iliupersis* (*Sack of Troy*), thought to have been written in the eighth and seventh centuries BCE. They are also covered in a much later work, dating to the fourth century CE, by an epic poet named Quintus Smyrnaeus (Quintus of Smyrna), who wrote a poem titled *Posthomerica* or the *Fall of Troy*, consisting of fourteen books (chapters) covering the time period from the end of the *Iliad* to the fall of Troy. Most modern scholars agree that Quintus probably used these earlier epics to compose his own work.

The *Aethiopis*

The *Aethiopis* picks up where the *Iliad* leaves off. Written by Arctinus of Miletus (a town on the western coast of Anatolia/Asia Minor/Turkey), perhaps as early as the eighth century BCE, at approximately the same time as Homer's writings, it consists of five chapters or books. The action begins immediately, when Achilles first kills the Amazon queen Penthesileia, and then kills Memnon, an Ethiopian prince who was the grandson of King Laomedon of Troy, predecessor of Priam, and therefore the nephew of Priam and cousin of Alexander/Paris and Hector. Both had brought armies to the aid of the Trojans.

Achilles is then killed by Alexander/Paris, aided by Apollo. Since we have only the brief summary of this epic, we are not told how Achilles was killed, but we know from other, later accounts— such as Ovid's *Metamorphoses* (12.580–619)—that he was shot with an arrow in his heel, the only place on his body where he was vulnerable. His mother had held him by the heel when she dipped him into the River Styx as a child, in order to make him invulnerable to wounding. Following a fight for Achilles's body, the Greeks brought him back to their ships, cremated him on a funeral pyre, and held games in his honor. Marring these events is a dispute between Odysseus and Ajax over the armor of Achilles, but this will not be resolved until the next epic in the cycle, namely the *Little Iliad*.

The *Little Iliad*

Proclus tells us that the *Little Iliad* was written by Lesches of Mytilene (a city on the island of Lesbos), in four chapters. He is usually thought to have lived and composed his works in the seventh century BCE. The epic begins with Odysseus triumphing over Ajax and winning the armor and weapons of Achilles. Following the resolution, Ajax committed suicide; an act that was later the subject of a play in its own right, written by Sophocles in the fifth century BCE. More fighting then takes place, and a number of deaths occur on both sides, including, most importantly, that of Alexander/Paris himself. He is killed by a man named Philoctetes, who later become the subject of plays written by Sophocles, Aeschylus, and Euripides. Following the death of Alexander/Paris, an otherwise-unknown man named Epeius built a wooden horse, following instructions given by Athena. It is noteworthy that this is the first time in the *Epic Cycle* that the idea of a wooden horse has been introduced.

The implication in the *Little Iliad* is that it is Epeius's idea ("Epeius, by Athena's instruction, builds the wooden horse"). This attribution is repeated in the *Odyssey* (VIII.492–94; see also XI.523–35): "But come now, change thy theme, and sing of the building of the horse of wood, which Epeius made with Athena's help, the horse which once Odysseus led up into the citadel as a thing of guile." Much later, however, Quintus Smyrnaeus gives credit for the idea to Odysseus, attributing to Epeius only the actual building of the horse:

The only one with a clever idea
Was the son of Laertes [Odysseus], who answered with this speech:
"Friend held in highest honor by the heavenly gods,
If it is really fated that the warlike Achaians
Should sack the city of Priam by means of trickery,
A horse must be constructed to contain the leaders,
An ambush that we will welcome." (Quintus Smyrnaeus,
Posthomerica XII.23–29)

The *Little Iliad* succinctly states what happened next: "Then after putting their best men in the wooden horse and burning their huts, the main body of the Hellenes sail to Tenedos [an island just off the coast]. The Trojans, supposing their troubles over, destroy a part of their city wall and take the wooden horse into their city and feast as though they had conquered the Hellenes." Later Greek authors, including Quintus Smyrnaeus (XII.314–35), usually put the number of men inside the horse at thirty (with some traditions upping the number to forty), and give their names, including Odysseus as the leader, Ajax the lesser, Diomedes, and Menelaus himself. However, the summary of the *Little Iliad* is brief and does not name even these, but instead comes to an abrupt end, with the story to be continued in the next epic, the *Iliupersis* or *Sack of Troy*.

The *Iliupersis*

The *Iliupersis* or *Sack of Troy* is composed of only two chapters, but it is full of action and brings closure to this phase of the epic tale. It was written by Arctinus of Miletus, the same man who had composed the *Aethiopis*. In this poem, we learn that the Trojans, even though they had already brought the wooden horse within their walls, are suspicious of it and debate what to do. Eventually they decide to dedicate it to Athena and "turned to mirth and feasting, believing the war was at an end." Some remain suspicious, however, and in Book II of the *Aeneid*, the Roman poet Virgil has Laocoön, the Trojan priest of Poseidon, warn his fellow citizens, "Trojans, don't trust this horse. Whatever it is, I'm afraid of Greeks, even those bearing gifts" ("Equo ne credite, Teucri. Quidquid id est, timeo Danaos et dona ferentes."). From this comes our saying "Beware of Greeks bearing gifts" and the idea of a Trojan horse as a computer virus, a plague of modern technology, particularly one that lets hackers in through a "back door" program installed surreptitiously on one's computer.

Laocoön's warning was prescient, for the *Sack of Troy* next reports that the Greek army sailed back from Tenedos under cover of night, while the warriors in the horse "came out and fell upon their enemies, killing many and storming the city." Priam was killed at the altar of Zeus, and Astyanax, the young son of Hector, was hurled from the city wall.

As a result of the Greek victory over the Trojans, Menelaus regained his wife, Helen, and took her to the Greek ships in preparation for the voyage home. After much additional killing and the dividing up of spoils, including female captives, the victorious Greeks sailed for home, not suspecting that Athena planned to destroy them enroute. At this point, the *Sack of Troy* ends, having presented the story of the Trojan horse and the Greek conquest of the city. It leaves the tale of the aftermath of the war to another epic poem, the *Nostoi* or *Returns*.

The *Nostoi*

According to Proclus, the five chapters of the *Returns* were written by Agias of Troezen, whom other sources date to the seventh or sixth century BCE. Troezen was a small town on the Greek mainland that also happens to be the hometown of the legendary hero Theseus. The *Returns* is the story of how the various Greek heroes, apart from Odysseus, made their way back home to their lands and kingdoms across the Aegean Sea.

In the *Returns*, both Nestor, the king of Pylos, and Diomedes, king of Argos and nephew of Heracles, reach home without incident. However, Menelaus, who had argued with Agamemnon about when to leave Troy, was caught in a storm while sailing home. He reached Egypt with only five ships left in his fleet. We are told nothing more of this in the *Returns*, but Homer in the *Odyssey* (III.299–304) fleshes out the story, including having Menelaus later tell Telemachus that he subsequently wandered for eight years in the Eastern Mediterranean, visiting Cyprus, Phoenicia, Ethiopia, and Sidon, in addition to Egypt, before continuing his journey home to Sparta: "For of a truth after many woes and wide wanderings I brought my wealth home in my ships and came in the eighth year. Over Cyprus and Phoenicia I wandered, and Egypt, and I came to the Ethiopians and the Sidonians and the Erembi, and to Libya, where the lambs are horned from their birth" (*Od.* IV.80–85).

Agamemnon, on the other hand, initially remained at Troy in order to appease Athena, and then finally sailed home, only to be murdered, along with his companions, by his own wife Clytemnestra and her lover Aegisthus. This episode, and the subsequent events involving his two children, Orestes and Electra, were greatly expanded upon by the later Greek playwrights of the fifth century BCE, including Aeschylus, Sophocles, and Euripides. The book ends with a brief mention that Menelaus finally returned home, presumably with Helen, only after the murder of Agamemnon.

The *Odyssey*

Homer's *Odyssey*, the only other complete epic from the *Cycle* that is extant, follows in sequence after the *Returns*. It is primarily concerned with the travels and travails of Odysseus, in his ten-year attempt to return home after the conclusion of the war. Like the *Iliad*, the *Odyssey* is composed of twenty-four books (or chapters).

The story is well known, having been told and retold in various forms down through the ages.

Odysseus's journey is essentially irrelevant to the tale of the Trojan War, but the epic does on occasion give him, or one of his comrades, the opportunity to reflect back upon the years of war and to give additional details that flesh out the picture presented only briefly in the summaries of the other epics. In the end, after many adventures, Odysseus was able to reach his home and, with the help of his son Telemachus, killed all of the suitors who had flocked around his wife, Penelope. He then resumed his role as king over the island of Ithaca.

The *Telegony*

After the *Odyssey* comes the final book in the *Epic Cycle*, the *Telegony*. Consisting of only two chapters, it was written by Eugammon of Cyrene, according to Proclus. Cyrene was a Greek colony founded in the seventh century BCE in what is now modern Libya. Eugammon is thought to have composed this work, essentially a postscript to the *Odyssey*, just a relatively short time later, in the sixth century BCE. It begins with the burial of Penelope's suitors and ends with the death of Odysseus at the hands of Telegonus, his other son, whom Odysseus had sired during a year of living with the goddess Circe while enroute home after the war.

Later authors

The later Greek playwrights, as well as Roman authors such as Ovid, Livy, and Virgil, continued to expand upon the details found in the *Epic Cycle*, especially on the events that took place in the aftermath of the war. The details found in the earlier epics may be more trustworthy than those in later works, since they are closer to the action of the Trojan War. But the reader should be aware that even these early epics were not written down until at least five hundred years after the original war, in the eighth century BCE, and may not have been formalized until two hundred years beyond that, in the sixth century BCE. The accuracy of their details is therefore of concern both to Homeric scholars and Bronze Age Aegean archaeologists, as is the question of whether Homer himself actually existed and was the author of both the *Iliad* and the *Odyssey*.

Chapter 2
The Trojan War in context: Mycenaeans, Hittites, Trojans, and Sea Peoples

If the Trojan War did take place, both ancient and modern scholars agree that it was fought toward the end of the Late Bronze Age, near the end of the second millennium BCE. This was a time when the Mycenaeans of mainland Greece and the Hittites of Anatolia were two of the greatest powers in the ancient Mediterranean, with the region of Troy and the Troad (the Biga Peninsula in Anatolia) caught in the middle. Both civilizations flourished from 1700 to 1200 BCE; the Trojan War, if it did take place, had to have been fought before the demise of these two groups. Although the Trojans themselves are known only from excavations at the site of Hisarlik (ancient Troy) in northwest Anatolia, both the Mycenaeans and the Hittites are by now fairly well known. The other group that may have been involved, the somewhat shadowy migratory Sea Peoples, is less known but still intriguing.

Mycenaeans

When Heinrich Schliemann began to excavate at the ancient site of Mycenae on mainland Greece in 1876, little was known about the civilization that inhabited the region during the Late Bronze Age. Schliemann had gone in search of Priam's city of Troy in 1870, and having fairly quickly ascertained its location in northwestern Turkey, he was determined to find the palace of Agamemnon.

His excavations at Mycenae gave a name to the civilization, the Mycenaeans, and his work there, as well as at the nearby site of Tiryns, was soon supplemented by other early archaeologists of various nationalities, who located and excavated additional Bronze Age sites across the Greek mainland, on Crete, and on the Cycladic islands. Within two decades, it was clear that the Mycenaeans had been established on the mainland of Greece from ca. 1700 to 1200 BCE. The first definitive volume on this subject, *The Mycenaean Age: A Study of the Monuments and Culture of Pre-Homeric Greece*, was published in 1896.

Mycenaean civilization can be reconstructed not only from the material remains that have been found during excavations at sites like Mycenae but also from a series of clay tablets that have been recovered from most of the major Mycenaean sites on mainland Greece and even on Crete. The tablets are inscribed with a writing system, known today as Linear B, with the characters scratched into the surface while the clay was still wet. Linear B was successfully deciphered in 1952; it is an early form of Greek and was used predominantly by an administrative bureaucracy that required permanent records of inventories and commercial transactions involving lists of people and goods.

The largest number of Linear B tablets has been found at Pylos, legendary home of the old and wise king Nestor, which was excavated in the 1930s by Carl Blegen of the University of Cincinnati. The city, located in the southwest of the Greek mainland, was destroyed about 1200 BC—part of the larger series of catastrophes that brought an end to the Mycenaean civilization. The fiery destruction accidentally baked the clay tablets, preserving them where they fell, to be discovered and deciphered thousands of years later.

The texts inscribed on these tablets are not literary masterpieces but simple economic texts. They consist primarily of mundane inventories of goods either entering or leaving the palace, with line after line of the number of chariot wheels that need to be repaired, the number of bolts of cloth sent to Mycenae, the number of slaves who need to be fed. Some of the female workers listed in the texts found at Pylos have ethnic names interpreted as western Anatolian in origin. These women came from Miletus, Knidus, and Halicarnassus on the western coast of Turkey; others from the Dodecanese Islands located just off this coast. They were probably slaves bought or captured by the Mycenaeans in the years before the Trojan War.

The Mycenaeans had an economy that was based on the so-called Mediterranean triad—grapes, olives, and grain. It was a primarily agrarian lifestyle, based on farming with a little fishing thrown in, at least for most of the people. The higher classes were able to indulge in a bit more luxury, owning goods and objects made of gold, silver, bronze, ivory, and glass. A middle class of merchants, artisans, and long-distance traders sustained and provided these indulgences. A textile industry and a perfume industry were among the most profitable, as was the production of olive oil and wine.

Some of these goods—especially textiles, perfume, and olive oil—were in demand not only in Greece itself but as far away as Egypt, Canaan (modern Israel, Syria, and Lebanon), and even Mesopotamia (modern Iraq). Mycenaean pottery was also in demand both at home and abroad, although it is not always clear whether it was valued in and of itself or for the contents that some of the vessels held. Several thousand Mycenaean jars, vases, goblets, and other vessels have been found in modern excavations, stretching from Egypt to Anatolia and beyond, with more being recovered each year, including at Troy.

The palaces of the Mycenaean kings were usually built on the highest hills in each area or section of Greece, as befitting the highest levels of authority of the land. They were heavily fortified, with thick walls and massive gates at the entrance to the citadel, such as the so-called Lion Gate at Mycenae. However, these palaces were much more than simply the residences of the kings; they also served as storage and redistribution centers for goods created at home or abroad and for agricultural products gathered at harvest time for later use. Around the palace, contained within the fortification walls of the citadel, were also the houses of the king's courtiers, administrators, and family members, as well as the workshops of the palace craftsmen.

On the slopes of the hill, spreading out below the citadel of virtually every Mycenaean palace in Greece, were the houses of the lower city. Here and in the surrounding smaller villages lived the everyday farmers, merchants, tradesmen, and craftsmen upon whom each kingdom depended. The majority of these people, both men and women, did not know how to read or write; probably less than 1 percent of the population was literate.

The Mycenaean civilization came to an end ca. 1200 BCE, or shortly thereafter, as part of the general collapse of civilizations that affected the entire Mediterranean region at this time. The cause is still not exactly clear, but there may have been a combination of factors involved, including drought, earthquakes, and invasion by outside groups.

Hittites

The Hittites were a civilization known by name, because of the Hebrew Bible, but were physically lost to the modern world until their rediscovery in the nineteenth century CE. The Bible refers

to the Hittites numerous times, primarily as one of the many
Canaanite tribes, which also included the Amorites, Hivites,
Perizzites, and Jebusites. There are also references to specific
Hittites, including Ephron the Hittite, from whom Abraham
bought a burial plot for his wife Sarah (Gen. 23:3–20), and
Uriah the Hittite, first husband of Bathsheba (2 Sam. 11:2–27).
King Solomon also had "Hittite women" among his entourage
(1 Kings 11:1).

Eventually it became clear, after investigations by pioneers such
as the Swiss explorer Johann Ludwig Burckhardt and scholars
such as the British Assyriologist A. H. Sayce, that the Hittites
were not located in Canaan but rather in Anatolia. One possible
explanation for the Bible's erroneous location is that the original
Hittites had disappeared by the time that the Hebrew Bible
was written down, between the ninth and the seventh centuries
BCE. Their successors—the so-called Neo-Hittites—were
firmly established in the northern part of Canaan by that point,
however, and it was they with whom the authors of the Bible
were familiar and to whom they referred anachronistically. In
addition, it also became apparent that the name "Hittites" is a
misnomer. Because the Bible referred to Hittites, the term was
simply adopted by scholars to refer to this Late Bronze Age
Anatolian kingdom. The Hittites, however, never referred to
themselves as Hittites; rather, they called themselves the "people
of the Land of Hatti."

By 1906, German archaeologists had begun excavating at
Hattusa, the capital city of the Hittites. Within a year they began
to uncover clay tablets, which recorded aspects of daily life as
well as official archival records and treaties. These were written
in several different languages, including Hittite, Akkadian,
and Luwian, all of which have now been deciphered to a large
degree. All of the texts dated to the Late Bronze Age, for the
Hittites, like the Mycenaeans, flourished from approximately
1700 to 1200 BCE.

We now know from those excavations and others at numerous additional sites throughout modern Turkey that the Hittites developed from smaller, little-known kingdoms into a fledgling empire in the mid-seventeenth century BCE, when they built their capital at Hattusa (modern Bogazköy, 125 miles east of Ankara). Some decades later they were already powerful enough to attack Babylon, bringing down the Old Babylonian dynasty begun by Hammurabi. Thereafter, until the collapse of the Hittite civilization in the twelfth century BCE, they rivaled Egypt as the main Near Eastern superpower.

We also know from documents found in modern Egypt, Syria, and Iraq as well as in Hattusa, that the Hittites traded, debated, and otherwise interacted with the other great powers of the Late Bronze Age. These included the New Kingdom Egyptians, the Assyrians, and the Babylonians, as well as smaller kingdoms at Ugarit and elsewhere in both north Syria and Anatolia, such as Troy (which the Hittites called Wilusa or Wilusiya). Overall, the Hittites seem to have been fairly self-sufficient, although we have textual evidence that they imported grain upon occasion, as well as probably olive oil and perhaps wine. After a century of excavation and study, scholars are now fairly confident about the reconstruction of Hittite society, religion, diplomacy, architecture, and material culture.

The high point of Hittite power came during the fourteenth and thirteenth centuries BCE, particularly during the reign of King Suppiluliuma I and the rulers who came after him, during which time the Hittite Empire expanded into northern Syria and came into repeated contact, and occasionally conflict, with the New Kingdom Egyptians. The last great Hittite king, Tudhaliya IV, who ruled from 1237 to 1209 BCE, claims to have conquered the island of Cyprus, carrying away gold and silver. The Hittite Empire collapsed soon thereafter, ca. 1200 BCE, perhaps because of the mysterious Sea Peoples who, according to Egyptian documents, destroyed the "Land of Hatti," or perhaps by unfriendly neighbors known as the Kashka, located just to the north of Hattusa.

Trojans

The region of Troy and the Troad was always a major crossroads from the Bronze Age on, controlling routes leading south to north and west to east, including the entrance to the Hellespont, the waterway leading from the Mediterranean to the Black Sea. Consequently, whoever controlled Troy also potentially controlled the entire region both economically and politically. It is not difficult to see why this region was so desirable for so many centuries to so many different peoples, from the time of the Trojan War right up to and including the Battle of Gallipoli during World War I. Thus, we should probably not be surprised that the Mycenaeans would also be interested in Troy and the western coast of Anatolia, especially since it was on the periphery of the region that they controlled in the Aegean, as well as on the periphery of the Hittite Empire.

Not much is known about the actual Trojans, though. Unlike the Mycenaeans and Hittites, who each had multiple sites in which their material culture and texts can be found, the Trojans occupied just one site, Troy, and its immediately surrounding area. Moreover, as scholars have pointed out, the Trojans were, literally speaking, anyone who happened to have been living in the city at a particular period in time. Since the city was destroyed and reoccupied several times during its history, with at least nine cities built one on top of the other within the mound of Hisarlik (identified as ancient Troy) in northwest Turkey, the ethnicity of the Trojans may well have been different in the third millennium BCE than it was a thousand years later, at the time of the Trojan War at the end of the second millennium BCE, and different again yet another thousand years later, when the Hellenistic Greeks and Romans occupied the site.

If we focus on the period of the Trojan War, however, we are able to glean some information not only from the four sets of excavations that have been conducted at Hisarlik/Troy over the past century and more but also from some of the texts found in other areas, belonging to civilizations dating to that time period. Thus, for example, we find Troy in the texts of the Hittites, assuming that we are correct in identifying it as the city that they call Wilusa. These show an ongoing relationship, sometimes hostile, sometimes peaceful, for several hundred years, with the Trojan kings frequently serving as vassal rulers to the Hittite Great King.

The Trojans were quite possibly also involved in the international trade that marked the cosmopolitan world of the Late Bronze Age. Numerous spindle whorls, associated with weaving, have been found during the excavations at Hisarlik, suggesting large-scale textile production. Homer also refers to the Trojans as breeders of horses, a valued commodity necessary for the chariots of the Bronze Age armies. However, both textiles and horses are perishable materials and little would remain of these in the archaeological record. Thus, we are hard-pressed to identify any Trojan goods that might have been exported to other parts of the Mediterranean at this time, including to the Mycenaeans, save for one particular type of pottery that has been identified as "Trojan Grey Ware," which may or may not have been produced in the Troad region.

Sea Peoples

We know of the Sea Peoples primarily from Egyptian records, for they attacked Egypt twice, in 1207 BCE during the reign of Pharaoh Merneptah, and again in 1177 BCE during the reign of Pharaoh Ramses III. They continue to perplex and mystify historians and archaeologists of the ancient Mediterranean, for they seem to come suddenly from nowhere, cause widespread disruption, take on some of the greatest powers of the region, and then abruptly disappear from history. It is the Egyptians who call them the "Peoples of the Sea," in inscriptions that describe them as coming from the north, from islands in the midst of the sea. Ramses III says specifically:

> The foreign countries made a conspiracy in their islands. All at once the lands were removed and scattered in the fray. No land could stand before their arms, from Khatte, Qode, Carchemish, Arzawa, and Alashiya on, being cut off at [one time]. A camp [was set up] in one place in Amor. They desolated its people, and its land was like that which has never come into being. They were coming forward toward Egypt, while the flame was prepared before them. Their confederation was the Peleset, Tjekru, Shekelesh, Denye(n), and Washosh, lands united. They laid their hands upon the lands as far as the circuit of the earth, their hearts confident and trusting: "Our plans will succeed!"

According to the traditional interpretation, the Sea Peoples brought an end to much of the civilized world at the end of the Late Bronze Age, ca. 1200 BCE, including the Hittites, Canaanites, Mycenaeans, and Minoans, but were then in turn brought to an end themselves by the Egyptians. The damage that they did during their marauding wave from west to east across the Mediterranean region was irrevocable.

According to more recent interpretations, however, the Sea Peoples are seen as much more than simply raiding parties and may actually have been more of a migration of entire peoples, complete with men, women, children, and possessions piled high upon carts pulled by oxen or other draft animals. Why they began their movements is a greatly debated question; the most likely scenarios involve natural catastrophes such as a prolonged drought or even earthquakes back in their homelands. They also may not have been responsible for as much of the damage observable at the end of the Late Bronze Age as has been thought, but rather they were only one of the many factors that caused the Mediterranean civilizations to come to an end at this time. And, it is not at all clear whether they attacked Troy or had anything to do with the Trojan War, although such scenarios have been suggested.

Literary warfare

Life was not always peaceful in the Late Bronze Age, nor were relations always friendly even between trading partners and neighboring civilizations. Especially during the years from 1500 BCE to 1200 BCE, there were a number of major battles in addition to the presumed Trojan War, fought either between the various great powers of the day or by them against lesser powers during periods of expansion. For instance, in addition to the battles against the Sea Peoples in 1207 and 1177 BCE, the Egyptians fought at Megiddo (biblical Armageddon), located in modern Israel, three centuries earlier, in 1479 BCE, against an army of Canaanite rebels. The battle ended in a decisive victory for the Egyptians, led by Pharaoh Thutmose III, and its details were duly inscribed on a wall of the Karnak Temple in Luxor, Egypt, making this the first recorded battle in history.

Similarly, the Egyptians also fought a major battle in 1286 BCE at the site of Qadesh in what is now modern Syria. This time they were led by Pharaoh Ramses II and were confronting the Hittites, led by King Mursili II. They were fighting over control of land in the region, in what was disputed territory between the Hittite Empire to the north and the Egyptian Empire to the south. The battle ended with both sides claiming victory and with a treaty signed by both parties. Copies of the treaty have been found both in Egypt and at Hattusa in Anatolia.

What these battles have in common is that although there is literary evidence that they took place, and no reason to doubt that they did, there is as yet absolutely no archaeological evidence for any of them. It can be argued that the same holds true for the Trojan War, for which we also have literary evidence but no definitive archaeological evidence (though even that may now be changing, depending upon how one interprets the recent finds from the site of Hisarlik). Thus, the Trojan War is not necessarily unique in the Late Bronze Age, neither in its occurrence in the first place nor in the literary manner by which its very existence has come down to us today.

Part II
Investigating the literary evidence

Chapter 3
Homeric questions: Did Homer exist and is the *Iliad* accurate?

Modern scholars studying the Greek literary evidence for the Trojan War are generally concerned with what is known as the "Homeric question." This actually consists of a multitude of smaller questions, of which the most relevant are: "Did Homer exist?" and "Does the information in Homer's *Iliad* and *Odyssey* reflect the Bronze Age (when the Trojan War took place), the Iron Age (when Homer lived), or something in between?" Although both questions are important, the latter has the more important implications for scholars studying the Trojan War, or excavating for the remains of Troy, or trying to re-create the world of the Bronze Age in the Aegean and eastern Mediterranean.

Homer

Not much is actually known about Homer or his life. The ancients held him in the highest regard as a bard—a traveling minstrel who sang of the heroic deeds of an age gone by—and he is still regarded as the first, and possibly the greatest, of the Greek epic poets. His genius reportedly lay in compiling, combining, and perhaps even ultimately writing down the story (or stories) of the Trojan War. One scholar, Barry Powell, has made the rather unusual suggestion that the Greek alphabet was invented so that the epics could be written down—that it was "invented by a single human being . . . to record the Greek hexameters of the poet we call Homer." Others have suggested that Homer may have created the epic poems but meant them to be passed along by an oral tradition, as had the earlier epics, until what we now know as the *Iliad* and the *Odyssey* were ultimately written down, perhaps as late as, or even later than, the sixth century BCE.

Assuming that Homer is a real person and the author of the epic poems, both of which are open to question, when and where did he live? Herodotus thought that Homer had lived approximately four hundred years before his own era, stating: "Homer and Hesiod . . . lived but four hundred years before my time, as I believe" (*Histories* II.53). Since Herodotus lived ca. 450 BCE, that would place Homer in the middle of the ninth century, ca. 850 BCE. However, after decades of discussion, scholars now generally place Homer about a century later, ca. 750 BCE, in part because one of his students, Arctinus of Miletus (composer of the *Aethiopis* and the *Iliupersis*) is said to have been born in 744 BCE (see Clement of Alexandria, *Stromata* 1.131.6).

Ancient Greek scholars, writers, and poets, among them Aristotle and Pindar, argued about Homer's origins. Some thought that Homer came from the city of Smyrna on the western coast of Anatolia (now Izmir in modern Turkey) and had worked for years on the island of Chios; others said that he had been born on Chios or on the island of Ios. In short, there has never been general agreement as to his origins. Indeed, there are many scholars who have insisted that he never existed, at least not as he is generally portrayed.

On the other hand, it has been suggested that Homer was not a single individual but was at least two people, Indeed, it was long thought, by German scholars in particular (among them Friedrich August Wolf in 1795), that the *Iliad* and the *Odyssey* were written by different people. At one point, a stylistic analysis of the texts by computer seemed to confirm this conclusion, but no general consensus has ever been reached. It has also been suggested that Homer was not a man, but a woman. Although the case for this hypothesis has recently been explored, the original suggestion goes back more than a century, to Samuel Butler, writing in 1897.

Perhaps most intriguing, and eminently plausible, is the suggestion that Homer was not a specific individual but was, instead, a profession. That is to say, there was no person named "Homer," but rather that one *was* a "Homer," a traveling bard who sang the epics of the Trojan War for his living. If so, then one or more of these professional bards may have written down the oral version of the story when a new writing system became generally available in the eighth century BCE. Overall, there is no shortage of suggestions, and books, about Homer. The simple answer, however, is that we actually know almost nothing about him, most importantly whether he actually wrote the two works, the *Iliad* and the *Odyssey*, which are generally attributed to him.

Bronze Age or Iron Age?

As for the second part of the Homeric question, we may well ask whether the information in the *Iliad* and *Odyssey* reflects events that occurred in the Bronze Age (1700–1200 BCE), the Iron Age (1200–800 BCE), or sometime in between. In order to answer this question, we must use information gleaned from the texts and compare it to information gained from archaeology.

We begin by testing the premise that the descriptions in the *Iliad*, the *Odyssey*, and elsewhere in the *Epic Cycle* are accurate representations of Bronze Age Greek society, and that they were handed down verbatim and without dilution by bards during the five hundred years between 1250 and 750 BCE. Could a single poet, or many poets, have accurately remembered, and transmitted, tens of thousands of lines of information over five centuries? What evidence, or examples, do we have that this might be the case?

Modern scholars using ethnographic analogies, such as Milman Parry in the 1920s, have documented that bards could indeed have accurately transmitted orally thousands of lines of epic poetry, for they recorded examples of modern poets and bards reciting and singing epics in Yugoslavia, Turkey, and Ireland. Clearly, it would have been no problem to accurately transmit such poems, especially if many of the lines or descriptions are stock, formulaic, and repetitive, such as "grey-eyed Athena," "swift-footed Achilles," and "rosy-fingered dawn."

The Catalogue of Ships from the *Iliad* (II.494–759), which mentions 1,186 ships in all, is considered by many scholars to be a reasonably accurate remnant from the Bronze Age, orally transmitted by generations of bards over the course of five centuries. Archaeological investigations have shown that many of the cities and towns listed in the catalogue as having sent men and ships were inhabited only in the Bronze Age and had long been abandoned by the time of Homer. Only ruins, if anything, would have been visible at these once-vital places during Homer's lifetime. Legends and stories could account for memories of some, but not for all; the only way for such a catalogue to be so accurate is if it had been composed at a time when the cities were flourishing, during the Late Bronze Age, and had then been handed down from bard to bard until finally inserted and written down as part of Book II of the *Iliad*. However, it is not a completely unblemished remnant from the Bronze Age, for there are cities present that should be absent and cities absent that should be present, if everything were strictly Bronze Age. Instead, it seems to be an amalgamation, with changes made over the centuries as the story was handed down orally by the bards.

Overall, the *Iliad* seems to be a compilation of details and data spanning the full range of time from the Bronze Age to the Iron Age. This may be expected, if changes and updates were constantly being made to the poem as it was handed down over the centuries, in order to keep it fresh and relevant. For instance, both Patroclus and Hector are said to have been cremated on funeral pyres following their deaths in battle (*Il.* XVIII.138–257 and XXIV.784–804, respectively): "they carried out bold Hector, weeping, and set the body aloft a towering pyre for burning. And set fire to it." Although the practice of cremation, rather than burial by inhumation, is much more typical of Iron Age Greece than of Bronze Age Greece, a cremation cemetery dating to the late fourteenth century BCE, in which the remains were buried in urns, was uncovered in level VIh at the site of Troy/Hisarlik.

In addition, the boars'-tusk helmets described in detail by Homer had gone out of use by the end of the Bronze Age. Boars' tusks from such helmets, and depictions of warriors wearing them, have been found at sites such as Tiryns on the Greek mainland, Knossos on Crete, and on the island of Delos, but they would no longer have been seen by the time of Homer, despite the knowledgeable description found in the *Iliad* (X.260–65):

> Meriones gave Odysseus a bow and a quiver and a sword; and he too
> put over his head a helmet fashioned of leather; on the inside the
> cap was cross-strung firmly with thongs of leather, and on the outer
> side the white teeth of a tusk-shining boar were close sewn one after
> another with craftsmanship and skill; and a felt was set in the center.

Similarly, the description that Homer gave of Ajax, and the large "Tower Shield" that he used is thought to be not only from the Bronze Age but from a period in the Bronze Age even earlier than the Trojan War:

45

> Now Ajax came near him, carrying like a wall his shield of bronze
> and sevenfold ox-hide which Tychios wrought him with much toil;
> Tychios, at home in Hylde, far the best of all workers in leather who
> had made him the great gleaming shield of sevenfold ox-hide from
> strong bulls, and hammered an eighth fold of bronze upon it. (*Il.*
> VII.219–23)

Such shields, and boars'-tusk helmets as well, can be seen in the
so-called Miniature Fresco painted in a house at Acrotiri on the
Greek island of Santorini, dating most likely to the seventeenth
century BCE, four hundred years before the Trojan War is said to
have been fought. Some scholars think that Ajax was a hero from
an earlier time, who was originally featured in another epic, now
lost, and was introduced into the *Iliad* as a character who would
already have been well known to the audience.

The Trojan hero Hector also wields a Tower Shield in one scene,
where his shield knocks against both his ankles and his neck (*Il.*
VI.117–18). Hector is also described as "complete in bronze armor"
(*Il.* XI.65). This, like similar descriptions elsewhere in the book,
is now thought to be validated by a discovery made at the site of
Dendra near Mycenae, which produced a full suit (panoply) of
armor reminiscent of Homer's description but dating to about
1450 BCE. This would make Homer's reference another example
of Bronze Age knowledge.

The more usual pieces of armor, including the leg greaves used by
the "well-greaved Achaeans" to protect their shins, are described
numerous times in the *Iliad* (e.g., III.328–39; IV.132–38; XI.15–45;
XVI.130–42; XIX.364–91) and also reflect Bronze Age items
rather than those of Homer's own time. The equipment is always
donned in the same order: greaves, corselet, sword, shield, helmet,
and then spears:

> Patroclus was helming himself in bronze that glittered. First he
> placed along his legs the beautiful greaves, linked with silver

fastenings to hold the greaves at the ankles. Afterwards he girt on
about his chest the corselet starry and elaborate of swift-footed
Aiakides. Across his shoulders he slung the sword with the nails of
silver, a bronze sword, and above it the great shield, huge and heavy.
Over his mighty head he set the well-fashioned helmet with the
horse-hair crest, and the plumes nodded terribly above it. He took
up two powerful spears that fitted his hand's grip. (*Il*. XVI.130–140)

Patroclus is also described in the *Iliad* as climbing the walls of
Troy three times, only to be knocked back by Apollo each time.
Homer's precise words are: "Three times Patroclus tried to mount
the angle of the towering wall, and three times Phoibos Apollo
battered him backward with the immortal hands beating back the
bright shield" (*Il*. XVI.702–3). The implication is that the walls
were climbable and, indeed, when archaeologists such as Heinrich
Schliemann, Wilhelm Dörpfeld, and Carl Blegen excavated the
remains of Hisarlik/Troy, they found that the walls of the citadel
of Troy VI were at such an angle and with enough spacing between
the stones that they could be readily climbed in at least one place.
At the time that Homer was writing, these walls may well have
lain buried deep under the surface, unseen for hundreds of years.
It seems likely, therefore, that Homer's description is an accurate
recollection of a Bronze Age fortification wall that had been
covered over long before Homer ever lived. And yet, Homer seems
to be describing the outer walls of Troy, rather than the walls of the
inner citadel, so there is some degree of confusion present in his
account.

Perhaps most telling is that Homer's warriors almost always use
bronze weapons, despite the fact that during his own age the
weapons were all made of iron. In the *Iliad*, few objects of iron are
mentioned, which is consistent with the fact that iron was known
but rare and valuable during the Bronze Age. In fact, one of the
few iron weapons known from the Bronze Age is a dagger found by
Howard Carter in the tomb of King Tutankhamun in Egypt, dating
to the fourteenth century BCE, which presents a possible parallel

for the iron knife held by Achilles as he mourned Patroclus (*Il.* XVIII.32–34).

Other details given by Homer confuse Bronze Age items and practices with those from the Iron Age. These are primarily minutiae, such as the number of spokes used in the wheels of the chariots used by Homer's warriors and the number of horses that drew those chariots. Bronze Age depictions, seen, for example, on grave markers found in the Shaft Graves at Mycenae and on gold rings found in other tombs at Mycenae and elsewhere, indicate that chariots at the time of the Trojan War had four spokes in their wheels, were pulled by two horses, and were used as moving platforms from which to fight. Homer's descriptions, however, indicate that his chariots had eight spokes in their wheels (*Il.* V.720–23), were frequently pulled by four horses, and were used as "battle taxis" to bring the warriors to the front lines, after which they dismounted to fight on foot—all of these are known characteristics of Iron Age chariots and fighting tactics, dating to long after the Trojan War.

Similarly, Homer's warriors usually carry two spears, which they used for throwing (*Il.* III.16–20, VII.244–48). This was a common Iron Age tactic, whereas warriors in the Bronze Age more often are shown with a long single spear, used for thrusting close-range at an opponent rather than throwing long distances. Such long spears are only infrequently described by Homer. However, he does mention an eleven-cubit-long spear wielded by Hector (*Il.* VI.318–20) and a single long spear belonging to Achilles (*Il.* XXII.273). Homer also frequently describes one-on-one fights or duels between major opposing heroes, designed to enhance the glory of the individual warriors; for example, Ajax and Hector (*Il.* VII.224–32) and Achilles and Hector (*Il.* XX). He also describes infantry marching in close formation (*Il.* III.1–9). Both the individual duel and the method of marching appear to be Iron Age methods of fighting, rather than those of the Bronze Age.

Additionally, Homer speaks frequently of weapons and other objects that are characteristic of the Mycenaean period as well as those that occur in the later Iron Age. He describes Mycenaean weapons like "silver-studded swords" (*Il.* XI.29–31)—that is swords with hilts riveted with silver or gold studs, such as have been found in the sixteenth to fifteenth century BCE Shaft Graves at Mycenae—as well as a scepter studded with golden nails (*Il.* I.245–46). He also describes Achilles's new shield (*Il.* XVIII.474–607) as made in a manner similar to the inlaid daggers that have been found in the Shaft Graves at Mycenae and elsewhere (using gold, silver, and a black gummy substance known as niello, inset into a base surface of bronze). All of these are proper Bronze Age artifacts. But Homer also describes Achilles's original shield (which was lost when Patroclus was killed in battle) as having a Gorgon face on it: "And he took up the man-enclosing elaborate stark shield, a thing of splendor. . . . And circled in the midst of all was the blank-eyed face of the Gorgon with her stare of horror, and Fear was inscribed upon it, and Terror" (*Il.* XI.32–37). Shields with such blazons, as they are called, did not come into general use until the Iron Age, reaching their peak usage during the Greek Hoplite phalanx warfare of the seventh century BCE.

In sum, Homer's recitation of the Trojan War and the minute details of the warriors, equipment, and fighting, as depicted in our version of the *Iliad*, contains a combination of Bronze Age and Iron Age practices. This amalgamation probably reflects the changes that were introduced into the original story as it was handed down over five centuries. Scholars, both archaeologists and ancient historians, are therefore very cautious about using the details provided by Homer when trying to reconstruct the Bronze Age in the Aegean. Indeed, it is partially this temporal combination, mixing different periods, that led earlier classicists to doubt that the Trojan War had actually happened.

However, one can obviously make the opposite argument. Homer's discussion contains much detail about the many objects and places that were only in use during the Bronze Age and that were not rediscovered until modern archaeologists began their excavations in the early twentieth century. It would not be surprising, therefore, if Homer's epic poems did reflect an authentic event that took place at the end of the Bronze Age, even if his account also includes some inaccuracies or details that were introduced during the centuries of oral transmission from one bard to another.

Neoanalysis

There is, however, one other point to consider, and that is the assessment by a number of scholars who argue that within the *Iliad*, the *Odyssey*, and the *Epic Cycle* are not only items from later in the Iron Age, but also people, places, and events that can be dated to earlier in the Bronze Age, that is, to before the thirteenth century BCE when the Trojan War is thought to have taken place. These scholars, who together comprise an informal grouping known as the German Neoanalysis School, argue that one can find bits and pieces of earlier epics that have been inserted into the Homeric epics.

For example, the first, ill-fated, Achaean expedition sent to rescue Helen at Troy, as recounted in the *Cypria*, reportedly resulted in Achilles and other Achaean warriors fighting in Teuthrania, an area in northwest Anatolia south of Troy, at some time immediately prior to the actual Trojan war. (Ancient and modern estimates for the elapsed time between the expeditions usually range from a few weeks to nine years.) The account of this expedition is seen by Neoanalysts as an excellent example of a pre-Homeric episode, most likely referring to an earlier "Trojan War." They also see the figure of Ajax, with his Tower Shield, as coming from a previous time and an earlier epic. The same might apply to the figures of Idomeneus, Meriones, and even Odysseus.

Neoanalysts and other scholars also point out that the *Iliad* itself mentions that the Greek hero Heracles sacked Troy in the time of Priam's father, Laomedon, using only six ships (*Il.* V.638–42): "Of other sort, men say, was mighty Heracles, my father, staunch in fight, the lion-hearted, who on a time came hither [to Troy] by reason of the mares of Laomedon with but six ships and a scantier host, yet sacked the city of Ilios and made waste her streets." (This previous expedition against Troy is depicted on the east pediment of the Temple of Aphaia on the island of Aegina, off the coast of Attica not too far from Athens.) At fifty men per ship, that would have been only three hundred men, which would have been a fairly small fighting force. However, an alternative tradition, mentioned by the later Greek authors Apollodorus and Diodorus, said that Heracles had eighteen, rather than six, ships under his command when he raided Troy, which would have meant that he had nine hundred men, a much more formidable army.

Clearly, there was a tradition in Greece, reflected even in the *Iliad* and the *Epic Cycle*, that Mycenaean warriors had been fighting and adventuring on the western coast of Anatolia for decades, and perhaps centuries, before the actual Trojan War, and that Troy itself may have been attacked by Mycenaeans almost a century before Agamemnon took on Priam. The ancient historian Moses Finley, in his book *The World of Odysseus* (1956), suggested that there were many "Trojan wars" during the Bronze Age.

The verdict

We are left with some fundamental, commonsense questions. Were the events and plot of the *Iliad* and *Epic Cycle* believable? Is it plausible that what Homer and the other epic poets describe actually took place and in the way that they say it did? Would an entire nation (or its ancient equivalent) really have gone to war over one person? Could Agamemnon really have been a "king of kings" who mustered so many men to retrieve his brother's wife? Was Mycenaean society of the Late Bronze Age really organized in that manner? And, what about the Trojan Horse—is it conceivable that such a machine was built and used successfully to end the war?

The answer to all of the above questions is yes. For instance, Homer's descriptions of the action, travels, battles, and other minutiae all ring true and the events depicted in the *Iliad* are believable, even if the arms, weaponry, and tactics come from a broad span of time, reflecting the oral transmission of the story over centuries. Furthermore, Bronze Age Greece was indeed split into a large number of what were essentially city-states, with each king ruling over a major city, such as Tiryns, Pylos, and Mycenae, and its surrounding region. And Mycenae certainly seems to have been more powerful and interconnected than the other cities of the time, especially if the foreign goods imported into the city and found by archaeologists are an indication of its international status.

It is unlikely that the war was actually fought because of Helen's kidnapping, even though that may have provided a convenient excuse. The real motivations were probably political and commercial, the acquisition of land and control of lucrative trade routes, as were most such wars in the ancient world. There are later historical examples, however, in which an action involving a single person was used as an excuse and catalyst to begin a war. The prime example is, of course, the assassination of Archduke Ferdinand that set off World War I. The war was probably destined to take place anyway, but the assassination served as the spark. A second example comes from the world of the Hittites, when the royal prince Zannanza, the son of king Suppiluliuma I, was killed by unknown attackers while on his way to marry an unnamed Egyptian queen in the fourteenth century BCE. His father used the death as an excuse to begin a war between the Hittites and Egyptians—a war that probably would have been fought eventually anyway, again for territorial reasons, which had nothing to do with the death of his son.

The Trojan Horse is among the least believable elements in the story, but even its presence can be explained. It is, frankly, unlikely that the Greeks would have built such a horse and hidden men in it; and it is even more unlikely that the Trojans would have been foolish enough to bring it inside their city. However, Homer and the other bards were poets, and as such, may be presumed to have taken some poetic license. It is not out of the question that the Trojan Horse represents some sort of siege engine, whether a huge battering ram, such as the Romans used in 74 CE to destroy the wall surrounding Masada in what is now modern-day Israel, or a tower from which the warriors could fight, like those depicted by Sennacherib in panels at his palace at Nineveh showing the siege of Lachish, just south of Jerusalem, in 701 BCE. It has also been suggested that the Trojan Horse is a metaphor for an earthquake that destroyed the city, for Poseidon was the Greek god of earthquakes and his symbol was a horse.

A final question relates to whether Homer was describing one Trojan war or several. The Greek epic tales document at least three Mycenaean attacks upon Troy and the region of the Troad during the Late Bronze Age; first, from the time of Heracles and Laomedon when Troy was sacked; then the mistaken attack on Teuthrania by Agamemnon and his men; and finally the battle for Troy as depicted in the *Iliad*. Which of these is Homer's Trojan War? Or are they all? Could Homer have telescoped these actions into a single great epic, a symbolic and poetic representation of numerous smaller conflicts that took place over several hundred years on the coast of western Anatolia? Indeed, there are additional indications, both archaeological and textual, that Greek warriors were fighting on the northwestern coast of Anatolia, and perhaps specifically at Troy, long before the thirteenth century BCE.

Chapter 4

The Hittite texts: Assuwa, Ahhiyawa, and Alaksandu of Wilusa

The Greeks recorded the Trojan War(s), but so too did the Hittites, located in central Anatolia. The Hittites controlled much of the region during the Late Bronze Age, from 1700 to 1200 BCE, all the way from the western coast where Troy lay to the eastern part of the country where Turkey now meets Syria. Clay tablets inscribed with texts in Hittite, Akkadian, and other contemporary languages have been found by German archaeologists at the capital city of Hattusa, located 125 miles (200 km) east of the modern city of Ankara.

Wilusa

Among these tablets are a number mentioning a city or area known to the Hittites as Wilusa, which was in frequent contact with the Hittite rulers over the course of at least three hundred years, including periods when the kings of Wilusa ruled at the pleasure of the Hittites, sometimes as puppet kings. It seems likely, according to most modern scholars, that the city of Wilusa is the same place that Homer and the Epic poets refer to as (W)ilios (that is, Troy). The Hittite archives contain details of at least four wars fought at this city during the Late Bronze Age. We even know the names of the kings concerned, including one named Alaksandu who was involved in a conflict dating to the early thirteenth century BCE and another named Walmu who was overthrown by an enemy force just a few decades later; both events took place during the same general time period as Homer's Trojan War and either or both could be related.

Beginning in 1911 and continuing until the present day, numerous scholars have suggested that Alaksandu is most likely the Hittite version of the Greek name Alexander. If this hypothesis is correct, one could tentatively identify the man known to the Hittites as Alaksandu of Wilusa as the same man known to the Greeks as Alexander/Paris of (W)ilios/Troy. If the two are not the same, then it would mean that two rulers with very similar names were ruling over two cities with very similar names at about the same time in northwestern Anatolia. Such a coincidence seems unlikely, and one can reasonably argue that it makes more sense to equate the two men.

Intriguingly, we also have the text of a treaty that was signed between Alaksandu, king of Wilusa, and the Hittite King Muwattalli II in the early thirteenth century BCE, in the aftermath of a war that was fought at Wilusa/Troy. We do not know which of the many battles fought at Troy might be referenced by this document, and so we cannot with certainty say whether the document supports or conflicts with the idea of the same individual playing a role in the literature of both cultures. We must, therefore, go back to a time before the thirteenth century war and then proceed forward in time in order to determine whether the battle described in the Hittite treaty is the same as the Trojan War described by Homer and the Greek poets. We are firmly within the realm of Hittite history here and have a wealth of detail available, even if the names are initially unfamiliar.

Ahhiyawa

We must first consider approximately two dozen texts discovered at Hattusa that mention a power and people known as Ahhiyawa. Scholarly quarrels about the identification of Ahhiyawa, and its possible relevance to the Trojan War, have now been ongoing for more than a century, ever since a Swiss scholar named Emil Forrer proposed that Ahhiyawa is a reference to the Bronze Age Mycenaeans, that is, the people whom Homer calls Achaeans (among other names). He went even further and identified specific people mentioned in the Hittite texts, linking them to Homer's warriors. For instance, Atreus and Eteokles of Homer were Attarissiya and Tawagalawa of the Hittites, in his view.

Others soon weighed in, including the German scholar Ferdinand Sommer, who in 1932 published a massive volume with all of the Ahhiyawa texts then known, with the primary intent of disproving Forrer's suggestions. The debate has continued ever since. It is now accepted by most knowledgeable authorities that Forrer was

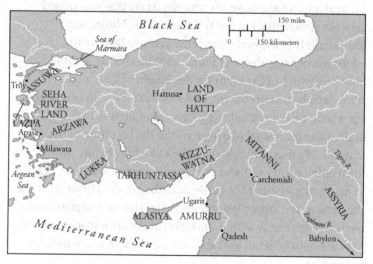

3. **Hittite Anatolia, ca. 1500–1200 BCE.**

correct in identifying Ahhiyawa as the Achaeans (Mycenaeans), most likely those from the mainland of Greece. If so, we can say that we have textual evidence for Mycenaeans involved in fighting and conflicts on the western coast of Anatolia as early as the fifteenth century BCE.

If Forrer is not correct, however, and the Ahhiyawans are not the Mycenaeans, then we have no textual evidence from the Hittites for any contact whatsoever between the two most powerful groups living on either side of the Aegean, themselves and the Mycenaeans. This seems unlikely, though, for if this were the case, we would have an important Late Bronze Age culture not mentioned elsewhere in the Hittite texts (the Mycenaeans) at the same time as having an important textually attested Late Bronze Age state or kingdom with no archaeological remains left whatsoever (Ahhiyawa). It makes far more sense to simply equate the two, as most scholars now agree.

Madduwatta and Attarissiya

One of the earliest of the so-called Ahhiyawa texts excavated at Hattusa dates to the time of the Hittite king Arnuwanda I but recounts an event that took place during the reign of his predecessor, Tudhaliya I/II, who ruled ca. 1450–1420 BCE. (It is uncertain whether there were one or two kings named Tudhaliya in this early period; hence the designation "I/II.") Known as the "Indictment of Madduwatta," because it concerns the activities of a Hittite vassal named Madduwatta, the text records the details of a direct engagement between the Hittites and a man named Attarissiya, described as "the ruler of Ahhiya" (Ahhiya being an early form of the word Ahhiyawa).

The text says plainly and without elaboration, that Attarissiya came to the western coast of Anatolia and fought against Hittite troops. We are told specifically that a Hittite officer named Kisnapili led thousands of infantry and a hundred chariots into battle against the forces of the Ahhiyawan ruler. We learn further that an officer on either side was killed, although there is no mention of the losses suffered by the regular infantry or the chariotry. This would have been nearly two hundred years before Homer's Trojan War. If one believes the numbers, the two opposing sides were substantial and were engaged in a real war, not merely a skirmish, for one hundred chariots was a large fighting force for that day and age.

Assuwa rebellion

Also among the texts discovered by the archaeologists at Hattusa are perhaps six that mention a rebellion in a region known as Assuwa—a region that can only have been located in northwestern Anatolia. This was a confederacy of twenty-two city-states that eventually gave its name to our modern geographical designation "Asia." It appears in the Hittite records primarily during the reign of the same Hittite king Tudhaliya I/II, during the latter part of the fifteenth century BCE.

At the time, Assuwa and its king rebelled against Hittite overlordship of the region, which had been established earlier. Among the twenty-two named members of the Assuwa coalition is Wilusiya, known to be an alternate name for Wilusa (i.e., Troy/Ilios). There is also a place called Taruisa, which appears on only one other Hittite text but here appears immediately next to Wilusiya. It also has been proposed as Troy or, more likely, the region of the Troad. If correct, it is interesting to note that these apparently alternative names for the same region in the Troad, Wilusa/Wilusiya and Taruisa, mirror the alternative names that the Greeks had for the same area, Ilios and Troy.

The Hittite records, specifically those known as the Annals of Tudhaliya, record that the Assuwa coalition began its rebellion as Tudhaliya I/II was returning from a military campaign against the west Anatolian polities of Arzawa, Hapalla, and the Seha

River Land, all known to lie on the western coast or immediately inland. Tudhaliya personally led his army against the coalition and defeated them. The annals state that ten thousand Assuwan soldiers, six hundred teams of horses and their Assuwan charioteers, as well as much of the population along with their animals and possessions, were taken back to the capital city of Hattusa as prisoners and booty. Included among these were the Assuwan king, named Piyama-Kurunta, his son Kukkulli, and a few other members of the royal family.

The order in which the events actually transpired is not completely clear, but Tudhaliya then apparently appointed Kukkulli as king of Assuwa, in place of his father, and allowed the coalition to be re-established, this time as a vassal state of the Hittite kingdom. Kukkulli himself then rebelled in turn, but this second attempt at revolt also failed. Kukkulli was put to death, and the coalition of Assuwa was destroyed. Thus the coalition was apparently rather short-lived, as a consequence of the intervention of Tudhaliya I/II. It appears to have existed primarily during the fifteenth century BCE.

Two additional points are relevant here. First, a bronze sword was accidentally found in 1991 at the capital city of Hattusa by a bulldozer operator doing repair work on a road leading into the ancient site. The sword has one line of writing on it, inscribed in Akkadian, the lingua franca of the day. It reads, in translation, "As Tudhaliya the Great King shattered the Assuwa country, he dedicated these swords to the storm-god, his lord."

Clearly, this sword was captured and dedicated by Tudhaliya after his victory over Assuwa, for such an inscription would have been carved on the blade only after the battle had been won. It is also clear that there was more than one sword originally dedicated, since we are told that "these swords" were dedicated. Most important, however, is that this is not a typical sword for anyone to have been using in Anatolia at that time, for it appears to be a type of sword specifically made and used by the Mycenaeans of mainland Greece only during the late fifteenth century BCE. The fact that it had been used, and captured, during the Assuwa rebellion means that either Mycenaeans themselves were also fighting in that conflict, against the Hittites, or that they had supplied weapons to, and been otherwise supportive of, the Assuwa coalition. This presents a unique instance of material evidence—as opposed to textual evidence—of Mycenaean involvement in a conflict fought in the region around Troy, fully two centuries before the date usually given to Homer's Trojan War.

Wilusa and Ahhiyawa

In addition, at least one city-state that belonged to the coalition, specifically Wilusa/Wilusiya, continued to exist for another two centuries. During that time, Wilusa not only interacted with the Hittites but was also clearly involved with the political entity known as Ahhiyawa, as well as with specific individuals from that entity, for among the twenty-eight known Hittite texts that mention Ahhiyawa or the Ahhiyawans are a few that specifically discuss their activities as related to Wilusa. If the Ahhiyawans are correctly identified as the Mycenaeans, as most scholars now agree, then we have textual evidence that Mycenaeans were involved in the affairs, and fighting on behalf of, the city-state of Wilusa (Troy), from the fifteenth to the thirteenth centuries BCE.

For instance, Mycenaean involvement with Wilusa in the Assuwa rebellion may be circumstantially indicated in a much later Ahhiyawa text, which is a translation into Hittite of a letter sent by the king of Ahhiyawa to a Hittite king, probably Muwattalli II, in the early thirteenth century BCE. Muwattalli, we know, ruled from approximately 1295 to 1272 BCE. The letter, which is partly concerned with much earlier events, was thought until recently to have been sent by Muwattalli to the king of Ahhiyawa, but has now been shown to have traveled in the opposite direction; as such, it is one of a very few letters to have been dispatched by an Ahhiyawan king to his Hittite counterpart.

The primary topic discussed in the letter is the ownership of a group of islands lying off Anatolia's Aegean coast, which had formerly belonged to the king of Ahhiyawa but had apparently been seized by the Hittites. Within the letter, we are told that sometime in the past a Hittite king named Tudhaliya had defeated the king of Assuwa and subjugated him. This matches the account found in the earlier Annals of Tudhaliya and is undoubtedly a reference to the Assuwa rebellion, so we know that the letter refers to events that had taken place about 150 years earlier.

The letter is damaged and incomplete, but it now seems, based on a new translation, that a diplomatic marriage had taken place between the current Ahhiyawan king's great-grandfather and an Assuwan princess, at a time prior to the Assuwan rebellion, and that the islands were transferred by the Assuwan king to the Ahhiyawan king as part of the dowry. The Hittites claimed that Tudhaliya's victory over Assuwa during the rebellion had given them possession of Assuwa's offshore territories, but according to the letter's author, the current king of Ahhiyawa, the victory had taken place only after these territories had already been presented to Ahhiyawa. Now the Ahhiyawan king was, a century and a half later, seeking to reaffirm his claim to the islands through diplomatic means.

The new translation of this letter indicates that there were good relations and, most intriguingly, apparently a dynastic marriage between the Ahhiyawans and the Assuwans during the mid-fifteenth century BCE. If we are correct in our identification of Ahhiyawa as the Mycenaeans and of the Trojans (Wilusa) as part of the Assuwa coalition, then we have in this document a good indication of relations between the two regions, marital and otherwise, beginning centuries before the presumptive time of Alexander/Paris and Helen's illegitimate affair. However, the letter does not indicate definitively that the Mycenaeans were actually drawn into the Assuwa Rebellion, as previous translations had possibly suggested, but the inscribed sword found at Hattusa does imply some sort of involvement, and a defeat suffered by the allied Mycenaeans and Trojans.

Additional Ahhiyawa texts, as well as pottery and other artifacts found on the coast of western Anatolia, indicate continued Mycenaean involvement in the region throughout the fourteenth century BCE. Still another series of texts specifically relevant to Wilusa date to the early and mid-thirteenth century BCE, approximately the time of Homer's Trojan War.

The Alaksandu Treaty and other Hittite texts

The first of these texts was sent to a Hittite king (probably Muwattalli II) by Manapa-Tarhunta, a king of the Seha River Land, located in western Anatolia just to the south of the region of the Troad. The letter, which is primarily concerned with the defection of a group of skilled Hittite craftsmen, specifically mentions a Hittite attack on Wilusa: "[Thus says] Manapa-Tarhunta, your servant: Say [to His Majesty, my lord]: [At the moment] everything is fine [in the land]. [Kassu] came (here) and brought the troops of Hatti. [And when] they went back to attack Wilusa, [I was] ill."

We do not know why Muwattalli and the Hittites attacked Wilusa at this time, early in the thirteenth century BCE. However, the treaty that Muwattalli subsequently drew up and signed with Alaksandu of Wilusa, generally dated to about 1280 BCE, makes it clear that the Hittites claimed control over the city and the region thereafter, just as they had in the time immediately following the Assuwa rebellion.

The Alaksandu Treaty, as it is called, outlines a defensive alliance between Wilusa and the Hittites. Here Muwattalli writes: "You,

Alaksandu, benevolently protect My Majesty. And later protect my son and my grandson, to the first and second generation. And as I, My Majesty, protected you, Alaksandu, in good will because of the word of your father, and came to your aid, and killed your enemy for you, later in the future my sons and my grandsons will certainly protect your descendant for you, to the first and second generation. If some enemy arises for you, I will not abandon you, just as I have not now abandoned you. I will kill your enemy for you."

It is this part of the treaty that is of the greatest interest, for here we are told by Muwattalli himself that he had, at some point earlier in his reign (1295–1272 BCE), come to the aid of Alaksandu and killed his enemy. This, we can conclude, is probably accurate information, since there is no reason for Muwattalli to have misstated or misremembered such current information, known to both parties. The question, however, is the identification of the enemy of Alaksandu, whose name or nationality—frustratingly— we are not given. Nor are we told any of the details regarding the circumstances surrounding this event. Instead, Muwattalli continues on and reiterates the mutual defense pact that they have in place.

In brief, we have evidence from the Hittite texts of at least two conflicts fought by Alaksandu, king of Wilusa, at some point immediately prior to 1280 BCE. In one, against an unknown enemy, Alaksandu was victorious, but only because Muwattalli and the Hittite army came to his aid. Although this is in the approximate era of Homer's Trojan War, we do not know for certain that it was the Mycenaeans who were the adversaries in this conflict. In the other, against the Hittites, he was defeated and forced to sign a treaty. Neither event is consistent with the story told to us in the *Iliad* or the *Epic Cycle*. Thus, however tempting it is to link Alaksandu of Wilusa to Alexander/Paris of (W)Ilios/ Troy, we cannot conclusively link these conflicts and this treaty to Homer's Trojan War, unless we posit that Homer has his details wrong.

The Tawagalawa Letter

Of the two additional Ahhiyawa texts that have some bearing on Wilusa, the so-called Tawagalawa Letter is of substantial interest. It is thought to have been written by a king of Hatti, probably Hattusili III, who ruled ca. 1267–1237 BCE, but possibly by Muwattalli II, who ruled slightly earlier. We possess only the third, and probably final, tablet of this letter, which is concerned with the activities of Piyamaradu, a "renegade Hittite" who was actively involved with Ahhiyawa. The letter does not give the name of the king of Ahhiyawa, but it does give the name of his brother, Tawagalawa, who was apparently present in person in western Anatolia, helping to transport local rebels to Ahhiyawan territory. Numerous scholars, beginning with Forrer, have suggested that Tawagalawa might be a Hittite representation of the Greek name Eteokles—Mycenaean *E-te-wo-ke-le-we*.

Within this letter, the Hittite king attempts to put words into the mouth (or onto the tablet) of the Ahhiyawan king, asking him to communicate specific topics to someone (probably Piyamaradu). He states, quite specifically, "O, my brother, write to him this one thing, if nothing (else): 'The King of Hatti has persuaded me about the matter of the land of Wilusa concerning which he and I were hostile to one another, and we have made peace. Now(?) hostility is not appropriate between us.' [Send that] to him." A few lines later, he says again, "And concerning the matter [of Wilusa] about which we were hostile—[because we have made peace], what then?"

This is one of the only instances in all of the Hittite texts thus far translated, and the first since the time of Tudhaliya I/II, where we have a specific reference to a conflict between Hatti and Ahhiyawa. Even in the Alaksandu Treaty, Alaksandu's opponent is unnamed and may not be the Ahhiyawans. And, we do not know the scale of the conflict described in the Tawagalawa Letter. Trevor Bryce of the University of Queensland points out that the Hittite word used in this text can be translated as meaning anything from "outright war, a skirmish or two, or merely a verbal dispute conducted through diplomatic channels." Nevertheless, this may be evidence that there was another hostile exchange between the Hittites and the Ahhiyawans (that is, the Mycenaeans) around the time that the events described in the *Iliad* were taking place.

Walmu of Wilusa

Finally, the last textual reference relevant to this topic is a letter probably written in the late thirteenth century BCE by one of the last Hittite kings, Tudhaliya IV, who ruled from ca. 1237–1209 BCE. It is known as the Milawata Letter, because of its principal concern with the city of Milawata (Miletus) as well as with the continuing activities of Piyamaradu (see table 1).

In the letter, the Hittite king notes that a king of Wilusa named Walmu, who had been driven from his land by unnamed forces, was to be reinstated, probably as a military vassal: "Now, my son, as long as you look after the well-being of My Majesty, I, My Majesty, will put my trust in your good will. Turn Walmu over to me, my son, so that I may reinstall him in kingship in the land of Wilusa. [He shall] now be King of the land of Wilusa, as he was formerly. He shall now be our military vassal, as he [was] formerly." Clearly the treaty signed with Alaksandu was still in force, for the Hittites had sworn to help his descendants to the first and second generations. One might speculate that this final conflict, during which the Wilusan king lost his throne as the result of an attack by a rebel force, only to have it restored to him by the Hittites, could have contributed to the later understanding by Homer that the Trojans had lost the war.

A Wilusiad?

Speaking of Homer and the Hittites, it was Calvert Watkins of Harvard University who first suggested, at a conference on Troy and the Trojan War held at Bryn Mawr College in 1984, that

Table 1. Known Trojan (Wilusa) Wars from Hittite records

Event	Wilusa ruler	Hittite king	Approx. date	Result
Assuwan revolt, two phases	Piyama-Kurunta and son Kukkulli	Tudhaliya I/II	1430–1420 BCE	Exiled to Hattusa (father) and put to death (son)
Attacked first by enemy and then by Hittites	Alaksandu	Muwattalli II	1280 BCE	Aided, then defeated, by the Hittites
Conflict over Wilusa between Hittites and Ahhiyawa	??	Hattusili III	1267–1237 BCE	Resolved
Attacked by enemy force	Walmu	Tudhaliya IV	1237–1209 BCE	Deposed by enemy, but then reinstated by Hittites

certain other Hittite texts might contain the remnants of what he called a possible *Wilusiad*. This would have been, he hypothesized, another historical epic about the Trojan War but one written from the perspective of the Trojans or the Hittites rather than the Greeks.

The *Wilusiad* will have been written in Luwian, a language or dialect spoken throughout Anatolia at the time, but we have only two possible lines left to us. One of the lines, inserted and quoted in a Hittite ritual text, reads quite simply: "[and they sing:] 'When they came from steep Wilusa.'" This language is reminiscent of Homer, who refers to Troy as "steep Ilios" no fewer than six different times in the *Iliad*. A second line, found inserted in another Hittite text, may be reconstructed to read: "When the man came from steep [Wilusa . . .]"

Unfortunately, we have nothing more than these two possible lines at the moment. But this could change, as additional Hittite tablets are currently lying undeciphered in collections throughout Europe and the United States, awaiting translation by scholars.

Speculations

A number of these suggestions are based on scholarly speculation, such as equating Wilusa with (W)ilios/Troy, Ahhiyawa with the Achaeans/Mycenaeans, and Alaksandu with Alexander/Paris. All of these are plausible, to a greater or lesser degree, with the consequence that some have been debated by scholars for more than a century. None is completely out of the realm of possibility, and some actually seem quite likely. Needless to say, if all were to turn out to be incorrect, we would be left with nothing substantial to point to, which remains a possibility. The majority of scholars, however, currently favor some or all of the above equations, especially the correlation between Ahhiyawa and the Achaeans, which allows us to utilize the Hittite texts as textual evidence with potential implications for several Trojan Wars.

So which of these four or more conflicts recorded in the Hittite texts is Homer's Trojan War? Are any of them? At least two, and possibly all, of these wars seem to have involved the Mycenaeans (Ahhiyawa) in some manner. At present, however, it is uncertain which, if any, of these conflicts is the Trojan War, as recorded by Homer and the Epic poets, or whether the Greek poems are a reflection of what seems to have been more than several hundred years of on-again, off-again conflict between the Hittites and the Ahhiyawans (Mycenaeans)—a telescoping of numerous events into a series of epic poems about the "war to end all wars."

Since the jury is still out, we must turn to the archaeological evidence that indicates several attacks, which resulted in destructions at the city of Hisarlik, identified as ancient Troy, during the Bronze Age. There are nine cities located one on top of another inside the ancient mound, and so here too we must consider which, if any, was the one immortalized by Homer in his grand epic of love and war, as recorded in the *Iliad*.

Part III
Investigating the archaeological evidence

Chapter 5
Early excavators: Heinrich Schliemann and Wilhelm Dörpfeld

The story of the search for Troy is inextricably intertwined in the story of the nineteenth-century businessman Heinrich Schliemann who is frequently referred to, albeit inaccurately, as the "father of Mycenaean archaeology." Schliemann was a German self-made millionaire who was among the luckiest individuals ever to put a shovel into the earth. His is a success story, for, as a self-taught "amateur" archaeologist, he was the first to comprehensively excavate at the site that most scholars now agree is probably ancient Troy. He did this against all odds and against the general thinking of the academics of his day, most of whom were convinced that the Trojan War had never taken place and therefore that there was no such place as ancient Troy. Schliemann also successfully excavated at the sites of Mycenae and Tiryns on the Greek mainland, searching for Agamemnon and his forces.

But, according to recent research, Schliemann was also apparently a scoundrel who falsified his excavation journals and who cannot necessarily be relied upon concerning details of either his professional or private life. For example, in his archaeology, he failed to give credit to Frank Calvert, the man who led him to the site of Hisarlik—ancient Troy. Moreover, Schliemann may have completely made up his account of finding "Priam's Treasure," which is neither Priam's nor a treasure per se but rather a collection of valuable artifacts that dates to fully a thousand years before the Trojan War.

Schliemann's search

Schliemann began his search for Troy after retiring from his business enterprises as a millionaire at age forty-five or so. He claims to have been waiting virtually all of his life, since the age of seven, to begin his search and prove that the Trojan War had taken place. In the introduction to his book *Ilios: the City and Country of the Trojans* (1881), he recounts seeing a woodcut engraving of Aeneas fleeing from the burning city of Troy, with his aged father upon his back and his young son holding his hand, in a book that he received in 1829 as a Christmas gift from his father.

Schliemann told his father that the story must have happened, and that Troy must have existed, otherwise the artist could not have known how to engrave the picture. (Such is the logic and reasoning of a seven-year-old.) He then informed his father that he would find Troy when he grew up. It is a marvelous autobiographical story, and one that is still frequently told about Schliemann. Unfortunately, it probably never happened. The story does not appear in any of Schliemann's writings, including his private journals and introductions to other books, until after he had already discovered Troy and announced to the world that the Trojan War had indeed happened. The scholarly consensus now is that Schliemann made up the tale much later in life, for reasons known only to himself.

Schliemann made his money as a successful businessman, who earned one fortune selling indigo, tea, coffee, and sugar in the

Crimea, and another during the California gold rush in 1851–52. It was in California that he served as a banker/middleman in Sacramento, buying gold dust from the miners and selling it to the Rothschild banking family, via its representative in San Francisco. He bought low and sold high—and, some say, kept his thumb on the scales while doing so. He may well have left California one step ahead of the law, perhaps with as much as $2 million in profits, amid charges concerning the amount of gold dust that he was shipping.

Schliemann kept journals throughout his life, and his time in the United States in 1851–52 was no exception. Unfortunately for Schliemann, several entries from this period show that even his private scribbling cannot be trusted. For instance, an ostensibly eyewitness account written by Schliemann of a great fire in San Francisco in June 1851 is highly suspect, for it appears that the fire actually took place a month earlier, in May, and that Schliemann was in Sacramento, not San Francisco, at the time. Detective work by David Traill, a professor at the University of California–Davis, has now shown that Schliemann had simply copied a newspaper account from the front page of the *Sacramento Daily Union* verbatim into his journal, changing the story slightly by inserting himself into it.

Additional "invented episodes," as William Calder III of the University of Illinois has termed them, probably include an entry for February 1851, in which Schliemann records that he was in Washington, DC and visited for an hour and a half with President Millard Fillmore during an extravagant reception. As both Calder and Traill point out, although this is not entirely out of the question, it seems highly unlikely that the president would have met with an unknown twenty-eight-year-old German, even one who spoke fluent English as did Schliemann. As with the San Francisco fire, the account was probably culled from a newspaper article, into which Schliemann placed himself.

While living in Sacramento in 1851, Schliemann filed a statement of intention to apply for US citizenship, although it was not until nearly twenty years later, arriving in New York City in late March 1869, that he did finally apply. In order to obtain it, however, Schliemann had to persuade a man named John Bolan to swear that Schliemann had been living in the United States for the five previous consecutive years, and that he had been living in New York State for at least a year, even though neither was true. Bolan had to perjure himself, but it worked. Schliemann received his citizenship, just two days after he arrived in New York.

A few days later, in early April 1869, Schliemann moved on to Indiana, which at the time had the most lenient divorce laws of any state. There, he applied to divorce his first wife, Katarina, who was back in Germany and with whom he had had three children, two of whom had survived childhood. By the end of June, having lived in Indiana for all of three months, he had received the divorce decree despite the requirement to have lived in the state for a year. Most likely he had found someone to testify to that effect, as he had just done in New York.

In the meantime, Schliemann had already begun to devote his life to finding the site of ancient Troy and proving that the Trojan War had taken place. A year earlier, in 1868, Schliemann had visited Ithaca and then Mycenae in Greece, before continuing on to Turkey. There, after fruitless visits to several ancient mounds favored by many others as the location of Troy, including sites known as Bunarbasi and Balli Dagh, Schliemann befriended the American vice-consul to Turkey, a man named Frank Calvert. Calvert believed that he himself had already discovered Troy. In fact, he had bought a portion of the ancient site—a mound called Hisarlik—and had already dug a few trial trenches. Calvert was by no means the first person to think that Hisarlik might contain the ruins of Bronze Age Troy; the suggestion had apparently first been made back in 1822, the year of Schliemann's birth, in a book published by the Scottish journalist Charles Maclaren, who was a member of several learned geographical societies. Calvert offered to join forces with Schliemann. It was an offer Schliemann gladly accepted, for he had money but no site, while Calvert had a site but no money. It promised to be a worthwhile partnership.

Upon his return from the United States, in September 1869, just a few months after procuring both his American citizenship and divorce through unorthodox and possibly illegal means, Schliemann married Sophia Engastromenos in Athens. He was forty-seven; she was sixteen. They had two children, whom they named Andromache and Agamemnon—but that would come later.

In April 1870, Schliemann began to dig at Hisarlik, ignoring the fact that he had not yet received an excavation permit from the Turkish authorities. He dug again at the site in 1871, but it was not until 1872 that he began his most audacious attack on the mound. Cutting a huge trench some forty-five feet deep right through the middle of the ancient hill, Schliemann had his workmen dig as quickly and as deeply as they could, for he believed that a city three thousand years old would be buried far below. He and his men cut through layer after layer of ancient settlements, first one, then two, then three cities, and more. Eventually, with the help of his architect, Wilhelm Dörpfeld, whose services he engaged ten years later, Schliemann identified remains from numerous cities built one on top of the other; he thought that there were six cities, or possibly seven. It is now clear, after more than a century of excavation at the site, that there were actually nine cities in all, with additional subphases and remodelings belonging to each. At the time, neither Schliemann nor Dörpfeld realized that there were so many layers.

Troy II and Priam's Treasure

Schliemann was convinced that the "Burnt City," as he called it, was Priam's Troy. It was unclear to him at first whether this was the second city built at the site—Troy II as it is now known—or the third city. Schliemann initially thought it was the second city but, persuaded by others, including Calvert, he mistakenly identified it as the third city throughout his book *Ilios* (1881). It was Dörpfeld who showed him, just one year later in 1882, that he had been correct in the first place; it was indeed the second city, rather than the third. Regardless of the label, Schliemann felt that this was the city that the Mycenaeans had taken ten long years to capture, using the stratagem of the wooden horse. The excavations of 1873, the year that Schliemann discovered Priam's Treasure, only served to convince him even more that he was correct in his identification.

Schliemann's own account of the discovery of Priam's Treasure says that he was wandering around the excavation one morning at the end of May, keeping an eye on all of the workmen, when he suddenly noticed one of them uncovering a large copper object, behind which he could see a glint of gold. Schliemann quickly announced to the workers that it was breakfast time, even though it was far from it, and while they were eating, he called for his wife and "cut out the Treasure with a large knife" (see fig. 4).

Schliemann says that he and Sophia unearthed the objects, including bronze, silver, and gold vessels, jewelry, and other artifacts. They did so at great personal risk, according to Schliemann, for towering above them was a high bank of earth, which threatened to come down upon them at any moment. Sophia gathered the smaller objects together in her apron or shawl and carried them into the house, and Schliemann followed with the larger objects.

Once inside, they made a quick inventory, noting that the treasure included a copper shield and vase; various vessels of gold, silver, or electrum; thirteen spearheads; fourteen battle axes; daggers, a sword, and other objects of copper or bronze; and numerous objects of gold, including two diadems, a headband, sixty earrings, and nearly nine thousand smaller ornaments. They then packed everything up in several large crates, and arranged for them to be

4. Pieces from "Priam's Treasure" were displayed by Heinrich Schliemann after their discovery at Troy. They were eventually shown to be from the Early Bronze Age, rather than the Late Bronze Age, and were a thousand years too early to have belonged to Priam.

smuggled out of Turkey and across the Aegean Sea to their house in Athens. When both they and the treasure were safely in Greece, Schliemann bedecked his wife in the gold jewelry and took her picture, before announcing to the world that he had found Priam's treasure (see fig. 5).

Knowing that Schliemann was untrustworthy in his personal life sends up a red flag that we might not want to take his word at face value when it comes to his professional life, especially the details recorded in his excavation journals. It is now clear that there are many problems with Schliemann's account of finding this treasure, first and foremost of which is the fact that Sophia was not even at Troy on the day that Schliemann said the treasure was found. His own diaries record that Sophia was in Athens at the time. He later admitted as much, saying that he just wanted to involve her in his life so much that he wrote her into the story, thinking that it would get her more interested in what had become his life's passion.

More recently, the treasure has been the focus of much scholarly investigation. It is abundantly clear that it cannot be Priam's treasure, for Schliemann identified its findspot as within the Burnt City, that is, Troy II, which we now know dates to about 2300 BCE. In fact, the items found in this "treasure" look remarkably like other items of jewelry found across a wide swath of territory, from the so-called Death Pits of Ur in Mesopotamia (modern Iraq) in the east to the site of Poliochni on the Aegean island of Lemnos in the west, all dating to the same approximate time period, just after the middle of the third millennium BCE and more than a thousand years too early to have belonged to Priam, Helen, or anyone else involved with the Trojan War.

Moreover, many scholars are convinced that Schliemann made up the entire story of its discovery—not only placing Sophia at the site when she was not there but making up the very existence of the treasure in the first place. Though there is little doubt that

5. Sophia Schliemann, shown in Athens wearing the jewels from "Priam's Treasure," which turned out to be from a period more than a thousand years before the time of Priam and the Trojan War.

Schliemann did find all of these objects at Troy, there is a good chance that he did not find them all together. Instead, many believe that he may have made a series of smaller discoveries all over the site throughout the excavation season, but held off announcing these finds until he had accumulated enough to put them together as one big "treasure" that would amaze the world when he announced its discovery. Ironically, if Schliemann had not erroneously labeled these items as "Priam's Treasure," they would not hold nearly the value nor interest that they do today. But Schliemann was a master showman and he knew that giving the items this label, whether accurate or not, would draw the world's attention to his site and his claim to have found the city of Troy, as indeed it did.

Eventually, Schliemann sent the treasure to Germany, where it was displayed in the Berlin Museum until near the end of World War II, when it simply disappeared for nearly fifty years. In the early 1990s, the Russian government admitted that the treasure had been taken to Moscow in 1945, as part of what they considered to be war reparations; it is now on display in the Pushkin Museum.

Since Schliemann thought that Priam's Troy was the Burnt City, the second of the nine cities that he had uncovered at the site, he and his men had dug hastily through the cities lying above, especially in the early 1870s. During his later campaigns, in 1879 and in the 1880s, he was far more careful, and often took the advice of scholars, but still much of the material from these upper, and later, cities was simply thrown out. This, as it turned out, was very unfortunate, for toward the end of his life, convinced by Dörpfeld and by his own findings at Mycenae and Tiryns on the Greek mainland, not to mention other scholars, Schliemann finally admitted that he had been mistaken. Troy II was indeed a thousand years too early and it was more likely that Troy VI or Troy VII—the sixth or seventh cities—were those belonging to the time of the Trojan War.

Schliemann eventually understood this, because he discovered the same sort of Mycenaean pottery at Mycenae and Tiryns as he had previously found at Troy VI and VII, meaning that these levels all dated to approximately the same time period during the Late Bronze Age. Others, including Frank Calvert, had for years been pointing this out to him and to anyone else who would listen. Unfortunately, it was too late. Schliemann's men had already destroyed or thrown away many of the very buildings and objects for which he had been searching. He had not realized that the later Greeks and Romans had already shaved off the highest part of the mound in order to build the temples and other structures of their own cities. Thus Priam's Troy—because of the earthmoving efforts of the Hellenistic Greeks and Romans—was much closer to the modern surface than Schliemann had suspected.

Schliemann began preparations for a new campaign at the site, but before he could begin, he collapsed on a busy city street in Naples on Christmas Day 1890. He died the next day. His body was sent to Athens, where he was buried in the First Cemetery, a place of honor. A monument was placed over his grave, in the form of a small Greek temple with various scenes relating especially to the Trojan War and his excavations at Troy, Mycenae, Tiryns, and elsewhere, complete with an image of Schliemann himself holding a copy of the *Iliad*.

Dörpfeld and Troy VI

After Schliemann's death, Wilhelm Dörpfeld, his architect, took over as director of the excavations at Hisarlik, financed in part by Sophia Schliemann. He dug for two seasons, in 1893 and 1894, this time focusing on the ruins of the sixth city at Troy. First settled about 1700 BCE, Troy VI had undergone many renovations, resulting in at least eight subphases, which were eventually detected by archaeologists and labeled a–h, before its final destruction several hundred years later.

Although Schliemann had excavated much of the central part of the citadel at Hisarlik, he had left the outer edges untouched, and it was here that Dörpfeld spent most of his time, money, and energy. His efforts paid off when he uncovered a tremendous fortification wall sweeping around the citadel of Troy VI, made of well-built limestone and worthy of Homer's heroic epics.

Dörpfeld uncovered three hundred yards of this wall, as well as entry gates and a watchtower still standing to a height of twenty-five feet. It is the remains of these fortifications that can be seen today when one visits Hisarlik/Troy (see fig. 6). Homer may have been accurately describing them in the *Iliad*, complete with the angle or "batter" mentioned in connection with Patroclus's attempt to climb the wall (*Il.* XVI.702–3), despite his possible confusion between the inner walls of the citadel and the outer walls of the city.

The final version of this city, Troy VIh, was the most impressive. Not only were there the high walls and towers of stone surrounding the citadel, but large houses and the palace graced the interior. This was a wealthy city, a desirable plum commanding the Hellespont—the passageway from the Aegean to the Black Sea— and growing wealthier from a combination of trade and taxation. At certain points during this period, its wealth and foreign contacts may have rivaled that of the larger Mycenaean palaces, though perhaps not that of Mycenae itself. The winds and the current in the Hellespont frequently presented adverse conditions for ships wishing to sail up to the Black Sea, and so these ships presumably would be forced to linger, sometimes for weeks on end, until the weather turned in their favor. Troy, and its nearby harbor facilities at Beşiktepe, would have played host to the crews of these ships and their passengers, be they merchants, diplomats, or warriors.

The goods found by archaeologists in the ruins of Troy VI provide evidence of the city's wealth. Imported objects from Mesopotamia,

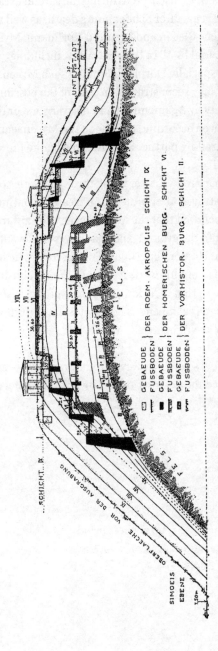

6. A schematic section of Troy, according to Wilhelm Dörpfeld, showing the nine major cities located one on top of another. The dotted lines at the top of the mound show where the Hellenistic Greeks and then the Romans shaved off the top of the mound, removing some of the Bronze Age material and thus leading Schliemann to miscalculate the level of Priam's Troy.

Egypt, and Cyprus were discovered during the careful excavations by Dörpfeld in the years after Schliemann's death, as well as by the later excavators, Carl Blegen and Manfred Korfmann. Mycenaean pottery was also found by all of the excavators, including Schliemann and especially Dörpfeld. Finding such Mycenaean objects in Troy VI may seem strange, in light of the possible ten-year siege of the city by Agamemnon and his warriors, until one remembers that, even according to Homer, the Mycenaeans and the Trojans were trading partners and friendly before the war.

Dörpfeld found that Troy VI, after going through a series of phases, was ultimately destroyed after hundreds of years of continuous inhabitation. He believed that the Mycenaeans had captured the city, burning it to the ground, and that it was this event that formed the basis of Homer's epic tales. This discovery, he believed, would end the debate. In his book *Troja und Ilion*, published in 1902, Dörpfeld wrote that "The long dispute over the existence of Troy and over its site is at an end. The Trojans have triumphed . . . Schliemann has been vindicated."

Contrary to Dörpfeld's belief, however, it may not have been humans who caused the destruction of Troy VI, but rather Mother Nature.

Chapter 6
Returning to Hisarlik: Carl Blegen and Manfred Korfmann

Carl Blegen began his excavations at Hisarlik on behalf of the University of Cincinnati in 1932, three decades after Dörpfeld published his words about "the end of the long dispute." Nobody had dug at the mound in the interim. Such a gap is not unusual at prominent sites, regardless of where they are in the world, for sustained excavations take a tremendous degree of commitment, funding, and preparation. There are also often months or years of negotiations involved, in order to procure the necessary permits from the proper authorities, who do not grant such permissions readily, especially if the site is deemed particularly significant.

Blegen disagreed with Dörpfeld's identification of Troy VI as Priam's Troy. He believed there was indisputable evidence that the final phase of Troy VI had been destroyed not by humans but by Mother Nature—specifically an earthquake. Instead of Troy VI, Blegen favored the next city, Troy VIIa, as Priam's Troy.

Blegen published a semi-popular book, *Troy and the Trojans* (1963), in which he described the situation at the site as his excavation team found it when they began reinvestigating the Troy VI phases. Despite the fact that the entire top of the mound had been shaved off during Hellenistic and Roman times as part of the construction for the Temple of Athena, and that what little survived was later removed by Schliemann, along the edges they found undisturbed deposits still remaining, 15 to 18 feet (5–6 m) deep, just inside the fortification wall. Within this "massive accumulation," as he called it, were the eight successive strata from Troy VIa to VIh (see fig. 7).

Blegen found that the eight layers contained the entire history of Troy VI without a cultural break, meaning that the inhabitants had simply been reorganizing and remodeling their city during the course of centuries without foreign interruption. Although the pottery changed over time, as did the architecture, overall it was clear that generation after generation of Trojans had lived in this city. There were some minor destructions and disturbances,

7. A plan of Troy I–IX, showing the different levels of the cities buried in the ancient mound of Hisarlik, with Troy VI expanded for a better view.

such as in phase VIf, dated to the late fifteenth or early fourteenth century BCE, when the remains of a fire were detected, but on the whole there was cultural continuity for the entire period of Troy VI, meaning no massive incursions of new residents or invaders.

Even the next phase in the site's history, known to archaeologists as Troy VIIa, showed similar cultural continuity with the previous city. In fact, both Dörpfeld and Blegen agreed that it was not really a new city—it was simply Troy VIh rebuilt, with the walls patched up and the houses restored. Even while Blegen was digging at the site from 1932 to 1938, Dörpfeld suggested (in 1935) that Troy VIIa should really be called Troy VIi, the ninth phase to this city, rather than the first phase of a new city. However, as Blegen stated, while this would "certainly correspond with the observed facts . . . we have kept the established terminology in order to avoid confusing those who have long been familiar with it." Manfred Korfmann, excavating again at the site fifty years after Blegen, made a similar comment: "It should be observed that even Dörpfeld had pointed out that, due to its close similarity to the preceding period, Phase VIIa really should be assigned to Period VI—that is, VIi. . . . On the basis of recent findings, we also prefer this classification."

Evidence for an earthquake

Blegen agreed with Dörpfeld in many instances, including that the site had been destroyed at the end of Troy VIh, for his excavations too yielded evidence of massive fire and destruction, although he disagreed as to how and why it had been destroyed. According to Blegen, there was no evidence of invaders, no new types of pottery, no major changes that might indicate the city had been destroyed by the Mycenaeans or anyone else.

There is even Mycenaean pottery found in Troy VIIa, much of it local imitations made by either Trojans or resident Mycenaeans, which would make no sense if the Mycenaeans had completely destroyed the city at the end of Troy VI and left it a smoking ruin, as Homer describes. Instead, it looks as if the Mycenaeans were still trading with the Trojans, or at least were still in contact with them during much of the time of Troy VIIa, which lasted for more than a century. All of this indicated to Blegen that the inhabitants—the survivors of whatever had destroyed the final city of Troy VI—had simply rebuilt the city and carried on, initiating the next phase of this long-lived sixth city, which had already been built and rebuilt in a series of different phases for more than four hundred years.

Thus, while Dörpfeld believed that the Mycenaeans had captured Troy VIh, burning it to the ground, and that it was this event that formed the basis of Homer's epic tales, Blegen, noting the continuity between Troy VIh and Troy VIIa, respectfully disagreed. He felt that Troy VIh had been destroyed by an earthquake, not by humans. If so, this would not have been the first time, for there is also evidence for earthquake damage in earlier cities—Troy III, IV, and V—and it is known that the site of Hisarlik is situated near the great North Anatolian fault line, which is still seismically active today, as shown by earthquakes that devastated the region in the late 1990s.

Blegen's evidence supporting his hypothesis that Troy VIh was destroyed by an earthquake is substantial—walls knocked out of kilter, huge towers collapsed, and everywhere the signs of tremendous force and upheaval (see fig. 8). As he noted in the final report published by the excavation team, "we feel confident in attributing the disaster to a severe earthquake.... A violent earthquake shock will account more convincingly than any probable human agency for the toppling of the city wall." A later re-examination by a respected geoarchaeologist agreed with Blegen's conclusion, stating, "the evidence supplied by the Cincinnati excavators . . . seems overwhelming."

Some scholars have argued that the Mycenaeans could have taken advantage of this earthquake that hit Troy, and that they may have

8. Collapsed stones and damaged walls indicate possible earthquake damage, in a photo taken during the excavations of Troy VI by Carl Blegen in the 1930s.

entered through the suddenly ruined walls which had fortuitously and dramatically been brought tumbling down. This in turn leads to an identification problem, for while Troy VI fits with Homer's description in many ways—its walls are big enough, its houses are grand enough, its streets are broad enough, it is wealthy enough—Homer makes no mention of an earthquake.

Enter the Trojan Horse. Although a number of scholars have suggested that the Trojan Horse was actually a battering ram or some other machine of war, the German academician Fritz Schachermeyr has proposed that the Trojan Horse was not a machine of war but was instead a poetic metaphor for an earthquake. His reasoning is simple: Poseidon was the Greek god of earthquakes; and Poseidon was usually represented by a horse (just as Athena was represented by an owl). The pounding of the horses' hooves, while pulling Poseidon in his chariot, not only created the crashing sound of the ocean's waves, according to the ancient Greeks, but also the sound that accompanies an earthquake. Therefore, the Trojan Horse may be Homer's way of depicting the earthquake sent by Poseidon to level the walls of Troy. The Trojan Horse is, quite literally, the earthquake, but only metaphorically speaking. This is an ingenious suggestion but is perhaps a bit farfetched. But if we put ourselves into Homer's position, it is one of the only ways to end the story without actually changing the real historical ending of the city. Besides, there is no other way, if one wants Troy VI to be Priam's Troy, to explain why the city fits Homer's description in every way except for the manner of its destruction.

Redating and reuse

A recent re-examination of the imported and local Mycenaean pottery found in the Troy VIh levels has redated the destruction of this city. Blegen had originally dated this pottery to ca. 1275 BCE, but later scholars argued about this date, with some even suggesting that it could be as late as 1130–1100 BCE. The new study was done in the 1990s by Penelope Mountjoy, a well-respected scholar and author of several authoritative volumes on Mycenaean pottery, who was able to handle and re-examine all of the sherds found by Blegen for the first time in many decades. In her detailed paper she concluded that Troy VIh was destroyed most likely ca. 1300 BCE. She also agreed with Blegen that it was probably ended by an earthquake, which had nothing to do with Agamemnon or the Mycenaeans.

Blegen noticed that the ruins of the large and prosperous houses located within the citadel of Troy VIh were either immediately rebuilt and reused in Troy VIIa, but now with many party walls subdividing their interiors, as if many families were living where a single family unit had lived previously, or else had ramshackle huts and houses built over their remains, using the stubs of the walls from the ruined fine houses. He also noticed other indications that he thought meant that the population of this fortified citadel had suddenly expanded to many times its previous size. A prime indication of this population explosion, to his mind, was the many storage jars—*pithoi* as they are known—not only within the houses but also buried beneath the floors so that only their tops were visible and accessible. By burying these jars, the inhabitants were able to keep some perishable items cold, even in an era that had no refrigeration, and they were also able to double or even triple their overall storage capacity for grain, wine, olive oil, and other necessities of life.

Destruction of Troy VIIa

Blegen was certain that he was excavating a city that had been besieged, and that the population from the lower city and perhaps from the surrounding villages had flooded the wealthy upper citadel of the town in the face of an advancing enemy force. His suspicions were confirmed, he believed, by the discovery that Troy VIIa had been destroyed by warfare, for he found skeletons, or portions of unburied bodies, in the streets within the citadel, as well as arrowheads, of specifically Aegean manufacture, and evidence of fire and of houses destroyed by burning. He and his fellow excavators wrote in their final report that the remains of Troy VIIa were "everywhere marked by the ravages of fire," adding that the "scattered remnants of human bones discovered in the fire-scarred ruins of Settlement VIIA surely indicate that its destruction was accompanied by violence (see fig. 9). Little imagination is required to see reflected here the fate of an ancient town captured and sacked by implacable foes."

Clearly, Blegen said, it was Troy VIIa, not Troy VIh, which had been put to the torch by the Mycenaeans. He dated this destruction to ca. 1260–1240 BCE, based on his dating of the pottery and perhaps on his desire to link this stratum to the Trojan War. He knew that if the Mycenaeans were involved in the Trojan War, as described by Homer, they would have had to participate before their own civilization was under attack and their own palaces on the Greek mainland were being destroyed—in some places, this began about 1225 BCE. In his 1963 book, *Troy and the Trojans,*

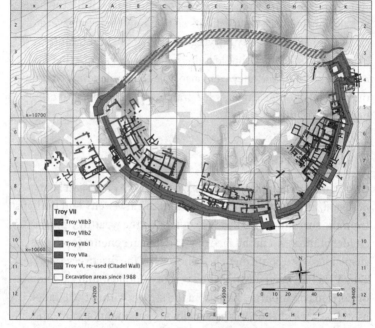

9. A plan of Troy VIIa, with the reused wall of Troy VI indicated, from the excavations at the site led by Manfred Korfmann from 1988 to 2005.

Blegen concluded: "The fire-blackened wreckage and ruins of the settlement offer a vivid picture of the harsh fate that was regularly meted out to a town besieged, captured and looted by implacable enemies, as is so graphically described in the accounts of marauding expeditions in the Homeric poems."

Having ascertained to his satisfaction that Troy VIIA was Priam's Troy, Blegen pointed also to the next city, constructed directly upon the ashes and burned debris, that previous excavators had already labeled Troy VIIb. Blegen was able to subdivide it into two separate phases, VIIb$_1$ and VIIb$_2$. The first of these two subphases, VIIb$_1$, showed great similarities to Troy VIIa, and Blegen therefore concluded that it was evidence for "an immediate reoccupation of the site by the survivors who somehow escaped the disaster that laid the citadel of Troy VIIa in smoldering ruins." At one point, in fact, he wrote again, "had we felt ourselves entirely free to modify Dörpfeld's numbering of the layers on the site, we should more properly have recognized the cultural connections of Troy VIIa and VIIb$_1$ by renaming them respectively Troy VIi and Troy VIj." The subphase lasted about a generation, according to Blegen, but he was not clear what caused it to come to an end ca. 1150 BCE, for he could detect no signs of violence, no burning, no looting, no sacking of the VIIb$_1$ city. He simply called it an unsolved mystery and left it at that.

The second of the two subphases, Troy VIIb$_2$, was completely different from everything that had come before. Had he been able to do so, Blegen would rather have called it Troy VIII because it was so different. Troy VIIb$_2$ was not simply the second phase of the same city; now the town plan was completely altered, the architecture of the houses unlike what had come before, and the pottery new and different. The inhabitants of Troy VIIb$_2$ were obviously different; it was as if the previous occupants of Troy VIIb$_1$ had totally vanished. This subphase, in turn, lasted for two or three generations before the site was again destroyed, perhaps by enemy action or another earthquake ca. 1100 BCE. Troy was then abandoned for several centuries, eventually to be re-inhabited later, starting in the Iron Age ca. 700 BCE and then continuing through the Roman period and beyond.

Problems with Blegen's interpretation

So had Blegen finally solved the mystery and identified the city of the Trojan War? Was it really Troy VIIa? There are several problems with his identification. For one thing, Troy VIIa does not fit Homer's description of a wealthy city—a city with towering gates, high walls, broad streets, large houses, and a magnificent palace. The city that Blegen excavated was a poor city, a reconstructed city, with its large houses subdivided by party walls and with storage jars buried underfoot. Blegen thought that it was a city under siege; Penelope Mountjoy has more recently suggested that it was simply a city trying to recover initially from a devastating earthquake, complete with temporary houses hastily erected amongst the ruins. Regardless, it was not a city that would have taken ten years to capture, and it certainly was not a city worth writing an epic about. In fact, the only way Troy VIIa matches Homer's story is in the manner in which it was destroyed—in a deliberate act of war. Perhaps Homer was writing about the magnificent city of Troy VI but also about the destruction of Troy VIIa—in other words, taking a poet's liberty by telescoping events in order to create a grand epic tale. But this is only one possible scenario.

In addition, Blegen's dating of the destruction of Troy VIIa has been challenged several times in the past half century, always on the basis of the pottery found in the settlement, with some scholars dating the destruction as late as 1050 BCE. Most recently it has been redated by Mountjoy to the last decades of the thirteenth century BCE and the first decades of the twelfth century BCE, sometime between 1230 BCE and 1190/80 BCE, based upon her personal re-analysis of the pottery. This might make it difficult to argue that the Mycenaeans were responsible for this destruction, unless the Mycenaean palaces back on the Greek mainland were being attacked and destroyed precisely because all of their warriors were away fighting at Troy. In fact, Mountjoy suggests that Troy VIIa was not destroyed by the Mycenaeans, but rather by the Sea Peoples, and that the city which the Mycenaeans destroyed is the much-later Troy VIIb$_2$ city, ca. 1100 BCE, although this latter suggestion is far too late to be likely.

The timing is certainly right for the Sea Peoples to have attacked and destroyed Troy VIIa, as part of their larger campaign of destruction, and some have suggested that survivors of the ravaged city joined the Sea Peoples in their subsequent activities. It is, however, not clear whether the Sea Peoples ever actually attacked Troy, and so the identity of the destroyers of Troy VIIa remains an open question, as does the destruction of Troy VIIb$_1$ and VIIb$_2$.

Korfmann at Troy

Exactly fifty years after Blegen's excavations at Troy ended, the next set began, in 1988. They were led by Manfred Korfmann of the University of Tübingen in Germany, who was interested in investigating the Bronze Age levels at the site. In coordination with Korfmann, investigations of the post–Bronze Age levels at the site (the Hellenistic and Roman remains) were also resumed, directed first by Stella Miller of Bryn Mawr College and then by C. Brian Rose of the University of Cincinnati.

Korfmann and his Bronze Age team started with a thorough re-examination of the Early Bronze Age remains in the center of the mound and also collected radiocarbon samples from all periods, the first time this had been done at the site. Later, they were primarily concerned with re-investigating the cities of Troy VI and VII in order to determine how large the cities were, what life was like there during the Late Bronze Age, and what exactly happened to these cities that brought each of them to dramatic endings.

Korfmann steadfastly maintained that he was not investigating the Trojan War, nor was he even interested in either proving or disproving the legend, but rather that he was investigating a very interesting Late Bronze Age city, one that had international connections and was a powerhouse in the region during the end of the second millennium BCE. By 2001, however, Korfmann was convinced that the city that he was excavating, Troia, as he called it in German, could be conclusively identified with the city known to the Hittites as Wilusa. From then on, his excavation reports refer to the site as Troia/Wilusa, an identification accepted by many other scholars.

Korfmann and his team made many discoveries, through both excellent excavation techniques and high-tech equipment. For one thing, they found and identified one more subphase, Troy VIIb$_3$, which lasted nearly a century and ended for an unknown reason about 1000 BCE, just before the site was abandoned for several hundred years.

They also found the first piece of writing ever discovered at the site—a biconvex bronze seal, inscribed on either side. Found in level VIIb$_2$ in 1995 and dating to ca. 1100 BCE, the seal has a man's name on one side and a woman's name on the other, and an indication that the man may have been a scribe.

The lower city

By far the most important of their discoveries, and certainly the largest, was made soon after the commencement of the project in 1988. Within a few years, Korfmann and his team were certain that they had detected, through the use of remote sensing equipment, the existence of an enormous lower city, stretching for more than 1,300 feet (400 m) south of the actual

Table 2. Chronology of Hisarlik/Troy Strata, ca. 1300–1000 BCE

Site Level	Approximate End Date	Probable Cause of Destruction	Aftermath
Troy VIh	1300 BCE	Earthquake	Continuity/ rebuilding
Troy VIIa	1230–1190/80 BCE	Attacked by enemy	Continuity/ rebuilding
Troy VIIb$_1$	1150 BCE	Unknown	New Culture
Troy VIIb$_2$	1100 BCE	Earthquake or Attacked by enemy	Continuity/ rebuilding
Troy VIIb$_3$	1000 BCE	Unknown	Abandoned for centuries

mound of Hisarlik. This discovery increases both the size and the population of Troy ten to fifteen times beyond that which was previously suspected. It also makes it clear that Late Bronze Age Troy was indeed a wealthy and prosperous city, covering 50 to 75 acres (200–300,000 sq m) and probably housing between four thousand and ten thousand inhabitants. As the investigation continued for more than a dozen years, through 2005, the archaeologists were able to confirm that virtually all of the fields surrounding the mound of Hisarlik covered this entire lower city, including levels dating to Troy VI and VIIa, in addition to later ruins above them laid out in an established north–south/east–west grid, dating to the Hellenistic and Roman periods. In fact, the remains from the later periods completely covered those of the Bronze Age lower city, leaving them "ill-preserved" and "excavated only with difficulty and in small patches," in the words of one expedition member.

Korfmann's team used several different types of magnetometers, a category of remote sensing equipment that has become popular because it enables archaeologists to peer beneath the ground before beginning excavation. By measuring the strength of the local magnetic field within the intended excavation area at specific points, the team was able to create images of what lay below: the local magnetic field varies depending upon whether a wall lies below, or a ditch, or nothing at all. Actual excavation was then conducted to confirm the initial remote sensing findings.

It was now apparent that Schliemann, Dörpfeld, and Blegen had all been excavating just the citadel or upper part of the city where the palace lay, which measured only about 656 feet x 656 feet (200 m x 200 m). In retrospect, it is not surprising that there is a lower city at Troy, for most of the contemporary Mycenaean palatial sites have both a citadel and a lower city. But it took modern scientific equipment and some educated guesswork on the part of Korfmann and his team to find the lower city of Troy.

This technology, or at least its interpretation, is not infallible, though, and at one point Korfmann and his team were led astray. In February 1993, they announced to great fanfare that their remote sensing equipment had indicated the presence of something deep underground, which was encircling the lower city more than a thousand feet away from the citadel. The team interpreted their discovery as a tremendous fortification wall. This made headlines around the world. Upon excavation during that summer, however, it turned out that it was not a fortification wall at all but a large defensive ditch dating to the time of Troy VI, cut into bedrock and measuring between 3 and 6 feet (1–2 m) deep and up to 13 feet (4 m) wide. The ditch had filled up with dirt and garbage over the millennia and thus appeared on their scans as a solid mass, which they had initially misinterpreted as a wall.

In the first two years after its discovery (1993 and 1994), the team traced this ditch for more than a thousand feet. They later discovered that there was a 30-foot-wide (10 m) gate present. They also discovered that there were two such ditches, one placed farther out from the citadel and in use later than the other, apparently as the population expanded outward during the later part of Troy VI. There may also have been a wooden palisade, or high fence, originally placed behind each ditch, but which has long since disintegrated. The archaeologists were also able to trace the remains of the massive Troy VI stone wall surrounding the citadel, first found by Dörpfeld, exposing more than had been found by the previous excavators.

Between 1997 and 2001, Korfmann's team also completely excavated the so-called Spring Cave—interconnected man-made tunnels, shafts, and galleries comprising a water system carved into the living rock. This lay outside the walls of the citadel, in the southwestern section of the lower city. The main tunnel had been discovered early on during the renewed excavations, but it was thought to date to the Roman period, because of the remains of fish ponds and other constructions in and near the entrance to the tunnel. These remains in front do indeed date to the Roman period, but by 2001 Korfmann and his team were able to date the construction of the tunnel system back to the Early Bronze Age, during the third millennium BCE, and to show that it had been in use for the better part of two thousand years. This was extremely important for Korfmann, especially in terms of connecting Hisarlik/Troy with the city of Wilusa known from Hittite records, for this may be the "underground watercourse of the land of Wilusa" mentioned in the Alaksandu Treaty.

Korfmann and Troy VIIa

Korfmann, as had Blegen and Dörpfeld before him, took pains to make clear that there was no cultural break between Troy VIh and Troy VIIa. Where Korfmann departed from his predecessors was in seeing Troy VIIa (or VIi) as having lasted for more than a century. Citing Penelope Mountjoy and her re-examination of the Mycenaean pottery, Korfmann declared that Troy VIIa begins about 1300 BCE and ends, after several building phases, ca. 1180 BCE "due to destruction caused by war."

Among the most dramatic of Korfmann's discoveries, as early as 1995, was evidence in the lower city that the Troy VIIa period had come to an end in fire and war. As he noted in a preliminary report, their excavations revealed a burned layer southwest of the citadel mound, dating to the end of Troia VIIa, which they believed was the result of "a military event." Later, in the popular magazine *Archaeology*, he noted that they had found some skeletons and "heaps of sling bullets" in this area, which eventually was shown to contain the remains of a large Courtyard House with storerooms. Interestingly, directly underneath this Troy VIIa Courtyard House is a building from phase Troy VIh, which was also completely burned and destroyed as the result of an earthquake, in Korfmann's opinion. Thus, in a single small area, Korfmann had found evidence for a Troy VIIa building destroyed by enemy action overlying a Troy VIh building destroyed by an earthquake.

Over the years, Korfmann's team discovered in the lower city bronze arrowheads, at least one skeleton from an unburied body of a young girl, and several piles of what may be sling stones ready to be used by the defenders (see fig. 10). One of his team members described the situation as indicative of a lost war and indeed, for Korfmann at least, all of this was clear evidence of a city under attack by enemy forces. At one point, in a BBC documentary broadcast in 2004, he reported: "Now the evidence is burning and catastrophe with fire. Then there are skeletons; we found, for example, a girl, I think sixteen, seventeen years old, half buried, the feet were burned by fire. Half of the corpse was underground. This is strange [that] a rapid burial was in [a] public space,

10. **Arrowheads recovered from the Troy VIIa stratum in the lower city at Troy indicate that the city was destroyed in battle by a hostile force.**

inside the city . . . and we found sling pellets in heaps. . . . It was
a city which was besieged. It was a city which was defended,
which protected itself. They lost the war and obviously they were
defeated." However, Korfmann does not specify by whom he thinks
the destruction was caused, nor does he comment on the fact that
the Mycenaean civilization was in an advanced stage of disruption
at that time.

In fact, it is not at all clear who caused the destruction of the
lower city. Such bronze arrowheads could have been used by the
Mycenaeans, but they could also have been used by the Sea Peoples
or someone else entirely. If the event that caused the destruction
of the city were to be dated as late as 1180 BCE, as Korfmann
indicated, then the destruction could as readily be linked with
the second invasion of the Sea Peoples during the time of Ramses
III as it could with the Mycenaeans. This dating, though, is based
on the latest possible date for the Mycenaean pottery analyzed
by Mountjoy, so the attack could just as easily have taken place a
few decades earlier, according to the same study. If that were the
case, then the destruction could be linked to the initial overthrow
of Walmu, king of Wilusa, as recorded in the Hittite tablets,
and could implicate the Mycenaeans after all. This hypothesis,
however, is highly speculative.

A new Trojan War

Although it is still not clear whether Troy VIIa was destroyed by
the Mycenaeans or by someone else, Korfmann's new findings may
eventually lead to an answer for the question of the Trojan War.
His data, like those of most archaeologists, are nonetheless subject
to interpretation. In this regard, Korfmann's work has already
come under attack from a surprising quarter—one of his own
colleagues at the University of Tübingen, Frank Kolb.

Beginning in the summer of 2001, during a large exhibit on Troy
that opened in Stuttgart, then went to Braunschweig and finally

to Bonn, Kolb accused Korfmann of exaggeration, misleading statements, and shoddy scholarship in connection with his excavations at Troy. Kolb claimed that there was no lower city at Troy and that both the lower city and the ditch hewn in the bedrock were figments of Korfmann's imagination, intended to deceive the general public.

The discussions grew in intensity and ultimately led to a two-day conference—almost a mock trial—at the university in February 2002. It was attended by more than eight hundred people per day. A three-hour general discussion during the second day was broadcast live on radio to a riveted audience throughout much of Germany. More than sixty journalists covered the proceedings. According to one reporter, the conference ended in a fistfight between Korfmann and Kolb, "an unseemly bout of fisticuffs," as the journalist called it, but the eventual ruling was in favor of Korfmann and his interpretation of Troy, supported soon thereafter by a long reassessment penned by some of the Bronze Age specialists who had been at the conference. Kolb did not give up the battle, however, and the debate has continued in the pages of academic journals.

Korfmann died suddenly in August 2005. With his death, Korfmann's banner has been taken up by his colleagues at Troy, Tübingen, Sheffield, and elsewhere. The Bronze Age excavations at Troy conducted by the University of Tübingen have continued, first during the summer of 2005 in the capable hands of Korfmann's deputy, Peter Jablonka, and since then under the leadership of Korfmann's senior colleague, Ernst Pernicka.

Epilogue

In the end, what do we know and what do we believe about
the Trojan War? Was Homer describing a real historical event
that took place toward the end of the Late Bronze Age, perhaps
the final conflict fought by the Mycenaeans on the coast of
Anatolia before their own civilization collapsed? Much has been
written about Troy and the Trojan War in both the distant and
the recent past. Assertions that Troy was located in England,
Scandinavia, or even Cilicia in Turkey, that the story was
actually a garbled version of the legend of Atlantis, and other
flights of fantasy have found their way into print, some even
in recent years. Scholars themselves are still arguing about the
historicity of Homer and the Trojan War, with some saying
that the Homeric poems should be regarded as mere fantasies
but others stating that it is inconceivable that "the Trojan War
motif . . . could have been invented out of nothing in the eighth
century."

Two questions remain paramount. Was there an actual war
fought in northwestern Anatolia on which Homer's *Iliad* was
based? Have we excavated the site where Priam's Troy once stood?
Naysayers aside, most scholars would agree that the answer to

both questions is yes, but a qualified yes. The problem in providing a definitive answer is not that we have too little data but that we have too much. The Greek epics, Hittite records, Luwian poetry, and archaeological remains provide evidence not of a single Trojan war but rather of multiple wars, which were fought in the area that we identify as Troy and the Troad. As a result, the evidence for the Trojan War of Homer is tantalizing but equivocal. There is no single "smoking gun."

How many wars?

According to the Greek literary evidence, there were at least two Trojan Wars (Heracles's and Agamemnon's), not simply one; in fact, there were three wars, if one counts Agamemnon's earlier abortive attack on Teuthrania. Similarly, according to the Hittite literary evidence, there were at least four Trojan Wars, ranging from the Assuwa Rebellion in the late fifteenth century BCE to the overthrow of Walmu, king of Wilusa in the late thirteenth century BCE. And, according to the archaeological evidence, Troy/Hisarlik was destroyed twice, if not three times, between 1300 and 1000 BCE. Some of this has long been known; the rest has come to light more recently.

Unfortunately, none of these individual events can be correlated to another with certainty. For instance, one would think that the overthrow of Walmu, seen in the relevant Hittite records, would be reflected in the destruction of Troy VIIa, but we cannot say with complete confidence that the two are definitely linked.

This, though, is a common problem in archaeology of these early periods—even when one has destructions attested archaeologically at a site on the one hand and written records documenting the capture and/or destruction of the same city on the other, it is frequently difficult to link the two. The best example that comes to mind is that of Megiddo in Israel, where we know, from written records, that the Egyptian pharaoh Thutmose III captured the city in about 1479 BCE. We also have several archaeological strata at the site that indicate destructions. However, it has proved impossible so far to correlate the written texts and the archaeological evidence.

It also must be made clear that any attempt to locate the Trojan War historically and archaeologically is still necessarily based on a circumstantial case, which invokes a series of assumptions and observations, resulting in a plausible but still hypothetical reconstruction. These include the following, some or all of which can be used:

- Wilusa is probably (W)ilios (Troy).
- Alaksandu, king of Wilusa, may be Alexander/ Paris of (W)ilios/Troy.
- Walmu, king of Wilusa, is deposed by enemy forces in the late thirteenth century BCE.
- Ahhiyawa probably is/are the Mycenaeans from mainland Greece.
- Troy VIh was destroyed but probably by an earthquake rather than by humans.
- Troy VIIa was destroyed by humans, in warfare.

Homer and history

One may argue that it is quite conceivable that Homer used literary license to telescope people and events, and several centuries of intermittent warfare, in order to create a compelling epic poem centered around a ten-year struggle. His poem was not meant to be a history book but rather an epic of national pride concerned with universal themes such as love and honor.

Among the material that Homer might have drawn upon, in addition to his understanding of the Bronze Age Aegean world of warriors and weapons, would have been tales of the Assuwa Rebellion, and probable Mycenaean involvement therein, in the time of Tudhaliya I/II ca. 1420 BCE, as well as knowledge of the wealthy city of Troy VIh, destroyed by an earthquake ca. 1300 BCE. The oral traditions might also have told of the rebuilt city of Troy VIIa, ruled over first by Alaksandu ca. 1280 BCE in the time of Muwatalli II and then by Walmu ca. 1225 or later in the time of Tudhaliya IV, as well as perhaps the animosity between the Hittites and Ahhiyawa over Wilusa in the time of Hattusili III in the middle of the thirteenth century BCE. He would also probably have heard of the destruction of Troy VIIa in warfare ca. 1230–1180 BCE, and perhaps even the later destruction of Troy VIIb$_2$ ca. 1100 BCE.

Thus, Homer's descriptions of Troy in the *Iliad* could be drawn from knowledge of Troy VIh, while the description of its destruction could be drawn from awareness of the fires that brought an end to Troy VIIa. If so, one could argue that Homer's Trojan War was a process rather than an event, incorporating details of people, places, and events taken from several hundred years during the Late Bronze Age, not to mention the subsequent five hundred years that lay between the war and Homer himself. Homer could have woven material from older epics into that of his own, incorporating boars'-tusk helmets, tower shields, and earlier figures such as Ajax, as well as updating the equipment and tactics used in some cases—to better fit his own time—and used descriptions of the lovely and forbidding city of Troy VI in place of Walmu's more ramshackle and rebuilt Troy VIIa.

Homer may not have had his facts straight, nor might he have cared. After all, some of the greatest epic poets and poetry since medieval times have altered the facts of history as we know them and sometimes a great heroic tradition is built around an event, which was of minor significance or which has been so distorted that it is no longer recognizable; one need only point to the *Chanson de Roland* and the *Niebelungleid*, both of which altered the details of actual historical events. Perhaps we should be content, therefore, with the knowledge that the basic parameters of the tale of the Trojan War can be confirmed, even if some of the details can be questioned, for we have come much farther than some might realize.

Since the days of Schliemann, we have confirmed the existence of the Mycenaeans and their civilization, even if we have not yet shown that Agamemnon once existed. We have confirmed that the city of Troy did once exist, even if we have not yet shown conclusively which level at the site belonged to Priam, or even if he too ever actually existed. We have confirmed, or at least can surmise with a great deal of confidence, that Mycenaean warriors were fighting on the coast of northwestern Anatolia, in the precise region of Troy, on and off again over the course of more than three centuries during the Late Bronze Age, even if we cannot point specifically to Achilles and Patroclus. And, we now know that Hittite records indicate numerous wars or conflicts fought at or over Troy during that same time period, even if we cannot definitively say that it was Agamemnon who fought Alaksandu in the early thirteenth century BCE or deposed Walmu in the late thirteenth century BCE. In other words, the basic outline of Homer's story rings true, whether or not Alexander and Helen, Agamemnon and Priam, or Achilles and Hector actually existed.

But would the Trojan War have been fought because of love for a woman? Could a ten-year war have been instigated by the kidnapping of a single person? The answer, of course, is yes, just as an Egypto-Hittite war in the thirteenth century BCE was touched off by the death of a Hittite prince, and the outbreak of World War I was sparked by the assassination of Archduke Ferdinand. But just as one could argue that World War I would have taken place anyway, perhaps triggered by some other event, so one can argue that the Trojan War would inevitably have taken place, with or without Helen. The presumptive kidnapping of Helen can be seen merely an excuse to launch a preordained war for control of land, trade, profit, and access to the Black Sea.

Would such a war have lasted for ten years? That seems unlikely, of course, and it may be that there are other factors in play here. Perhaps there was a nine-year gap between the initial raid on Teuthrania and the final attack on Troy, as some have suggested. Perhaps it is as Barry Strauss, a classics professor at Cornell University, has suggested, that the ten years simply reflect a Near Eastern expression, "nine times and then a tenth," meaning simply a very long time. Or perhaps it really did last ten years. We may never know.

In addition, it may be that the real basis for the Trojan War had nothing to do with the Trojans themselves. Troy lay on the edge of both the Mycenaean Empire and the Hittite Empire, in what one might call a "contested periphery," and was caught in between two of the great powers in the ancient Mediterranean world. Both sides thought that they should possess Troy, and both sides were willing to go to war for control of the city. What the Trojans themselves wanted would have been irrelevant, or at least of little consequence. Thus, we have the distinct possibility that the Trojan War was actually fought between the Mycenaeans and the Hittites, with the Trojans being the hapless peoples caught in the middle (but whom both Homer and the Hittite records saw as being on the side of the Hittites, against the Mycenaeans/Ahhiyawa).

A war for the ages

And, of course, artistic and literary reinterpretations of the Trojan War and the fate of its better-known participants, including Odysseus, have been produced and reproduced over the centuries, up to and including the present. Thus, we have not only the later Greek playwrights and the Roman poets but also Chaucer's *Troilus and Criseyde*, Shakespeare's *Troilus and Cressida*, Camille

Saint-Saëns's opera *Hélène* (1904), James Joyce's *Ulysses*, and the silver screen's various takes on the epic, with numerous films appearing since the early twentieth century featuring the Trojan War, Helen, Achilles, Odysseus, and/or the Trojan Horse.

Some of these later works contain parts that may be considered inaccurate or unfaithful to Homer in details or plot—the 2004 Hollywood blockbuster movie, for instance, has no gods or goddesses in sight; Brad Pitt anachronistically placing coins on the closed eyes of dead Patroclus five hundred years before such currency is invented in Lydia ca. 700 BCE; and both Agamemnon and Menelaus killed at Troy while Paris/Alexander is not, thereby changing the familiar Homeric/*Epic Cycle* version—but this is a long-standing tradition going back to the Greek playwrights who followed Homer and who also felt free to change some of the details. More importantly, each has reinterpreted the story in its own way, with changes and nuances frequently reflecting the angst and desires of that particular age, such as medieval Christianity for Chaucer, the Elizabethan worldview for Shakespeare, and the Iraq war for *Troy* director Wolfgang Peterson.

The relevance to wars of all ages is obvious, and is perhaps most exemplified by an untitled poem by Patrick Shaw-Stewart, a classics scholar from Oxford who fought at Gallipoli in World War I, just across the Dardanelles from Troy. He wrote in part:

O hell of ships and cities,
Hell of men like me,
Fatal second Helen,
Why must I follow thee?

Achilles came to Troyland
And I to Chersonese;
He turned from wrath to battle,
And I from three days' peace.

Was it so hard, Achilles,
So very hard to die?
Thou knewest, and I know not—
So much the happier I.

In 1964, the eminent historian Moses Finley suggested that we
should move the narrative of the Trojan War from the realm of
history into the realm of myth and poetry until we have more
evidence. Many would argue that we now have that additional
evidence, particularly in the form of the Hittite texts discussing
Ahhiyawa and Wilusa and the new archaeological data from
Troy. However, we have seen that there was no specific "Trojan
War" that one can definitively point to, at least not as Homer has
described it in the *Iliad* and the *Odyssey*. Instead, we have found
several such Trojan wars and several cities at Troy, enough that one
can conclude there is a historical kernel of truth—of some sort—
underlying all the stories.

The lines between reality and fantasy might be blurred,
particularly when Zeus, Hera, and other gods become involved
in the war, and we might quibble about some of the details, but
overall, Troy and the Trojan War are right where they should be,
in northwestern Anatolia and firmly ensconced in the world of the
Late Bronze Age, as we now know from archaeology and Hittite
records, in addition to the Greek literary evidence from both
Homer and the *Epic Cycle*. Moreover, the enduring themes of love,
honor, war, kinship, and obligations, which so resonated with the
later Greeks and then the Romans, have continued to reverberate
through the ages from Aeschylus, Sophocles, and Euripides to
Virgil, Ovid, and Livy, and thence to Chaucer, Shakespeare, and
beyond, so that the story still holds broad appeal even today,
more than three thousand years after the original events, or some
variation thereof, took place.

Glossary: characters and places

Achilles: Greek hero

Aeschylus: Greek playwright; lived in the fifth century BCE

Aethiopis: part of the Epic Cycle

Agamemnon: brother of Menelaus; king of Mycenae on mainland Greece

Agias of Troezen: probable author of the *Returns*

Ahhiyawa: probable Hittite name for Mycenaean Greece

Ajax: Greek hero; possibly from even earlier Greek myths

Akkadian: language spoken and written in the second millennium BCE ancient Near East; the diplomatic *lingua franca* of the time

Alaksandu: king of Wilusa; ruled ca. 1280 BCE

Alaksandu Treaty: lengthy treaty signed between Alaksandu of Wilusa and the Hittite king Muwattalli II, ca. 1280 BCE

Alexander: alternate name for Paris, prince of Troy; son of Priam; lover of Helen

Aphrodite: Greek goddess of love and beauty

Arctinus of Miletus: probable author of the *Aethiopis* and the *Sack of Troy*

Arnuwanda I: Hittite king, successor of Tudhaliya I/II; ruled ca. 1420 BCE

Assuwa: confederacy of twenty-two city-states in western Anatolia ca. 1420 BCE

Athena: Greek goddess of wisdom, courage, and other attributes

Attarissiya: a ruler of Ahhiya (Ahhiyawa)

Clytemnestra: wife of Agamemnon

Cypria: part of the Epic Cycle

Cyprias of Halicarnassus: possible author of the *Cypria*
Epeius: Greek warrior who had the idea for the Trojan Horse
Epic Cycle: fragmentary collection of epic tales about the Trojan War
Euripides: Greek playwright; lived in the fifth century BCE
Hattusili III: Hittite king; ruled ca. 1267–1237 BCE
Hector: Trojan hero
Hecuba: wife of King Priam of Troy
Hegesias of Salamis: possible author of the *Cypria*
Helen: wife of Menelaus; queen of Mycenaean Sparta; lover of
    Alexander/Paris
Hera: wife of Zeus
Heracles: Greek hero; attacked Troy in the generation before the
    Trojan War
Herodotus: Greek historian; lived in the fifth century BCE
Hisarlik: mound most likely containing the ancient site of Troy
Hittite: language spoken and written in second millennium BCE
    Anatolia (Turkey)
Hittites: major power in Anatolia (modern Turkey),
    ca. 1700–1200 BCE
Homer: purported author of the *Iliad* and the *Odyssey*;
    lived ca. 750 BCE
Iliad: Homer's epic of the final days of the Trojan War
Ilios: alternate name for Troy; originally spelled (W)ilios
Iliupersis (Sack of Troy): part of the Epic Cycle
Iphigenia: daughter of Agamemnon; sacrificed at Aulis to ensure
    favorable winds for the Mycenaean fleet
Kukkulli: king of Assuwa, son of Piyama-Kurunta, ruled ca. 1420 BCE
Laomedon: king of Troy at the time of Heracles's attack; predecessor
    of Priam
Lesches of Mitylene: probable author of the *Little Iliad*
Little Iliad: part of the Epic Cycle
Luwian: language spoken and written in second millennium BCE
    Anatolia (Turkey)
Madduwatta: Hittite vassal who features prominently in the
    Ahhiyawa correspondence
Manapa-Tarhunta: king of the Seha River Land, south of the Troad;
    ruled in the thirteenth century BCE
Menelaus: husband of Helen; brother of Agamemnon; king of
    Mycenaean Sparta
Milawata: Hittite name for the city of Miletus, on the coast of Asia
    Minor/Anatolia

Milawata Letter: letter probably written and sent in the late thirteenth century BCE by the Hittite king Tudhaliya IV (ruled ca. 1237–1209 BCE); concerned with the city of Milawata (Miletus) as well as with the continuing activities of Piyamaradu, a "renegade Hittite" involved with Ahhiyawa.

Minoans: inhabitants of Bronze Age Crete, in the Aegean

Muwattalli II: Hittite king; ruled ca. 1295–1272 BCE

Mycenae: major city of the Mycenaeans, in the Peloponnesus region of the Greek mainland; inhabited ca. 1700–1100 BCE; first excavated by Schliemann in the 1870s

Mycenaeans: Achaeans; inhabitants of the Greek mainland from 1700–1200 BCE

Nestor: king of Pylos on the Greek mainland

Odysseus: Greek hero

Odyssey: Homer's epic of Odysseus's journey home after the Trojan War

Ovid: Roman poet; first century BCE to first century CE

Paris: alternate name for Alexander, prince of Troy; son of Priam; lover of Helen

Patroclus: faithful friend of Achilles; dies while fighting wearing Achilles's armor

Philoctetes: kills Achilles by shooting him in the heel with an arrow

Piyama-Kurunta: leader of the Assuwan Confederacy, prior to ca. 1420 BCE

Piyamaradu: a "renegade Hittite" who was involved with the Ahhiyawans in the thirteenth century BCE

Priam: king of Troy at the time of the Trojan War

Proclus: editor of the *Epic Cycle*, (i.e., the *Chrestomatheia Grammatiki*); lived in either the second or fourth century CE

Quintus Smyrnaeus: epic poet of the fifth century CE

Returns: part of the Epic Cycle

Sea Peoples: roving/migrating groups that came through the Mediterranean region twice, in 1207 and 1177 BCE; may have contributed to the end of the Late Bronze Age in the region

Sophocles: Greek playwright; lived in the fifth century BCE

Stasinus of Cyprus: possible author of the *Cypria*

Suppiluliuma I: one of the greatest Hittite kings; ruled ca. 1350–1322 BCE

Tawagalawa: brother of king of Ahhiyawa, mid-thirteenth century BCE; named in Hittite letter

Tawagalawa Letter: written by a king of Hatti, probably Hattusili III (ruled ca. 1267–1237 BCE), the letter is concerned with the activities of Piyamaradu, a "renegade Hittite," who was actively involved with Ahhiyawa (probably the Mycenaeans)

Telemachus: son of Odysseus

Teuthrania: area south of Troy, which Achilles and other Mycenaeans mistakenly attacked

Trojans: inhabitants of ancient Troy

Troy: Ilios; home to Priam, Alexander/Paris, and Hector; site of the Trojan War; probably to be identified with the site of Hisarlik in modern Turkey

Tudhaliya I/II: Hittite king who ruled ca. 1450–1420 and put down the Assuwa Rebellion

Tudhaliya IV: Hittite king; ruled ca. 1237–1209 BCE

Virgil: Roman epic poet; first century BCE

Walmu: king of Wilusa, late thirteenth century BCE

Wilusa: probable Hittite name for Troy (Ilios)

Zannanza: Hittite prince, son of Suppiluliuma I; killed enroute to Egypt in mid-fourteenth century BCE

Zeus: head of the pantheon of gods worshipped by the ancient Greeks

References

Throughout, translations from the *Iliad* follow A. T. Murray, *The Iliad, Books 1–12*; revised by William F. Wyatt (Cambridge, MA: Harvard University Press, 1999); Richmond Lattimore, *The Iliad of Homer* (Chicago: University of Chicago Press, 1961); or Robert Fagles, *Homer: The Iliad* (New York, Penguin, 1991). Those from the *Odyssey* follow A. T. Murray, *The Odyssey* (Cambridge, MA: Harvard University Press, 1984); from the *Epic Cycle* follow H. G. Evelyn-White, *Hesiod, the Homeric Hymns and Homerica* (London: W. Heinemann, 1914); from *Quintus Smyrnaeus* follow Alan James, *Quintus Smyrnaeus: The Trojan Epic (Posthomerica)* (Baltimore: Johns Hopkins University Press, 2004); from Herodotus follow George Rawlinson, *Herodotus: The Histories* (New York: Random House, 1997); and from the Hittite Ahhiyawa texts follow Gary Beckman, Trevor Bryce, and Eric H. Cline, *The Ahhiyawa Texts* (Atlanta: Society of Biblical Literature, 2011). Information regarding the finds from the recent excavations at Troy comes primarily from articles in the periodical *Studia Troica*, published annually from 1991 to 2009; many are in English but most are in German.

Chapter 2: The war in historical context

"The foreign countries made a conspiracy in their islands": Translation following W. F. Edgerton and J. A. Wilson, *Historical Records of Ramses III: The Texts in Medinet Habu*, vols. 1 and 2 (Chicago: University of Chicago Press, 1936), 53, pl. 46; revised translation found in J. A. Wilson, "The War Against the Peoples of the Sea," in *Ancient Near Eastern Texts Relating to the Old Testament, Third*

Edition with Supplement, ed. J. Pritchard, 262–63 (Princeton, NJ: Princeton University Press, 1969).

Chapter 3: Homeric questions

"invented by a single human being": Jay Tolson, "Was Homer a Solo Act or a Bevy of Bards? Classicists Have Few Clues but Lots of Theories," *US News and World Report,* July 24, 2000, 39; available online at: http://www.usnews.com/usnews/doubleissue/mysteries/homer.htm (last accessed November 4, 2012).

Chapter 4: The Hittite texts

"As Tudhaliya the Great King shattered the Assuwa country": Translation following Ahmet Ünal, A. Ertekin, and I. Ediz, "The Hittite Sword from Bogazkoy—Hattusa, Found 1991, and Its Akkadian Inscription," *Muze* 4 (1991): 51.
"When They Came from Steep Wilusa": Calvert Watkins, "The Language of the Trojans," in *Troy and the Trojan War: A Symposium Held at Bryn Mawr College, October 1984,* ed. Machteld J. Mellink, 45–62, esp. pp. 58–62 (Bryn Mawr, PA: Bryn Mawr College, 1986).
"outright war, a skirmish or two, or merely a verbal dispute": Commentary by Trevor Bryce, in *The Ahhiyawa Texts,* ed. Gary Beckman, Trevor Bryce, and Eric H. Cline, 121 (Atlanta: Society of Biblical Literature, 2011).

Chapter 5: Early excavators

"cut out the Treasure with a large knife": David A. Traill, *Schliemann of Troy: Treasure and Deceit* (New York: St. Martin's Griffin, 1995), 111, quoting Heinrich Schliemann, *Troy and Its Remains: A Narrative of Researches and Discoveries Made on the Site of Ilium, and in the Trojan Plain* (New York: Benjamin Blom, Inc., 1875).
"The long dispute over the existence of Troy": Michael Wood, *In Search of the Trojan War,* 2nd ed. (Berkeley: University of California Press, 1996), 91, citing and translating Wilhelm Dörpfeld, *Troja und Ilion: Ergebnisse der Ausgrabungen in den vorhistorischen und historischen Schichten von Ilion, 1870-1894* (Athens: Beck & Barth, 1902).

Chapter 6: Returning to Hisarlik

"correspond with the observed facts": Carl W. Blegen, *Troy and the Trojans* (New York: Praeger, 1963), 145.

"even Dörpfeld had pointed out": Manfred Korfmann, "Die Arbeiten in Troia/Wilusa 2003; Work at Troia/Wilusa in 2003," *Studia Troica* 14 (2004): 5 and 14.

"we feel confident in attributing the disaster": Carl W. Blegen, John L. Caskey, and Marion Rawson, *Troy III: The Sixth Settlement* (Princeton, NJ: Princeton University Press, 1953), 331.

"the evidence supplied by the Cincinnati excavators": George Rapp Jr., "Earthquakes in the Troad," in *Troy: The Archaeological Geology*, ed. G. Rapp and J. A. Gifford, 55–56 (Princeton, NJ: Princeton University Press, 1982).

"everywhere marked by the ravages of fire": Carl W. Blegen, Cedric G. Boulter, John L. Caskey, and Marion Rawson, *Troy IV: Settlements VIIa, VIIb and VIII* (Princeton, NJ: Princeton University Press, 1958), 11–12.

"The fire-blackened wreckage": Carl W. Blegen, *Troy and the Trojans* (New York: Praeger, 1963), 162.

"an immediate reoccupation of the site": Carl W. Blegen, Cedric G. Boulter, John L. Caskey, and Marion Rawson, *Troy IV: Settlements VIIa, VIIb and VIII* (Princeton, NJ: Princeton University Press, 1958), 142.

"had we felt ourselves entirely free": Carl W. Blegen, Cedric G. Boulter, John L. Caskey, and Marion Rawson, *Troy IV: Settlements VIIa, VIIb and VIII* (Princeton, NJ: Princeton University Press, 1958), 144.

"excavated only with difficulty": Peter Jablonka, "Troy," in *The Oxford Handbook of the Bronze Age Aegean*, ed. Eric H. Cline, 853 (New York: Oxford University Press, 2010).

"a military event": Manfred Korfmann, "Troia—Ausgrabungen 1995," *Studia Troica* 6 (1996):7, see also 34–39.

"heaps of sling bullets": Manfred Korfmann, "Was There a Trojan War?" *Archaeology* 57/3 (2004): 37.

"due to destruction caused by war": Manfred Korfmann, "Die Arbeiten in Troia/Wilusa 2003; Work at Troia/Wilusa in 2003," *Studia Troica* 14 (2004): 15, table on 16.

"Now the evidence is burning and catastrophe with fire": Korfmann, in the transcript of the BBC documentary *The Truth of Troy*; http://www.bbc.co.uk/science/horizon/2004/troytrans.shtml (last accessed November 4, 2012).

"an unseemly bout of fisticuffs": Philip Howard, "Troy Ignites Modern-Day Passions," *Australian*, February 26, 2002, 12.

Epilogue

"the Trojan War motif": Susan Sherratt, "The Trojan War: History or Bricolage?" *Bulletin of the Institute for Classical Studies* 53.2 (2010):5. See also similar statements by Kurt A. Raaflaub, "Homer, the Trojan War, and History," *Classical World* 91/5 (1998): 393.
"altered the details of actual historical events": Suzanne Saïd, *Homer and the Odyssey* (Oxford: Oxford University Press, 2011) 76–77.
"Was it so hard, Achilles, So very hard to die?": originally published in the *London Mercury* 1:3 (January 1920): 267; reprinted in Elizabeth Vandiver, *Stand in the Trench, Achilles: Classical Receptions in British Poetry of the Great War* (Oxford: Oxford University Press, 2010), 270–71.

Further reading

The Trojan War

Alexander, Caroline. *The War that Killed Achilles: The True Story of Homer's Iliad and the Trojan War*. New York: Viking, 2009.

Blegen, Carl W. *Troy and the Trojans*. New York: Praeger, 1963.

Bryce, Trevor L. "The Trojan War." In *The Oxford Handbook of the Bronze Age Aegean*, ed. Eric H. Cline, 475–82. New York: Oxford University Press, 2010.

Castleden, Rodney. *The Attack on Troy*. Barnsley, UK: Pen & Sword Books, 2006.

Dickinson, Oliver. "Was There Really a Trojan War?" In *Dioskouroi. Studies presented to W. G. Cavanagh and C. B. Mee on the anniversary of their 30-year joint contribution to Aegean Archaeology*, ed. C. Gallou, M. Georgiadis, and G. M. Muskett, 189–97. Oxford: Archaeopress, 2008.

Fields, Nic. *Troy c. 1700–1250 BC*. Oxford: Osprey Publishing, 2004.

Finley, Moses I. "The Trojan War." *Journal of Hellenic Studies* 84 (1964):1–9.

Graves, Robert. *The Siege and Fall of Troy*. London: The Folio Society, 2005.

Korfmann, Manfred. "Was There a Trojan War? Troy Between Fiction and Archaeological Evidence." In *Troy: From Homer's Iliad to Hollywood Epic*, ed. Martin M. Winkler, 20–26. Oxford: Blackwell, 2007.

Latacz, Joachim. *Troy and Homer: Towards a Solution of an Old Mystery*. New York: Oxford University Press, 2004.

Raaflaub, Kurt A. "Homer, the Trojan War, and History." *Classical World* 91/5 (1998): 386–403.

Sherratt, Susan. "The Trojan War: History or Bricolage?" *Bulletin of the Institute for Classical Studies* 53.2 (2010): 1–18.

Strauss, Barry. *The Trojan War: A New History*. New York: Simon & Schuster, 2006.

Thomas, Carol G., and Craig Conant. *The Trojan War*. Westport, CT: Greenwood Press, 2005.

Thompson, Diane P. *The Trojan War: Literature and Legends from the Bronze Age to the Present*. Jefferson, NC: McFarland, 2004. [Accompanying and updated website: http://novaonline.nvcc.edu/Eli/Troy/BbVersion/Troy/index.html]

Winkler, Martin M., ed. *Troy: From Homer's Iliad to Hollywood Epic*. Oxford: Blackwell, 2007.

Wood, Michael. *In Search of the Trojan War*. 2nd ed. Berkeley: University of California Press, 1996.

Homer and other early literary sources

Burgess, Jonathan S. *The Tradition of the Trojan War in Homer & the Epic Cycle*. Baltimore, MD: Johns Hopkins University Press, 2001.

Dalby, Andrew. *Rediscovering Homer: Inside the Origins of the Epic*. New York: W. W. Norton, 2006.

Finkelberg, Margalit, ed. *The Homer Encyclopedia*. 3 vols. Oxford: Wiley-Blackwell, 2011.

James, Alan. *Quintus Smyrnaeus: The Trojan Epic (Posthomerica)*. Baltimore, MD: Johns Hopkins University Press, 2004.

Lord, Albert. With Steven Mitchell and Gregory Nagy, ed. *The Singer of Tales*. 2nd ed. Cambridge, MA: Harvard University Press, 2000.

Nagy, Gregory. *The Best of the Achaeans: Concepts of the Hero in Archaic Greek Poetry*. Baltimore, MD: Johns Hopkins University Press, 1979.

Parry, Adam, ed. *The Making of Homeric Verse: The Collected Papers of Milman Parry*. Oxford: Oxford University Press, 1971.

Powell, Barry B. *Homer*. 2nd ed. Oxford: Wiley-Blackwell, 2007.

Powell, Barry B. *Homer and the Origin of the Greek Alphabet*. Cambridge: Cambridge University Press, 1996.

Saïd, Suzanne. *Homer and the Odyssey*. Oxford: Oxford University Press, 2011.

Thomas, Carol G., ed. *Homer's History: Mycenaean or Dark Age?* Huntington, NY: Robert E. Krieger, 1977.

West, Martin L. "The Invention of Homer." *Classical Quarterly* 49 (1999): 364–82.

Willcock, Malcolm. "Neoanalysis." In *A New Companion to Homer*, ed. Ian Morris and Barry B. Powell, 174–92. Leiden: Brill, 1997.

Achilles and Helen of Troy

Austin, Norman. *Helen of Troy and Her Shameless Phantom*. Ithaca, NY: Cornell University Press, 2008.

Hughes, Bettany. *Helen of Troy: Goddess, Princess, Whore*. New York: Knopf, 2005.

Maguire, Laurie. *Helen of Troy: From Homer to Hollywood*. Oxford: Wiley-Backwell, 2009.

Shay, Jonathan. *Achilles in Vietnam: Combat Trauma and the Undoing of Character*. New York: Simon & Schuster, 1995.

Archaeology of Troy

Blegen, Carl W. *Troy and the Trojans*. New York: Praeger, 1963.

Blegen, Carl W., John L. Caskey, and Marion Rawson. *Troy III: The Sixth Settlement*. Princeton, NJ: Princeton University Press, 1953.

Blegen, Carl W., Cedric G. Boulter, John L. Caskey, and Marion Rawson. *Troy IV: Settlements VIIa, VIIb and VIII*. Princeton, NJ: Princeton University Press, 1958.

Dörpfeld, Wilhelm. *Troja und Ilion: Ergebnisse der Ausgrabungen in den vorhistorischen und historischen Schichten von Ilion, 1870–1894*. Athens: Beck & Barth, 1902.

Jablonka, Peter. "Troy." In *The Oxford Handbook of the Bronze Age Aegean*, ed. Eric H. Cline, 849–61. New York: Oxford University Press, 2010.

Mountjoy, Penelope A. "The Destruction of Troia VIh." *Studia Troica* 9 (1999): 253–93.

Mountjoy, Penelope A. "Troia VII Reconsidered." *Studia Troica* 9 (1999): 295–346.

Schliemann, Heinrich. *Ilios: the City and Country of the Trojans*. New York: Benjamin Blom, Inc., 1881.

Schliemann, Heinrich. *Troy and Its Remains: A Narrative of Researches and Discoveries Made on the Site of Ilium, and in the Trojan Plain*. New York: Benjamin Blom, 1875.

Heinrich Schliemann

Allen, Susan Heuck. *Finding the Walls of Troy: Frank Calvert and Heinrich Schliemann at Hisarlik*. Berkeley: University of California Press, 1999.

Boedeker, Deborah, ed. *The World of Troy: Homer, Schliemann, and the Treasures of Priam*. Proceedings from a Seminar sponsored by the Society for the Preservation of the Greek Heritage and held at the Smithsonian Institution on February 21–22, 1997. Washington, DC: Society for the Preservation of the Greek Heritage, 1997.

Calder, William A. III, and David A. Traill. *Myth, Scandal and History: The Heinrich Schliemann Controversy and a First Edition of the Mycenaean Diary*. Detroit, MI: Wayne State University Press, 1986.

Schuchhardt Carl. *Schliemann's Excavations: An Archaeological and Historical Study*; New York: Macmillan and Co., 1891.

Traill, David A. *Excavating Schliemann: Collected Papers on Schliemann*. Atlanta: Scholars Press, 1993.

Traill, David A. *Schliemann of Troy: Treasure and Deceit*. New York: St. Martin's Griffin, 1995.

Hittites

Bryce, Trevor. *The Kingdom of the Hittites*. New ed. New York: Oxford University Press, 2005.

Bryce, Trevor. *Life and Society in the Hittite World*. Oxford: Oxford University Press, 2004.

Bryce, Trevor. *The Trojans and Their Neighbors*. London: Routledge, 2006.

Bryce, Trevor. *The World of the Neo-Hittite Kingdoms: A Political and Military History*. New York: Oxford University Press, 2012.

Collins, Billie Jean. *The Hittites and Their World*. Atlanta: Society of Biblical Literature, 2007.

Mycenaeans

Castledon, Rodney. *The Mycenaeans*. London: Routledge, 2005.

Dickinson, Oliver T. P. K. *The Aegean Bronze Age*. Cambridge: Cambridge University Press, 1994.

Finley, Moses I. *The World of Odysseus*. New York: Penguin, 1956.

French, Elizabeth. *Mycenae: Agamemnon's Capital*. Oxford: Tempus, 2002.

Schofield, Louise. *The Mycenaeans*. Malibu, CA: J. Paul Getty Museum, 2007.

Sea Peoples

Cline, Eric H., and David O'Connor. "The Sea Peoples." In *Ramesses III: The Life and Times of Egypt's Last Hero*, ed. Eric H. Cline and David O'Connor, 180–208. Ann Arbor: University of Michigan Press, 2012.

Roberts, R. Gareth. *The Sea Peoples and Egypt*. PhD diss. Oxford: University of Oxford, 2008.

Sandars, Nancy. *The Sea Peoples: Warriors of the Ancient Mediterranean, 1250–1150 B.C.* 2nd ed. London: Thames and Hudson, 1985.

"牛津通识读本"已出书目

古典哲学的趣味	福柯	地球
人生的意义	缤纷的语言学	记忆
文学理论入门	达达和超现实主义	法律
大众经济学	佛学概论	中国文学
历史之源	维特根斯坦与哲学	托克维尔
设计,无处不在	科学哲学	休谟
生活中的心理学	印度哲学祛魅	分子
政治的历史与边界	克尔凯郭尔	法国大革命
哲学的思与惑	科学革命	民族主义
资本主义	广告	科幻作品
美国总统制	数学	罗素
海德格尔	叔本华	美国政党与选举
我们时代的伦理学	笛卡尔	美国最高法院
卡夫卡是谁	基督教神学	纪录片
考古学的过去与未来	犹太人与犹太教	大萧条与罗斯福新政
天文学简史	现代日本	领导力
社会学的意识	罗兰·巴特	无神论
康德	马基雅维里	罗马共和国
尼采	全球经济史	美国国会
亚里士多德的世界	进化	民主
西方艺术新论	性存在	英格兰文学
全球化面面观	量子理论	现代主义
简明逻辑学	牛顿新传	网络
法哲学:价值与事实	国际移民	自闭症
政治哲学与幸福根基	哈贝马斯	德里达
选择理论	医学伦理	浪漫主义
后殖民主义与世界格局	黑格尔	批判理论